COGNITION
TO LANGUAGE

COGNITION TO LANGUAGE
Categories, Word Meanings, and Training

by

Mabel Rice, Ph.D.
Department of Human Development and Family Life
and
Bureau of Child Research
University of Kansas

University Park Press
Baltimore

UNIVERSITY PARK PRESS
International Publishers in Science, Medicine, and Education
233 East Redwood Street
Baltimore, Maryland 21202

Composed by University Park Press Typesetting Division.
Manufactured in the United States of America by The Maple Press Company.

Library of Congress Cataloging in Publication Data
Rice, Mabel.
Cognition to language.
Bibliography: p.
Includes index.
1. Cognition in children. 2. Children—Languages. I. Title.
BF723.C5R52   155.4'13   79-23267
ISBN 0-8391-1548-2

CONTENTS

FOREWORD

There are two continuing challenges confronting specialists in child language. One challenge is to comprehend the increasingly numerous organizing theories and frames of reference that are evolving. The other challenge is to design the functional systems for operationalizing the work that one wants to undertake. The work may be in a clinic with handicapped children, in a preschool classroom, or in a language laboratory. The worker may be a linguistics scientist, a language teacher, an application researcher, or a student in an academic program. All of these workers must understand the source material that is available on any problem before they attempt to achieve a desired language objective.

There appear to be few shortcuts to competent and humanistically effective ends. Workers in child language simply must do their homework on critical topics of child language or they will not keep up with the progress of the academic field and may find themselves formulating answers for yesterday's theoretical problems. At the same time the researchers and clinicians who need better research or clinical designs and technologies must also study a range of application literature to find the precedents, the models, the techniques, and the substantiating data for the work area under study.

Both activities are intensive and call for considerable skill at the analysis and integration levels. The analyses are often rendered more difficult by work schedules that allow limited time for reading and integrating and by access problems that may not permit the worker to know about critical information.

Aside from these work-a-day problems of information processing there are the challenging issues of interpretation and judgment. Child language is an interdisciplinary field of study. Few child language specialists can manage to be knowledgeable about all of the basic disciplines in order to mold them into a comprehensive plan for research or clinical intervention. However, the possibility that individual scientists can intensively study and master a critical topic area is much greater. There is even the excellent possibility that the topic can be given competent theoretical, methodological, and operational attention. If so there is great need for such published statements.

Available reports of research and of theoretical treatments of current knowledge are available in ever increasing volume. There is also an impressive number of workbooks that provide details about materials, lesson plans, writing aims, objectives, and evaluation services. The material that is scarce is the bridging information between the theoretically based research and the actual practical design used to teach the child. The issue holds for both the experimental and the clinical worker.

This volume, *Cognition to Language: Categories, Word Meanings, and Training,* is a prototype of the needed bridging designs. Dr. Rice has capitalized on her background in speech pathology and psycholinguistics to create an authoritative statement for both researchers and clinicians. The topical area is complex but timely and practical. The book essentially explores the role of cognition in language training. In critical respects, the book examines the historical approaches and provides the bases for a close relationship between the acquisition of cognition and language and the means for teaching meanings.

The author explains that the questions implied in the content of the respective chapters grew from her own experience in teaching language. She further explains that the questions had not been answered in previous writings and that as she sought the answers it was necessary to integrate information from a number of sources. The implication from this experience is that clinicians and applied psycholinguists may not find easy answers to the questions they raise. It may indeed be necessary to integrate information to serve the special demands for teaching.

In critical respects this effort reverses the procedure usually followed in language publications. Beginning with the training context, Dr. Rice has sought and refined the means for instruction, and in so doing she has further clarified the language issues involved. In my opinion, this is the reverse of the usual procedure for studying a critical area of language. The common practice is to begin with the basic research on key psycholinguistic issues and use that as a source for generating speculations about teachability. In contrast, Rice has expanded the teachability functions and speculates about further researchability. She has contributed important knowledge to be incorporated in a complete design for first-language instruction. This knowledge involves the specification of one kind of linkage between cognition and language. In the language literature, this linkage is a theoretical issue, but in the context of training it becomes an immediate problem. When the training problem is solved, the findings refine the language issues involved.

I should point out that clinicians, teachers, and other "on line" professionals are likely to find help from the approach and the content that Dr. Rice has developed. Her work provides an important beachhead for interventionists into a critical area of language leading to a comprehensive design for first-language instruction. Furthermore, the data generated by her instructional design raise new questions for further theoretical and basic research.

Richard L. Schiefelbusch, Ph.D.
University Professor, and
Director, Bureau of Child Research
University of Kansas
Lawrence, Kansas

PREFACE

This book began in 1969 when a 6-year-old little boy whom I will call "Stevie" looked at me and asked, "Why you call that red?" He was a child who was developmentally delayed in cognition and communicative skills. The teacher of his special class had asked me, his speech clinician, to teach him the correct use of color terms since he had shown no progress in the classroom activities directed to that goal. Reflecting my training as a behaviorist, I began with careful delineation of the desired response and the associated stimuli: "red" for a small collection of red objects familiar to a young child. After many trials and repeated failures, I decided the reinforcer, verbal praise, was not sufficiently powerful. So I switched to red licorice. Sure enough, he began to say "red" when asked "What color is this?" and rewarded by a small piece of red licorice to eat. The next step was to introduce a contrast for discrimination training, i.e., to ensure that the response "red" was tied to the visual stimuli and not just a matter of "this is what you say after the clinician says something." Relying on the same line of inspiration, I introduced "black" in response to black licorice, again with a small piece of the candy as reinforcer. Once again he quickly learned to say "black." However, when I tried to intermingle red and black, the number of correct responses dropped to chance levels. Both he and I became very frustrated—over hundreds of trials we had each given the task our best effort, but we were obviously getting nowhere. Then, during one session, I picked up a piece of red licorice in yet one more try when Stevie looked at me, pointed to the candy, and said, "Why you call that red?"

I had no ready answer, beyond "because it *is* red." I put the red and black licorice away. It seemed to me that trying to teach Stevie to say "red" was not only pointless but probably futile when he had not grasped the essence of it. We never worked on color names again. Instead, I closely observed his classroom performance in activities where color names were required. Much to my surprise, after a few weeks' interim, Stevie began to master the color names in a spontaneous fashion although the classroom activities were not qualitatively different from those he had failed earlier. Furthermore, when he did learn them, the first few color names were quickly followed by the other ones.

As I observed Stevie's pattern of learning these relatively few words, I began to wonder about some questions: What did he need to know before he could learn the names of colors? He had a number of related skills: he could match colors correctly; he knew and used correctly hundreds of other words, including correct pronounciation; and he wanted to learn. So what was special about color words? It was obvious that the methods of instruction that I had used had not supplied the information that he needed. It was apparently more than a matter of matching a name to a referent (in this case, a particular attribute of objects). Some deeper insight, some cognitive knowledge, was involved that he managed to acquire on his own during the classroom activities. Once he had arrived at this understanding, the linguistic learning seemed to come easily.

I now realize that this book is a culmination of my efforts to answer Stevie's question and the many other related ones that it prompted. His question was not at the front of my consciousness during the decade between our encounter and the work reported here. Indeed, it was submerged in a wave of new information molded by the constraints of formal, logical reasoning. It wasn't until my intellectual search led me back to the acquisition of color terms that I realized I had come full circle. I was once again face-to-face with Stevie's question, but this time there was much more available knowledge to draw upon for an answer.

During the intervening years I had learned that my questions corresponded to those addressed by scholars in the emerging field of developmental psycholinguistics. The issue of the nature of the relationship between children's nonlinguistic knowledge (cognition) and their language acquisition had been the focus of much new and exciting work. I approached the literature from the perspective of one who wishes to identify principles for the remediation of children with language disorders. My questions distilled to one: How does underlying cognition influence language acquisition? I discovered that when this issue is approached from the context of training circumstances, there are two consequences: 1) questions arise that have not appeared in previous writings, and 2) many areas of knowledge that have yet to be integrated in scholarly writings begin to converge.

The content of this book reflects these two consequences. The sequential organization corresponds to a series of questions: Why should we take into account a child's nonlinguistic knowledge when we train language skills (Chapter 1)? How can cognitive and linguistic skills be measured in such a way that a direct link can be observed in the behaviors of a particular child (Chapter 2)? What specific knowledge is amenable to being observed both nonlinguistically and linguistically (Chapter 3)? Does nonlinguistic knowledge facilitate the subsequent mastery of related linguistic forms (in a training situation) (Chapter 4)? My search for answers to these questions led me to information scattered in an unrelated fashion across several different disciplines.

When the training study reported in Chapter 4 was completed, some questions were answered, but other unexpected ones arose. Some aspects of the cognition/language relationship were clarified while other new and more subtle complexities emerged. The clarification was in regard to the facilitative effects of a child's preexisting cognitive knowledge upon his subsequent mastery of linguistic forms. The additional complexities were apparent in the observation that the relationship between cognition and language was not the same for comprehension and production. That is, if one observed only production accuracy, one received an entirely different impression of the relationship than if one also looked at comprehension skills (Chapter 5). An interpretation and explanation of these serendipitous findings led me into yet another body of literature that had not previously been related to the cognition/language issue—the nature of the difference between the production and comprehension modes of responding. Both the developmental psycholinguistic literature and the training literature reported relevant findings. The scope of this work was beginning to stretch the limits of the neat and tidy traditional format for presenting one's findings.

Yet still other questions began to trouble me. The unexpected intricacies were incongruous with the nature of the training tasks. Color terms were the linguistic forms trained. They were selected because it was possible to observe a rather direct link between preexisting cognitive (categorical) knowledge and subsequent linguistic learning. Inherent in this characteristic is their apparent simplicity of training. One can carefully specify many of the dimensions of training when teaching color terms, certainly more so than most other linguistic and nonlinguistic content. This presumption of simplicity is evident in the widespread practice of teaching color terms early in language programming for children having problems, as in the example of Stevie. However, the findings revealed such assumptions to be naive. If what we assume to be a simple training task turns out to be far from easy to understand (as was the case of Stevie), what about more complex word meanings? Do not most of our present language-training practices presume a general "we know enough about it to manage" attitude toward the training of word meanings? Is that assumption valid?

The last section of this book takes up the issue of training word meanings in general. The scope of the content is enlarged far beyond that of a more orthodox presentation, and the form changes from the report of one particular investigation to a mosaic-like presentation of interrelated questions. Nonetheless, the final section is a logical extension of the earlier chapters, a bridge between the relatively narrow confines of training for research purposes and the wide range of considerations evident in the clinical situation. Furthermore, the content of the earlier sections of the book establishes the full context for the final section: the general philosophy of integrating training issues with the developmental psycholinguistic and related literatures; the rationale for looking more closely at how to train word meanings; and the implication of the issues and findings from the study reported here for training word meanings in general.

This book has another uncommon characteristic: it is not a summary of things proved or known to be true. Indeed, the general thrust is that of question generation rather than question resolution. My primary purpose is not to disseminate known or newly-arrived-at information as in a textbook or research monograph. Rather, my intention is to explore how what we know can be rewoven into new patterns—patterns that reflect the real world in such a way that previously unrecognized gaps in our knowledge can be identified and investigated.

Just as the content ranges across academic disciplines, so does the intended audience. While the book is directed to those professionals who have a direct involvement in training children having difficulty acquiring language (such as speech/language pathologists), another audience was also in mind—my academic colleagues in the areas of developmental psycholinguistics, cognitive development, applied behavioral analysis, and children's memory.

There were others in addition to Stevie who contributed to the recognition of questions and guided the intellectual insights and reasoning that form the framework for this book. Three of my professors and colleagues at the University of Kansas have been particularly helpful: Melissa Bowerman, who introduced me to the field of developmental psycholinguistics and the elegance of specificity in one's thought and writing; Ken Ruder, who supported my pursuit of the initial question when others considered it to be a fruitless proposition, and who continues to offer reassurance, feedback, advice, and intellectual stimulation; and Richard Schiefelbusch, who has provided a sense of how it all fits together—theoretical and applied, normative and disordered. By his example, he has also conveyed a sense of professional identity, a recognition of the small group of investigators who pursue an as-yet-unnamed hybrid area of study that combines the area of speech/language pathology and developmental psycholinguistics.

During the time of the study reported in the book, I received financial support provided by DHEW Research Service Award HD07066 from the National Institute of Child Health and Human Development to the Kansas Center for Mental Retardation and Human Development.

COGNITION
TO LANGUAGE

Chapter 1
INTRODUCTION
Why Get Involved with Cognition?

The relationship between nonverbal mental functioning and the use of language has been a matter of considerable interest to philosophers for hundreds of years. More recently, psychologists and linguists have sought to unravel the relationship by means of scientific, empirical inquiries. While researchers and theoreticians have struggled with describing and defining how language and thought are interrelated, those professionals who teach children various communication skills have proceeded on the basis of their own notions of what mental processing relates to what language skills or behaviors, or vice versa. This knowledge is more likely to be intuitive than explicit (comparable to a "naive" or "common-sense" theory of learning, described by Carroll, 1976). To describe such knowledge as intuitive is not to suggest that it is unsystematic or of little significance. On the contrary, each language interventionist[1] may well have a systematic set of underlying assumptions that exerts powerful influence upon the content and procedures of language training. Such notions as "teach basic concepts first" or "children talk about what they know" or "teach the meaning of a word by defining it in terms of other simpler words" reflect some strong underlying assumptions.

Recent theoretical developments and experimental findings have immediate implications for the assumptions and strategies underlying language training, particularly at the earliest stages of acquisition. The time has come for systematic, empirical investigations of how a child's cognitive knowledge and linguistic knowledge interrelate when his[2] task is to learn certain language skills within a structured training experience.

---

[1]The choice of terms to refer to those professionals who provide training or educational experiences for children demonstrating language disorders calls for some clarification. Unfortunately, there is no one term that adequately encompasses the diversity of professional expertise and training contexts that are currently evident in the management of children with language disorders. Throughout this writing, "language interventionist" is the generic term, i.e., any professional (or paraprofessional) who teaches a language-disordered child how to communicate. "Speech clinician" refers to a subset of those who provide language training, i.e., those who have completed a degree in speech and language pathology. While the "official" title of such professionals was recently changed to "speech-language pathologist" ("Report of the Legislative Council," 1977), the traditional and easier to process title of "speech clinician" is the preference of this author, even though the more awkward hyphenated term may be referentially more accurate.

[2]Masculine pronouns are used throughout this volume for clarity and ease of reading. They are not meant to be discriminatory or exclusionary.

This book explores the role of cognition in language training. Several questions are considered: Why should those who provide language training get involved in the unobservable mental phenomena that are the "stuff" of cognition? How can we go about empirical investigation, e.g., *how* do we *measure what* cognitive content is directly tied to *which* linguistic skills? When such problems of operationalization are mastered and the relationship between cognition and language is empirically studied within the context of training, what are the results? Do prior concepts facilitate language acquisition? Does cognitive organization have a different influence upon language acquisition than heretofore recognized? What are the more general implications for language training?

Speech clinicians have traditionally relied upon the literature from other disciplines, such as cognitive psychology, for information about the relationship between mental processing and organization and verbal symbolic communication. However, recent changes in the responsibilities of speech clinicians, coupled with recent developments in the theoretical literature, have led to a realization that a more active involvement in the quest for knowledge is appropriate, that there are questions specific to the concerns of those who are responsible for applying scientific theories and knowledge within a training context. This involvement may appear to be so sudden, unexpected, and pervasive that it may be characterized by some as yet another one of the waves of faddish flirtation with a related discipline that appear to periodically wash over the field of speech pathology. However, I agree with those who argue that this concern for the relationship between cognition, language, and training will lead to fundamental changes in perspective that are not temporary phenomena. The next section traces the historical and theoretical developments that account for this present change in perspective.

HISTORICAL PERSPECTIVE

Two separate and unrelated disciplines experienced profound changes during the early 1960s. These changes converged upon the field of speech pathology with an impact great enough to change its entire focus. The first change with future implications for speech clinicians was in the emerging field of psycholinguistics. Unbeknownst to most speech clinicians, three linguists and three psychologists interested in language were brought together at a summer seminar at Cornell University in 1951 by the Social Science Research Council. This interaction led to a new area of research—"psycholinguistics" (Brown, 1958b, p. x). The scientific study of language as a means of furthering our understanding of mental processes has proved to be overwhelmingly productive for those interested in how children acquire language. Chomsky's (1957, 1965) contributions to this new field inspired an explosion of studies investigating children's language acquisition. He introduced such powerful and provocative notions as:

1 . Human language is creative, "open ended," and rule governed. Behaviorism, as an account of learning, is totally incapable of explaining the creativity inherent in language.
2. There are linguistic universals. The general principles that determine the form of grammatical rules in particular languages are to a considerable degree common to all human languages.
3. The role of the environment is minimal in accounting for how children acquire language. This conclusion is based on two inferences: since all children readily learn a highly complex, formally constrained language system in similar sequences of acquisition and at the same ages, irrespective of environmental differences, that learning must be controlled by biological determinants. Furthermore, the adult speech that children hear is so haphazard, random, and often disfluent and ungrammatical that a child could not make enough sense of it to induce rules of grammar.

Much of the expanding body of child language literature, which has grown to formidable proportions within the past 10 years, is in response to these claims of Chomsky's. There has been a marked shift in focus of inquiry during this time, however. The earlier studies concentrated primarily on Chomsky's notions of formal syntactic configurations and operations. Later studies reflect a reaction to Chomsky's nativist position. A growing group of psycholinguists have argued that the formal structure of language is not totally distinct from cognitive organization, and that the acquisition of syntax cannot be adequately explained without reference to the meanings children intend to express. Questions regarding the contributions of underlying cognitive organization, intentions, and meanings in early language acquisition have dominated the psycholinguistic literature for the past 5 years (see Bowerman, 1976, 1978b, for excellent reviews).

The second change during the early 1960s with implications for speech clinicians was in the field of special education. The concern for civil rights for minority groups that generated profound social and political upheavals in the United States during the 1960s led to an increased awareness of the rights of handicapped adults and children. The adequacy, appropriateness, and availability of treatment and rehabilitation for even the most severely and multiply handicapped individuals became a matter of general concern. During the early 1960s attention was focused on categorical conditions such as mental retardation. Various advocates emerged, such as photo-journalists, organizations of parents, professional groups, and concerned politicians. The result was federal legislation to provide funds for the education of professionals to rehabilitate handicapped children, research monies to explore improved methods of prevention and treatment, and financial support for direct services.

The trend during the 1970s has been to emphasize the commonalities among disabilities, with less interest in defining particular categories and more attention to merging training and service programs with similar goals. The interdisciplinary team has progressed from a desirable model of service to a functional reality. The increased advocacy efforts for appropriate treatment programs for handicapped children during the 1970s culminated in the passage of the Education for All Handicapped Children Act (PL 94-142) in 1975. This legislation, frequently referred to as the "Bill of Rights for the Handicapped," guarantees the right of all handicapped children to receive a free appropriate public education, meaning special education and related services that are provided in conformity with an individualized education program (IEP). As of September 1, 1978, every public education agency must now make available a free appropriate public education to all children identified as handicapped and eligible for service under federal and state law. The majority of these handicapped children will demonstrate communication disorders requiring the services of a speech clinician.

How have these changes in other fields influenced speech clinicians? The growing involvement of speech clinicians with severely handicapped children during the 1960s served as a pivotal point for changes in perspective that have eventually amounted to a complete restructuring of the field of speech pathology. The work with mentally retarded children was a central focus of much of the change. Prior to the 1960s, the research in speech and language of the retarded focused upon the incidence of impairments and the relation of such impairments to organicity, a perspective that reflects the medical model that dominated speech pathology at that time. The prevailing assumption was that, since the underlying organicity was irreversible, the likelihood of effecting meaningful changes in social or cognitive behaviors, such as verbal communication, was very limited. However, the application of behavior modification technology to the training of mentally retarded children and adults in the early and mid 1960s demonstrated that the verbal behavior of retarded persons could be modified. The possibilities inherent in such a discovery generated a great deal of excitement and optimism among some scientists and educators, which in turn contributed to the growing number of advocates for increased services to the handicapped.

After 10 years of rapid change, during which "language" and "multiply handicapped" have become the catchwords for a new approach to clinical services, what is the current status of speech pathology? It appears that nothing less than a fundamental restructuring of the discipline has occurred.[3] Siegel and Spradlin (1978) suggest that language has replaced articulation as the central focus for the academic curriculum and clinical preparation of speech clinicians. Psycholinguistics and language development will not only serve as the central core for academic preparation in the future but will also provide the basis for communicating across related disciplines (pp. 363-364).

This assimilation of psycholinguistics and language development presents a powerful set of new challenges to language interventionists, not the least of which is the immediate and sometimes overwhelming responsibility to be knowledgeable of the burgeoning body of literature in such fields as psycholinguistics, and developmental and cognitive psychology. Our increasing appreciation for alternative theoretical accounts of language acquisition has combined with our clinical observations and training experiments to challenge some of the initial postulates of language training. The nature of the relationship between cognition and language and its significance for language-training programs are central issues in important matters of current debate.

Two differing rationales have emerged in the language-training literature that reflect different perspectives on the language/cognition/training relationship. The initial dominant influence was that of the behaviorist theoretical position. Indeed, the power of the operant training techniques was responsible for establishing the important fact that mentally retarded children could be taught functional communication skills. Radical behaviorism has traditionally dismissed concepts of inferred mental processing as unobservable and therefore inaccessible and untrainable. The emphasis is upon the manner in which the environment affects behavior. The basic premise is that logically defined sequences of training can develop functional communication for a child, irrespective of how well the training content matches his prior nonverbal concepts. It is assumed that any specific word labels can be trained at any time, in any order, if the procedures are sufficiently powerful. Language-training programs developed by Guess, Sailor, and Baer (1974) and Gray and Ryan (1973) exemplify this position. (See Harris, 1975, for a review of the literature

---

[3]Confirmation of the emerging significance of language is evident in the recent change of the name of the dominant professional organization, from the American Speech and Hearing Association to the American-Speech-Language-Hearing Association ("Report of the Legislative Council," 1979).

reporting the use of operant conditioning techniques for teaching language to nonverbal children.)

The behaviorist approach to language training was immediately challenged by another group of speech clinicians inspired by psycholinguistic writings, including Chomsky's reply (1959) to Skinner's (1957) account of language behavior. The behavioral training programs were characterized as limited in scope, developing only topographical language responses, instead of the spontaneous, creative, rule-governed, contextually sensitive language responses that characterized the verbal communication of young normal children. Miller and Yoder (1974), Bricker and Bricker (1974), and MacDonald and Blott (1974) were among the earliest advocates of what has been described as a "psycholinguistic" or "developmental" approach to language training. Among the distinguishing features of such an approach are:

1 . A synthesis of psycholinguistic and behavioral models: the former to determine content and a model for underlying linguistic processes, and the latter to provide instructional procedures.
2. Adherence to the normal sequence of language development as the most effective content sequence for language-training programs.
3. Training within an appropriate communicative context to ensure "meaningfulness."
4. Training content selected so as to facilitate underlying linguistic processing. For example, particular items are selected as exemplars of linguistic rules that the child can infer and assimilate into his own linguistic structures.
5. The child's underlying concepts provide the basis for early language acquisition; language development is intimately tied to nonlinguistic representational abilities. Training begins with the behaviors that the child already exhibits, since these presumably reflect cognitive readiness for linguistic marking or representation.

A primary distinction between the behaviorist and developmental approaches to language training is the relative importance attributed to nonlinguistic cognitive processes and structures. The behaviorists simply do not address such notions. For example, in Harris's (1975) review and discussion of the language-training literature, she never mentions any aspects of meaning or underlying cognition as factors to be considered in teaching a child functional language skills. The developmentalists argue that such conceptual organization is of central significance; indeed, that it accounts for the meaningful use of appropriate novel utterances across different contexts.

A feature common to language programs, developed by either behaviorists or developmental adherents, is the use of applied behavior analysis procedures as the most efficient and appropriate means of establishing changes in communicative behaviors. However, even this tenet is showing erosion from the influence of those who regard cognition as important to language acquisition. Developmental psycholinguists have for some time maintained that a normal child's language development cannot be accounted for by differential feedback from others in his environment (see Bowerman, 1976, pp. 169–173). What is new are recent statements by those directly involved in language programming that reveal a change in their perspective. For example, Schiefelbusch (1978a, p. 6) concludes that "applied behavior analysis (behavioral learning theory) in its current state of technical development does not serve as a complete system for language instruction." He recommends an amalgam of features of naive (natural, common sense) learning theory, behavioral learning theory, and cognitive learning theory as a basis for developing language programming. Recent writing by such language programmers as Waryas and Stremel-Campbell (1978) indicate a more eclectic approach to training procedures and techniques than is evident in earlier writings (Stremel and Waryas, 1974).

To summarize, speech clinicians have found themselves riding currents of change during the past 15 years. The type of clients to be served has changed to embrace an increasing proportion of younger children who in turn demonstrate a wider range of communication difficulties. The types of programming being regarded as appropriate are changing to include ever-widening considerations of all parameters of communicative performance. The theoretical issues and models involved are new to speech clinicians and changing rapidly. In light of such rapid developments, practicing clinicians must keep abreast of the relevant theoretical literature in order to judge the appropriateness of various tests, assessment procedures, and language-training materials. Not only is the relevant literature rapidly broadening in scope, but it is also subdividing into intricate webs of complexity.

The nature of the relationship between cognition and language acquisition is a particularly complex issue. Its subtle convolutions have fascinated philosophers and psychologists for centuries. There was a considerable degree of comfort in the earlier position that speech clinicians were only responsible for observable communication behaviors; unobservables, such as thinking processes and mental organization, were in the province of cognitive and developmental psychologists. But the management of children with language disorders has pulled speech clinicians inexorably into a consideration of how what a child knows relates to what he can communicate. Indeed, some authors (Morehead and Ingram, 1976; Leonard, 1978, 1979) propose that children with language disorders may be cognitively disordered, with underlying specific deficits in mental representation abilities that are manifest in language difficulties, along with other problems in symbol manipulation.

The nature of the influence of cognition upon language acquisition has become a matter of immediate relevance for language intervention-ists. It affects what is taught in language-training programs, how it is taught, and our conception of the nature of the problem. It is time for a careful consideration of some of the issues involved in the relationship be-tween cognition and language; time to formalize some of the intuitive clinical knowledge that has been guiding language training.

The relevant theoretical literature is also in a time of transition with new explanations and models appearing frequently, each with what seems to be a relatively short period of scientific consideration before another alternative is proposed that diverts attention to itself. While such fluidity generates intellectual interest and excitement, it also makes it difficult to keep abreast of developments, especially when one is a practicing clinician with many demands on one's time. It is sometimes difficult to justify a weighty and time-consuming consideration of theoretical literature that may or may not directly relate to clinical issues when there is plenty of reading to be done that does have immediate significance. However, this happens to be an occasion where a look at some of the theoretical contro-versies has a direct bearing on language-training issues. A selected review of one of the relevant theoretical issues is presented in the following sec-tion.

THEORETICAL PERSPECTIVE

The literature concerning the relationship between the acquisition of lan-guage and cognitive development is extensive (even when only the last 20 years are considered), ranging across many disciplines and many topics. Only one issue is discussed here—the question of whether or not early lan-guage development is a matter of the child's learning to map language skills onto preexisting nonlinguistic cognitive structures, meanings, or in-tentions. This issue was selected because it is a hypothesis that has recently received wide acceptance among psycholinguists. It has in turn been directly applied to language programming, remains a matter of consider-able debate among theoreticians, and is wide open for empirical investiga-tion. A further, although incidental, reason for focusing on the role of underlying cognitive structures, meanings, and intentions is that this aspect of cognitive development is generally less familiar to speech clinicians than other cognitive processes that influence language development, such as short- and long-term memory span, sequencing abilities, production span, and auditory processes, all of which have received scientific scrutiny in the speech pathology literature almost entirely in connection with motor/phonological performance. (For a psycholinguistic perspective, see Cromer, 1976a, pp. 311–316 for a brief review, and Cromer, 1976b, pp. 316–334 for a more detailed look at related perceptual processing strategies.)

The debate concerning the significance of underlying cognition for language acquisition has a long and interesting history (see Cromer, 1974, for an excellent review). This discussion picks up the controversy in the mid 1960s. The various theoretical positions presented below differ with respect to the relative significance attributed to cognition in accounting for early language acquisition. The positions can be roughly characterized as: language and cognition are independent of one another in both source and development; language development is dependent upon prior cognitive development (in both a "strong" and a "weak" form); language and cognition share a common source and develop along parallel lines; language development and cognitive development interact with each other; and cognition is dependent upon language.

Language and Cognition Independent of Each Other

The first position, that asserting an independence of language and cognition, is essentially what Chomsky (1957) argued (allowing for some oversimplification of Chomsky's rather complex theoretical formulations). The formal structure of language is independent of cognition. The child's ability to acquire the formal structures is attributed to species-specific innate linguistic processing mechanisms that are unique and distinct from other more general intellectual processes.

Language Development Dependent upon Cognitive Development

Many students of child language found the notion of an innate linguistic processing mechanism, separate from other intellectual abilities and subject to some kind of "activation" instead of principles of learning, difficult to accept. Yet another of Chomsky's tenets, that of commonalities in linguistic acquisition across children and across languages, was receiving increasing empirical support, particularly in terms of striking similarities in the meanings expressed in the earliest utterances. If these common features were not attributable to innate linguistic mechanisms, there had to be another factor common to all children. Many investigators began to link the universality of expressed meanings to universally acquired cognitive concepts. Piaget's theory of cognitive development appeared to be a particularly suitable alternative to a "language acquisition device." In what has since been referred to as the "strong cognition hypothesis," language acquisition was regarded as a matter of the child's figuring out which linguistic devices to use to express what he already knew nonlinguistically. Within such a position, concepts are regarded as prerequisite for subsequent language skills. Language builds on a cognitive base.

One of the earliest representatives of this position was Sinclair-de Zwart (1971, 1973), who has served as a leading interpreter of Piaget's theory. She has argued that the child's initial construction of grammar is directly linked to his earlier sensorimotor learning, which is in turn based upon his actions on the environment. In another widely cited article, Macnamara (1972) asserted that children first learn meanings and then later work out the correspondences between meanings and linguistic expression. Meaning is used to decipher language. Slobin (1973) concurred that cognitive development was worked out independently of language, and was a prerequisite for the development of grammar; the child's problem was that of finding a means to express what he already knew. A number of writings appeared with a shared thesis—that cognition accounted for linguistic meanings. For example, Bloom (1973) asserted that object permanence is a prerequisite for stable word meanings; both Clark (1973, 1977) and Nelson (1974, 1977, 1978) argued that it is the child's a priori conceptual knowledge that determines his first meanings for words; Brown (1973, p. 198) concluded that Stage I meanings are an extension of sensorimotor intelligence; Bates (1976) advocated a cognitive basis for sociocommunicative events, implying that physical-cognitive behaviors were prerequisite to sociocommunicative behaviors.

The strong cognition hypothesis is supported by a number of empirical findings. Bowerman (1978b, pp. 103–105) summarizes the evidence as follows:

1. "New forms and old functions; old forms and new functions." Slobin (1973, pp. 184–185) first observed that children will use a new form to express a meaning or function that has previously been expressed with a simpler form, and vice versa. The child is aware of certain concepts before he marks them in his speech.
2. "Use of a form over a non-adultlike semantic range." The child's own concepts seem to direct his use of words, not the way he has heard the words used by adults.
3. "Nonlinguistic strategies for the interpretation of language." Children's early comprehension of various language forms reveals systematic errors that indicate strategies based upon the child's knowl-

edge of the nature of things in the real world (cf. Cromer's reviews of evidence for this position, 1974, pp. 199–235; 1976a, pp. 291–316).

However, there has been growing dissatisfaction with the strong cognition hypothesis. The first reservations concerned the claim that cognition accounted for all of language. Slobin (1973) made it clear that "cognitive development and linguistic development do not run off in unison. The child must find linguistic means to express his intentions" (pp. 182–183).[4] Cognition could account for meanings, but the child also had to address certain specifically linguistic skills in order to figure out how to map meanings into language. This position was more fully developed by Cromer (1974, 1976a), who dubbed it the "weak form of the cognition hypothesis." Bowerman (1976, pp. 140–141) has also challenged the idea of direct mapping of cognition into language in her criticism of Macnamara (1972). She felt that the strong cognition hypothesis was unable to account for how children get from their understanding of sentences in concrete situations to their correct production of more abstract relational categories. She argued that sensorimotor intelligence does not directly translate into linguistic categories.

Cromer (1974, pp. 235–245; 1976a, pp. 316–325) and Bowerman (1978b, pp. 105–107) cite a number of examples of linguistic phenomena not accounted for by cognition alone. The evidence that is most inconsistent with the strong cognitive hypothesis is the observation that children who have already acquired a linguistic means of encoding a particular meaning subsequently learn other more complicated linguistic devices for expressing the same meaning. These advances in linguistic skill do not depend on changes in underlying cognition. Another example offered by Bowerman (1978b, p. 106) is the child's mastery of formal linguistic devices that are not linked to meaning at all, such as McCawley's (1974) example of "Put the hat on," "Put it on," and "Put on the hat" as grammatically acceptable whereas "Put on it" is not. Such advances in linguistic sophistication are not explained by changes in meaning or underlying cognitive developments. Instead, specific linguistic abilities appear to be involved. This conclusion carries an implicit recognition of biologically

---

[4]It is necessary to specify how terms such as *meanings* and *intentions* will be used in this discussion. As Dore (1975, p. 36) has pointed out, in the psycholinguistic literature the term *intention* has been used to refer to two aspects of meaning: underlying semantic categories (Schlesinger, 1971, p. 66) and the pragmatic functions of language (requests, comments, denials, etc.). The former corresponds to the "what" of communication whereas the latter refers to the "why." Slobin's (1973) use of *intentions* is in the context of semantic categories. In the following discussion the use of the term *intention* is limited to the pragmatic functions, the "why" of communication, and the term *meanings* refers to the "what," e.g., categories of semantic relations, semantic information encoded in lexical items.

based linguistic competencies, an implication that has been explicitly acknowledged and supported in recent work by Cromer (1979).

Language and Cognition Share a Common Source

Another modification of the strong cognition hypothesis has been directed toward the claim that particular cognitive achievements are prerequisites for particular language developments. The work of Bates (1976) and her colleagues (1977a, 1977b) illustrates the shift in theoretical explanation. Bates's earlier investigations were directed to establishing cognitive and social prerequisites to communication developments. The cognitive prerequisites were defined in terms of particular cognitive tasks that measured cognitive structures defined by Piaget. Bates (1976) concluded that the cognitive prerequisite for preverbal, intentional communication is sensorimotor Stage 5, the invention of new means to familiar ends. However, in a following paper, Bates et al. (1977a) modified their earlier theoretical position on the basis of a slightly different interpretation of Piaget's theory and additional evidence. The notion that "performance on cognitive tasks should precede performance on linguistic tasks appropriate to the same cognitive level" (1977a, p. 262) was rejected on both theoretical and empirical grounds. It was dismissed as a misreading of Piaget's position, and furthermore it was not supported by a growing body of evidence collected by Bates and her colleagues and other investigators. While one-way influence was not evident, the correlations found between cognitive behaviors and language behaviors suggested some kind of connection. Bates et al. (1977a) proposed a "homologue" model for the interdependence of cognition and communication, in which both derive from a common, deeper underlying system of cognitive operations and structures that is biased toward neither. Such a model, argues Bates and her fellow workers, is a more accurate interpretation of Piaget's theory than the earlier, more literal model of cognitive behaviors as a direct prerequisite for language behaviors.

Bates et al. (1977b) have since refined the notion of underlying common cognitive structure to differentiate "local homologies," or specific underlying schemes that define a particular domain, from "deep homologies," or general operative schemes that cut across sensorimotor developments in various domains (pp. 38–39). They note that the "local homology" or "skill-specific" interpretation of cognitive development can be regarded as "neo-Piagetian," i.e., not entirely consistent with the orthodox Piagetian view (p. 39). They conclude that "the relationship between language and cognitive development is one of local, specific homologies between domains, rather than a single, homogeneous shared structural base" (abstract).

Up to this point in the discussion, two major revisions of the strong cognition hypothesis (language development depends on prior cognitive development) have been described. The "weak cognition hypothesis" allows that cognition accounts for meanings, but not for the way those meanings are mapped into linguistic forms. The second modification addresses the nature of the cognitive organization underlying utterances. The "local homologies model" proposes that cognitive performances and language achievements share a common source, i.e., specific underlying cognitive schemes.

Language and Cognition Interact

Another challenge to the strong cognition hypothesis has focused on the claim that concepts account for meaning. Some investigators have suggested that a child's experience with language may introduce him to certain concepts. It is important to note that the issue here is not whether language *ever* plays a role in introducing concepts but instead at what level of language acquisition is the influence apparent. Even those who advocate the strong cognition hypothesis acknowledge that at some point in the child's language development words begin to serve as a means of acquiring concepts. However, some investigators argue that the influence of language on concepts is apparent from the very beginning of language acquisition.

Schlesinger (1974, 1977b) proposed an "interactionist position" characterized by a two-way influence of cognition on language and vice versa. Blank (1974) had also argued that very early on children use language to determine meanings, especially for those meanings not accessible visually, e.g., meanings of "how" and "why." Wells (1974) has posited that linguistic input affects the child's earliest constructs. Bowerman (1976, pp. 135–136) presented evidence from her daughters' utterances consistent with the notion that language can serve to influence conceptual development. Her position is that while language can "get a concept started," the concepts are the child's own invention (not directed solely by linguistic input), reflecting his own system of creating equivalences that may be constrained by certain "universally shared categorizational propensities" (1977b, p. 26). Further evidence in support of the interactionist position is reported by Gruendel (1977) and Braunwald (1978).

Cognition Depends on Language

Schlesinger (in preparation) has recently moved a step further in his criticism of the cognition-first position. He postulates that concepts are formed as a concomitant of learning words. He argues that "our perceptual world has what may be called texture, which constrains but does not fully determine the formation of concepts...texture suggests concepts; it does not create them...." A child's first nonlinguistic conceptual groupings are "evanescent," returning readily to their natural textural bundles. The child "singles out objects, actions, and properties from reality, but for the results to be permanent, they must be firmly anchored to relatively invariant linguistic responses." This notion of words as an anchor for concepts is a full departure from the Piagetian claim that language is rooted in underlying cognitive operations and structures.

To conclude, a number of different theoretical positions have recently been proposed to account for the relationship of cognitive development and language acquisition at the earliest stages of language development. Each theory seems to explain some of the phenomena of language acquisition, but none appears to account for all of the complexities that are emerging from new observations of children's language skills and performances. The relationship between nonlinguistic meanings and their representation in linguistic forms continues to be an issue of considerable interest to current investigators of child language.

IMPLICATIONS FOR LANGUAGE INTERVENTIONISTS

The issues raised in the theoretical work have often been implicit assumptions in language-training content and procedures. There has been a recent trend to build language-training programs on an explicit psycholinguistic theoretical base.

The earlier programs designed to teach language skills were consistent with the notion that language and cognition are independent. They were addressed only to verbal communication behaviors; conceptual development was virtually ignored. However, this circumstance could more accurately be described as a reflection of the behaviorist influence than that of the psycholinguistic position of Chomsky.

The strong cognitive hypothesis has been evident in recently developed language programs. The hypothesis that conceptual learning precedes and serves as a prerequisite for language acquisition has led to language programs that include considerations of cognitive development. Behavioral evidence of related cognitive structures may be regarded as a prerequisite for initiating training on a particular structure. For example, Stremel and Waryas (1974) state that "a child is not introduced to negation training until he has given some indication of denial or rejection, such as a head shake in response to some event" (p. 99). If such cognitive prerequisites are not evident in the child's behaviors, some authors (Bricker and Bricker, 1974, pp. 447–449; Miller and Yoder, 1974, p. 507; MacDonald, 1976; Bloom and Lahey, 1978, pp. 395–415; Leonard, 1978,

p. 92) suggest that the training of certain nonverbal concepts presumed to relate directly to early language development, such as object permanence and the categorization of objects by actions, may be necessary before initiating verbal communication training. In these programs the nonverbal conceptual training is regarded as a secondary, or supplemental, but necessary preliminary to verbal training, particularly for such populations as mentally retarded children. Other remediation programs give a greater emphasis to the development of more general intellectual processes as essential for language programming, e.g., Cooper, Moodley, and Reynell (1978). The goal of such language-training programs is intellectual as well as verbal development.

None of the subsequent modifications of and counterproposals to the strong form of the cognition hypothesis has yet been cited as a rationale for language-training programs. This is undoubtedly a function of the time lag involved between an author's initial consideration of a theoretical position and its operationalization into a working program design. However, many of the theoretical points are implicit in commonly used training techniques and procedures. For example, the notion that meaning does not account for all of language acquisition is inherent in the frequent use of rote teaching techniques that have no tie to meaning. One example is the use of imitation and repetition, combined with reinforcement, without contextual cues, for teaching grammatical constructions that are difficult to depict, such as the perfect verb tenses.

Clinicians have long acted on the assumption that words can introduce concepts. A common activity is to teach a child to name a particular referent (such as a cup) and then to show the child referents with slight variations (slightly different cups) and require the same verbal name for each referent. It is generally assumed that by naming each of the items with the same name the child now "knows" that they are equivalent, even if he did not know at the beginning of the activity. Bloom and Lahey (1978, p. 406) have stated this assumption clearly: "In the course of intervention, a child will be helped to acquire different underlying concepts as new words are presented in appropriate contexts." Miller and Yoder (1974, p. 520) have presumed such a direction of influence in regard to the relational meanings between words and their underlying cognitive underpinnings: "By pairing explicit environmental experiences with their linguistic referent, the child will note these relations and begin to express them." They have reported that they taught the semantic relations of recurrence, nonexistence, and disappearance by tying a word to appropriate contexts.

The only available means of determining the merit of such alleged "principles" as "train cognitive prerequisites first" has been each clinician's intuitive and professional judgment, combined with an assessment of the reasonableness of the theoretical rationale. No studies have been reported in the language-training literature that have directly investigated the training performance of children at the earliest stages of language acquisition who do or do not indicate the attainment of prior concepts.

It is the purpose of this book to present evidence bearing on the relationship between cognition and language acquisition in training circumstances. The question addresses the strong form of the cognition hypothesis: do prior nonlinguistic concepts facilitate subsequent language acquisition? Before this question can be investigated, there is the matter of operationalizing the link between nonlinguistic concepts and particular linguistic performances. A discussion of measurement considerations appears in Chapter 2. The *how* to measure leads to the question of *what* to measure, and *what* to train. The acquisition of word meanings provides an appropriate linguistic domain for the purposes of the investigation. One particular area of word meanings, that of color terms, is especially suitable. The special features of color term acquisition are described in Chapter 3. An experimental training study that compared the language performance of children who demonstrated prior nonlinguistic concepts (that were linked to the linguistic form to be trained) with those who did not have such prior concepts is reported in Chapter 4. Some interesting evidence of an interaction among cognitive organization and the production and comprehension of color terms is explored in Chapter 5. In Chapter 6 different factors involved in the training of word meanings are examined. Various theoretical issues in the psycholinguistic literature are related to the clinical questions of what vocabulary items to teach, how to teach word meaning, and how to assess word meaning.

Chapter 2
CATEGORIZATION UNDERLYING LANGUAGE
Measurement Considerations

Suppose we want to conduct our language training according to the principle that "nonlinguistic cognitive achievements are necessary precursors to linguistic acquisition for children at the earliest stages of language development." First, we would be dealing with children who were very young or had a severe disorder, or both, since these are the children who would be at the earliest stages of acquisition. We would be interested in identifying a particular linguistic skill that they did not demonstrate in their linguistic repertoire that could serve as a target behavior for training. Next, we would need to determine a nonlinguistic concept that is directly related to that linguistic skill, one that can be measured for its presence or absence. Following the initial measurement of linguistic and conceptual behaviors to determine a baseline for training, the actual training could begin. It would be necessary to train to some level or criterion or goal, and use corresponding measurements to conclude that the goal had been reached. It would also be desirable to be able to demonstrate that the changes in linguistic performance were the result of the intervention procedures, not a consequence of fortuitous coincidence with other effects, such as a change in the parents' behaviors, or the work of another teacher, or "maturation." If we wanted to establish that the changes in language performance were directly tied to underlying conceptual functioning, we could compare the performance of two groups of children, those demonstrating conceptual attainments before training and those without such knowledge. The children would have to be matched for their need of training for a particular linguistic skill, and receive the same training. It would also be appropriate to match the children for other factors related to training performance, such as age, intellectual abilities, related problems (if any), and prior training experiences.

At first glance the situation appears to be analogous to several studies reported in the Piagetian literature. A number of investigators have looked at how the acquisition of one nonlinguistic concept affects the acquisition of other nonlinguistic concepts. The studies have focused on acquisition within a training situation.

17

COMPARISON OF NONLINGUISTIC
TO OTHER NONLINGUISTIC CONCEPTS

A central tenet of Piaget's theory of intellectual development is that the child's acquisition of knowledge is based upon underlying self-discovered cognitive operations that become progressively more abstract with further development. The most important factor in shaping intellectual development is the child's self-regulation, referred to as "equilibration." The child's cognitive learning is based upon his interactions with the world and his internal interpretations and reconstructions of those experiences. The child's physical experiences, per se, are not the determinants of "meaningful" knowledge; his internal experiences, his logical-mathematical inductions, are the basis for his "knowing." The child's self-regulated learning proceeds through a series of natural stages, with later learning dependent on the mastery of earlier, simpler kinds of knowledge. A corollary of this position is that certain knowledge cannot be taught to a child until he has attained the prerequisite level of internal cognitive organization: "Learning is subordinated to development and not vice versa" (Piaget, 1964, p. 18). While he may be taught to perform certain behaviors, these behaviors will be superficial in nature and lacking in real understanding. Indeed, Piaget asserts that "teaching children concepts that they have not acquired in their spontaneous development... is completely useless" (1970, p. 30).[1]

The claim that training is "useless" unless combined with a particular state of conceptual readiness has inspired a series of experiments by other investigators to test the hypothesis that children's concept learning is constrained by their stage of cognitive development. Almost all of these experiments have focused on conservation learning, one of the mental operations described by Piaget. The notion of conservation refers to the child's ability to recognize that the weight, volume, number, or continuous quantity of objects or substances remains the same when the stimulus properties are transformed, such as by pouring liquid from a short, wide container to a tall, thin one, or by manipulating a ball of clay into different shapes (Ginsburg and Opper, 1969).

One example representing a typical design for the studies that have investigated the influence of prior cognitive knowledge on subsequent training is that reported by Curcio et al. (1972). They looked at the rela-

---

[1]It is important to note that Piaget does not assert that all efforts to teach are useless, that children should be left entirely to their own devices in acquiring knowledge. He argues that the child will benefit from adult-directed education "only if he is in a state where he can understand this information" (1964, p. 13). Given this context, Piaget's theory can be regarded as "interactive."

tionship between the attainment of compensation knowledge and the subsequent training of conservation. Piaget had observed that compensation precedes and is a prerequisite for conservation. Compensation was defined as "the recognition that material undergoing a perceptual transformation in one dimension is accompanied by a specific change in another dimension" (Curcio et al., 1972, p. 259). For example, when liquid is poured from a short, wide container to a tall, thin one, the child who can compensate recognizes that the height of the liquid will be greater in the tall, thin container; the child who conserves will also recognize that the amount of water remains the same.

Curcio et al. (1972) used the same procedures to train a group of compensators and a group of noncompensators on a continuous quantity (liquid) conservation task, with a control group paired with each of the experimental groups. Posttests indicated significant conservation gains among trained compensators relative to either untrained compensators or trained noncompensators. The authors concluded that the general import of the findings was "that preexisting skills systematically interact with experiential factors to produce cognitive change" (Curcio et al., 1972, p. 264).

The conclusion of Curcio et al. (1972) that their findings supported Piaget's hypothesis is consistent with the conclusions reported by many other investigators. However, this judgment of support of Piaget is far from unanimous and is attracting a growing chorus of criticism. Brainerd (1976) repeated the Curcio et al. (1972) study with a different training procedure. He found that his experimental subjects' knowledge of compensation did not predict their responsiveness to the training procedures. He concluded that the presence of a compensation-trainability relationship may depend on the training procedure used: "When the procedure is either based on the compensation rule or imparts information that is more easily understood by compensators, compensation may be an excellent predictor of learning. But when the training procedure is neither directly based on compensation nor imparts compensation-related information, conservation learning may be independent of compensation knowledge" (Brainerd, 1976, p. 4).

Brainerd's (1976) observation raises an issue of immediate import to those investigators dealing with the problem of how to measure concepts that are said to underlie language skills for the purpose of serving as a baseline for language training. If the training procedures are directed to the preexisting conceptual performance, an interaction may be observed that would not have been present with other, nonbiased training procedures. Brainerd (1977a, 1977b) has cast this criticism in broader terms, arguing that it is a weakness of all the conservation experiments:

In all of the conservation experiments, the only evidence about subjects' stages of cognitive development has come from scores on conservation tests. The only evidence that learning has occurred has come from scores on the same tests. Therefore, to say that children learn more about conservation than others because they are at more advanced stages of cognitive development is not an explanation at all. It is a circular statement masquerading as an explanation'' (1977a, p. 936).

Brainerd's recognition of these problems with the measurement and training of behaviors presumed to represent cognitive learning is central to his criticism of Piaget's stage theory of cognitive development. He raises two very important points:

1. Performances on the various concept tests are dependent variables. However, age-related changes in performance on these tests are interpreted by Piaget as evidence for underlying cognitive structures. The test scores (behavioral performances) have served as both phenomena to be explained and explanations of cognitive development (Brainerd, 1977a, p. 936).

2. Concepts associated with one stage are usually defined entirely in terms of the other, i.e., the later-appearing concept contains the earlier-appearing one plus some other things. Given such a state of affairs, the prediction that children who demonstrate prior cognitive acquisition, i.e., subjects who pass some pretest items, train more easily than children without such knowledge reduces to the less profound prediction that children who start with partial knowledge of the task to be trained will train faster than children with no knowledge. Such an observation is as acceptable to most learning theories as it is to Piagetian theory (Brainerd, 1977b, pp. 97–100).

Let's return to the problem of nonlinguistic concepts and the training of related language skills. Since the hypothesis that underlying cognitive acquisition accounts for early language development is rooted in Piagetian theory, a first glance at the Piagetian experiments in other cognitive domains, such as conservation, suggests that their methodologies might be useful for investigations of language training. An initial conclusion that emerges from a review of this literature is that one of Piaget's cardinal premises, that of cognitive prerequisites for learning, is far from confirmed by this line of experimentation. Furthermore, the logical deficiencies evident in the designs of the experiments hinge on questions of measurement—measurement of the cognitive skills before training and measurement of the performance on training tasks. The problem is that the one is defined in terms of the other, that is, the concept to be achieved at the conclusion of training is the concept apparent at the beginning of training plus some additional knowledge.

Will this confounding of pre- and posttraining concepts be a problem for the investigations of the effects of underlying cognitive knowledge on subsequent language training? A careful consideration of what is involved in a study of language training indicates that the problems involved in comparing one nonlinguistic concept to another nonlinguistic concept do not apply when nonlinguistic concepts are compared to linguistic concepts. Instead, there is a different and no less challenging difficulty in operationalizing the cognition-language question.

COMPARISON OF NONVERBAL AND VERBAL CONCEPTS

When the question is moved to the linguistic domain there are some additional complexities. The experimental problem unique to the linguistic domain is in finding a means of measuring a prior concept in a nonverbal domain that has immediate links to a particular linguistic competency. It is this bridge between cognition and language that has been missing in the language programs based upon the cognition hypothesis. How does one know when a child has a "prior concept"? How does one know that the mastery of a given concept, such as "object permanence," is directly linked to a particular linguistic competence in a prerequisite relationship?

Answers to these questions may vary according to the nature of the many different kinds of constructs to which the term *concept* has been applied in the context of cognition underlying language. Two types of relevant cognitive processing have been differentiated (Cromer, 1976a; Bowerman, 1978b): a superficial level of thoughts, intentions, and meanings, and a deeper level of cognitive structures. The two levels present different problems for answering the questions of measurement. The "superficial" level is obviously relevant for language, since it is defined specifically in terms of what one must know to use language appropriately, but how can it be measured? The problem with the deeper level is exactly the reverse, i.e., we can measure it, but we don't know if it's really relevant or a prerequisite for language.

Intentions and Meanings Underlying Language

Much of the recent literature has addressed the first level of underlying cognition, the cognitive processing underlying intentions or meanings. The diversity of such proposed "cognitions" can be illustrated by a few examples:

1. Causal intentions for making verbal utterances, such as requests versus comments, before the child has acquired his first words (Bates, 1976)
2. Meanings underlying the productive use of first words that are unlike the corresponding adult semantic category, e.g., unadultlike meanings for the words "off" and "hi" (Bowerman, 1976, pp. 135–136), and a number of other words (Clark, 1973)
3. The relational categories of agent, action, object, negation, and so forth, underlying children's first word combinations (Bloom, 1970; Schlesinger, 1971; Bowerman, 1973; Brown, 1973, pp. 111–146; and Braine, 1976, provide detailed discussion of the notions involved in such categories.)
4. Time relationships underlying verb tenses and lexical items expressing temporal notions, such as "current relevance" or "relevance from the past," discussed in detail by Cromer (1976a, pp. 299–304).

The question that is difficult to answer with regard to these proposed cognitions is, how does one know that a child has a prior concept (e.g., the intention of requesting), a meaning for "off" unlike that of adults, the notion of "agentness," or the idea of "current relevance"? There are two aspects to this question. The first is the problem of assessing whether a child "has" a concept. As Schlesinger notes (1977b, p. 156), "a concept has been acquired only to the extent that one knows what belongs to it and what does not." As an operational definition, "for someone to have a concept entails that all instances of the concept elicit a common response" (Schlesinger, 1977b, p. 157). In the case of the putative underlying cognitions cited above, the assessment of whether a child "has" these concepts in past studies has involved looking at his verbal output, combined with related contextual cues. The important point is that none of the measures used have been independent of verbal output. If the child has not mastered the relevant aspects of language, such language-dependent measures will not reveal underlying concepts that may be present prior to the acquisition of the particular language form.

Several authors have commented on this state of affairs. Concern has been expressed about the grounds for labeling particular putative underlying categories and for assigning particular utterances to particular categories. For example, Cazden (1977) discussed these problems with regard to identifying categories of underlying communicative intentions and attributing particular utterances to particular intentional categories. The question of the "psychological reality" of proposed categories of semantic relations has been raised by Brown (1973, p. 146), Bowerman (1975,

p. 84), and Braine (1976, pp. 58–63). The current debate about what kinds of concepts underlie children's earliest word meanings and the manner in which children determine whether an object, event, etc., is an instance of a certain lexical category (Clark, 1973; Nelson, 1974, 1978; Rosch et al., 1976; Anglin, 1977; Nelson and Bonuillian, 1978; see Bowerman, 1978b, pp. 120–127, for a review of these positions) is fueled by a lack of language-independent measures of conceptual categories proposed as a basis for word meanings.

The second aspect of the measurement question concerns what should be measured. In addition to the problems of how to measure such cognitions as intentionality and meaning, Schlesinger (1977b) points out that there is a problem of determining if those cognitions are directly related to particular linguistic forms. While children may be able to categorize the world around them for nonlinguistic purposes, it does not guarantee that they have drawn the distinctions required for the appropriate use of words and linguistic devices such as word order and intonation. This was also the point raised by Bowerman (1976, pp. 140–141) in her criticism of Macnamara (1972), which was cited earlier (p. 11). She argued that a child's sensorimotor understanding of notions of causality and location do not directly translate into corresponding categories of semantic relations such as "agent" and "location." The linguistic concepts encoded in semantic relations presuppose different groupings of experiences on a higher level of equivalence, a more abstract notion of symbolic similarities than is evident in sensorimotor interactions.

Cognitive Structures Underlying Language

There are similar problems of measurement associated with the second, deeper level of cognitive structures underlying language. Piaget's theory of cognitive development is the source of the particular cognitive structures that have been proposed as prerequisites for language. Mental representation, i.e., memory for absent objects and events, is a cognitive structure often held to be prerequisite for the beginnings of language (Sinclair, 1971; Morehead and Morehead, 1974). The scheme of the permanent object, that is, the realization that the universe consists of permanent objects that do not disappear when out of sight, is the form of mental representation most specifically and most often tied to early linguistic acquisition. Some examples are: Bloom (1973) argued that attainment of object permanence was necessary for learning the meanings of object words but not function words, and also for learning how to combine words; Ingram (1978) tied the emergence of semantic relations to the attainment of sensorimotor Stage 6 intelligence (the full mastery of object permanence); Bates et al. (1977a, p. 296) reported that the ability to use words referentially, i.e., to stand for or represent objects and events, appeared as the child demonstrated Stage 6 behaviors. These hypotheses and evidence from studies of normal language acquisition have been applied to matters of language intervention. A clear example is offered by Leonard (1978), who specifies that mastery of sensorimotor Stage 6 skills, that is, a complete mastery of object permanence, is a prerequisite for introducing words as semantic roles, such as agents and objects of actions.

How do cognitive structures such as object permanence relate to the problem of measuring a prior concept in a nonlinguistic domain that has immediate links to a particular linguistic competency? Unlike the assessment problem with intentions and meanings, there are ways of measuring "object permanence" in terms of objective, observable behaviors, well suited to serve as baselines for training (e.g., Uzgiris and Hunt, 1975; see, also, Bower, 1974, pp. 180–241, for some ingenious experimental tasks measuring substages in the acquisition of object permanence). Rather than a measurement problem, then, the question confronting the researcher is how does one know that the mastery of a particular concept is a prerequisite to a particular linguistic competence?[2]

The hypothesis that object permanence is a prerequisite for establishing the meanings of words has been challenged on differing grounds. Huttenlocher (1974) found that children could correctly comprehend the meanings of words for some time before this knowledge became manifest in correct productions of those words. She argued that such correct comprehension depends upon the child's accurate mental representation of events. This was especially evident when a child was able to locate and retrieve objects that were out of sight and in a temporary or atypical location. In view of Huttenlocher's findings, evidence for mental representation that is based upon children's verbal productions, such as the data reported by Bloom (1973), would be biased in the direction of underestimating a child's ability to mentally represent objects.

Corrigan (1978) questions the accuracy of the claim that sensorimotor Stage 6 skills are necessary for the acquisition of specific language behaviors such as a semantic class. She addressed some of the method-

---

[2]The question raised here is more specific than the related question of "does object permanence predict language development?" in which case the dependent variables are defined in broader terms than particular linguistic skills. For example, Corrigan (1978) used mean length of utterance as a measure of language acquisition. She found no relationship between object permanence and MLU. Bates et al. (1977a, 1977b) used nine measures of communicative language, including both comprehension and production. They reported that object permanence was not a good predictor of communicative development.

ological weaknesses of earlier studies in her 18-month longitudinal study of three children. The studies of Bates (1976; Bates et al., 1977b) and Ingram (1978) were correlative in nature; that is, they sought to establish temporal relationships between the acquisition of particular cognitive and linguistic performances. For example, do children first display behaviors indicating mastery of object permanence, then start to use words (productively) in a referential manner, or do these emerge concurrently or in a reversed order? Corrigan (1978, p. 174) pointed out that what had been lacking in earlier studies were measures of object permanence that were independent of language and that also indicated the degree of object permanence, i.e., the attainment of which levels of various kinds of object permanence tasks. She used a modified form of the Uzgiris and Hunt (1975) scale as the measure of object permanence (Corrigan, 1978, pp. 178–179). Stage 6 object permanence encompassed six ordinal behaviors on the scale. The three subjects remained in Stage 6 for 5, 6, and 7 months. The onset of single-word utterances generally corresponded to the onset of search for an invisibly displaced object (early Stage 6, without full mental representation of an object's actions). During this time the child spoke only about objects that were present. There was a general correspondence between the final rank of the object permanence scale and an increase in total vocabulary. Also at this time was the first evidence in the children's spontaneous verbal productions of the semantic categories of nonexistence and recurrence. Corrigan (1978, p. 188) concludes that hypotheses that predict that Stage 6 is related to specific language behaviors need to be revised for greater specificity in the definition of Stage 6, that is, to indicate which performance levels on which tasks are to be tied to which language skills.

The issues raised by Huttenlocher (1974) and Corrigan (1978) are of immediate relevance to the question of how does one know that the mastery of a particular concept is a prerequisite to a particular linguistic competence. Huttenlocher (1974) reminds us that established relationships at the earliest stages of acquisition between particular cognitive achievements and verbal productions represent only part of the cognition/language relationship—that represented by production but not the more advanced knowledge represented in comprehension. Corrigan tells us that it is not very meaningful to cast our cognitive prerequisites for a particular linguistic skill in such broad terms as "attainment of stage 6 sensorimotor intelligence." Both of these methodological concerns are considered in the most recent work of Bates et al. (1977b). They used measures of both production and comprehension of language in their assessment of overall language acquisition. They used items from the six Uzgiris and Hunt Ordinal Scales of Infant Development (Uzgiris and Hunt, 1975) to measure performance on various kinds of cognitive tasks. One of the scales used was that of object permanence, composed of different tasks representing various levels of difficulty. Furthermore, Bates et al. (1977a, 1977b) concluded that the search for prerequisite relationships between Piagetian cognitive tasks such as those measuring object permanence and specific linguistic behaviors is theoretically unjustified. Both kinds of behaviors are surface manifestations of a deeper, underlying cognitive structure or of a specific cognitive scheme that unites a particular cognitive domain (Bates et al., 1977a, 1977b). Therefore, the theoretical prediction shifts from a particular order of emergence to a concurrent appearance within roughly the same age range (Bates et al., 1977a, p. 270).

The feasibility of tying a measure of object permanence to a particular linguistic skill that is to be trained appears to be nonexistent, on both empirical and theoretical grounds. Other cognitive structures have not fared any better as established prerequisite links to a particular form. Bowerman (1978b, pp. 111–120) reviewed the evidence linking language development and the concrete operational period. She concluded that "success on particular cognitive tasks (e.g., tests for the tool-using capacity, for object permanence, for reversible operations) are not in themselves prerequisites for particular linguistic achievements, such as intentional communication, the acquisition of a stable vocabulary of object words, word combination, an understanding of the relationship between active and passive sentences, and so on" (p. 120). Moore and Harris (1978) arrived at a similar conclusion.

To summarize, the constructs to which the term *concept* have been applied in discussions of cognition underlying language development have been difficult to apply to the problems of developing language-training programs. Of the two types of cognitions described in the literature, the deeper level of cognitive structures is ruled out because of the lack of evidence for a direct, prerequisite relationship to linguistic acquisition. The more superficial level of thoughts, meanings, and intentions presents measurement problems for the particular concepts that have been described in the literature. However, it is possible to pursue this latter level of cognitive processing from a different angle by focusing upon the measurement of nonverbal concepts first, then finding a corresponding linguistic form. This strategy is, in effect, the reverse of that reported in previous studies, where evidence for underlying concepts was dependent upon verbal output which in turn defined the underlying concepts.

HOW TO MEASURE NONLINGUISTIC CONCEPTS

There is a long tradition of concept measurement in nonlinguistic domains reported in the psychological literature. In their investigations psychologists have worked out operational definitions of a concept and have devised a number of experimental tasks to measure conceptual equivalences. There is considerable evidence reporting how children of various ages perform on these measures of conceptual functioning; that is, there is evidence to support some general notions of how young children acquire certain kinds of concepts. It is very appropriate to take a careful look at this literature as we consider how to go about measuring nonlinguistic concepts that could eventually be tied to particular language forms.

Definitions and Sorting Tasks

Evidence of a concept is generally defined as the same response (action or word label) for a series of discriminably different events (stimuli). A concept is more than a particular, isolated response, however. As Bruner, Goodnow, and Austin (1956) emphasize, a concept represents a dynamic process:

> ...when one learns to categorize a subset of events in a certain way, one is doing more than simply learning to recognize instances encountered. One is also learning a rule that may be applied to new instances. The concept or category is, basically, this rule of grouping, and it is such rules that one constructs in forming and attaining concepts (p. 45).

The "rule of grouping" is generally referred to as the *intension* of the concept, that is, the properties that define the concept or word, in contrast to the *extension* of the concept, that is, the set of objects that are instances of the concept. When applied to verbal concepts the distinction between extension and intension corresponds to the distinction between reference and meaning (Anglin, 1977, pp. 3–4).

Concepts have typically been measured by sorting tasks whose purpose is to externalize into observable behavior the internal strategies for equating objects (the intensions of the concepts). What kinds of sorting tasks are appropriate for very young children? Different tasks have been used by different researchers. Some features are shared by many of the studies. The child is instructed to group or select objects that he regards as equivalent with such instructions as, "Put together the things that go together," or "Here's an X; find another X," or "Point to the two that are the same." The format can be either expressive, where the child selects and manipulates the stimuli, or receptive, where the stimuli presentation is controlled by the experimenter. The stimuli used in such sorting tasks have been predominantly of two types: 1) geometric forms varying in dimensions such as form, color, and size where each attribute occurs with all combinations of all others (e.g., Vygotsky, 1962; Inhelder and Piaget, 1964; Denney, 1972a, 1972b; Denney and Acito, 1974), or 2) representational stimuli such as toys or pictures of real world objects (e.g., Inhelder and Piaget, 1964; Olver and Hornsby, 1966). Given such sets of stimuli, concepts are generally defined in terms of shared attributes common to all instances, at the level of either perceptual attributes or criteria for superordinate groupings.

A look at individual studies reveals considerable variation in the procedural specifics. Piaget used free-sorting tasks, with geometric shapes of various colors and, later, with small toy objects, introduced by the instructions "Put together things that are alike" (Inhelder and Piaget, 1964). Vygotsky (1962) named a selected sample block, then asked the subjects to pick out all the blocks (that varied in color, shape, height, and size) they thought would have the same name. Feedback was provided as to the accuracy of choices. Denney (1972a) replicated the procedures of both Vygotsky and Inhelder and Piaget. Sigel's Categorization Test (as reported in Kogan, 1976, pp. 72–73) also involved a free-sorting procedure. Twelve common objects were placed before the child. The examiner selected one as a standard and asked the child to choose all of the remaining objects that belong with the standard and to describe the basis for the selection.

Olver and Hornsby (1966) used both verbal and pictured equivalence tasks. For the verbal task, subjects as young as 6 years were presented with various words such as "banana" and "peach" and asked to tell how the words were alike and, along with subsequent items, how they were different from the preceding items (p. 70). The pictured task consisted of an array of 42 drawings of familiar objects, with the instructions to select from this array a group of pictures that "are alike in some way" (p. 79).

Rosch et al. (1976) used oddity problems consisting of triads of color photographs of animals and vehicles that were presented to a subject one at a time with the instructions to put together or point to "the two that are alike, that are the same kind of thing." A similar procedure was used by Marquesen (1975), who presented pictured stimuli within a match-to-sample format (i.e., the subject was given two choice stimuli and asked to find the one like a third picture). Faulkender, Wright, and Waldron (1974) adapted the experimental procedures of the infant habituation studies to infer conceptual categories, by measuring looking times of children ages 29 to 44 months to slide-projected stimuli representing the categories of fruits, animals, and environmental patterns.

Ricciuti (1965) modified the usual concept measurement procedures to determine whether there was evidence of grouping strategies used by prelinguistic infants, ages 12 to 24 months. He set an arrangement of geometric forms in front of the child that could be grouped into two contrasting sets on the basis of form, color, or size. The instructions were "See these? You play with them; you fix them up." The child was then allowed to play with the objects. There were two criteria for determining conceptual groupings: 1) the order in which objects were touched or displaced, and 2) the spatial grouping of objects. Nelson (1973a) used a similar procedure with children ages 19 to 22 months.

The various tasks represent a wide range of sorting procedures and elicited behaviors, ranging from free-sorting tasks to carefully controlled and limited stimulus presentation. The child's conceptual groupings are generally determined by comparison with the experimenter's predetermined definitions, or by post-hoc analysis in which the experimenter organizes the child's responses into descriptive categories that appear reasonable from an adult's perspective.

Findings: How Do Children Perform on Sorting Tasks?

How do young children categorize objects? Kogan (1976, pp. 87, 91–95) notes the distinction between cognitive abilities, i.e., the kinds of groupings children are capable of making (implicit in the stage theories of Piaget and Vygotsky), and cognitive style, or preference for one out of several available ways of grouping in either categorization behavior or in the rationales offered to account for categorization, or both. The question at this point addresses cognitive abilities. The information that is available is characterized by inconsistent findings and controversy. Much of the controversy centers around a comparison between children's and adults' categorical groupings. Vygotsky (1962) and Inhelder and Piaget (1964) reported that children between the ages of 2 and 5 years do not group geometric stimuli according to one common perceptual attribute, such as color, which is a common grouping strategy of adults. Instead, children's groupings were described as "complexive" (Vygotsky, 1962; Bruner, Greenfield, and Olver, 1966), consisting of grouping by associations, stories, or chaining of adjacent choices by shared attributes instead of by maintaining a single attribute common to all choices. From such evidence it was concluded that children could not abstract out a single defining attribute common to all objects, and, therefore, that their categorization behavior was qualitatively different from adults'.

The characterization of young children's conceptual groupings as being different from adults' has recently come under attack from several sources. Denney (1972b; Denney and Acito, 1974) has reported that many children in the 2- to 5-year age group do group geometric stimuli according to one common perceptual attribute; Ricciuti (1965) and Nelson (1973a) suggest that there may be grouping of objects by single attributes in subjects as young as 12 to 24 months, depending on the sorting task procedures and materials. This directly contradicts the earlier findings of Inhelder and Piaget (1964) and Vygotsky (1962). Another source of criticism has focused upon the characterization of children's groupings as "complexive," in contrast with those of adults as "noncomplexive." Rosch and her colleagues (Rosch et al., 1976) have pointed out that in traditional sorting tasks the stimuli are such that they can only be grouped on a superordinate level. They showed that children as young as 3 years of age classify in an adult taxonomic manner, at a ceiling level of accuracy, when they are presented with pictures of objects that can be equated at the level of basic objects. Furthermore, Rosch and Mervis (1975) have also determined that adults use "family resemblances," a form of complexive grouping, in the organization of semantic classes. The use of complexive classes is thus neither unique to children nor indicative of inferior processing abilities. A third source of questioning is the evidence from children's early use of words, in their inferred categorization abilities as revealed by their extension of words to novel referents. Bowerman (1977b) presents longitudinal data indicating that children can link words to noncomplexive categories as early as 13 to 14 months of age.

Three conclusions from these recent findings are particularly relevant to the development of an assessment of nonlinguistic concepts for the purposes of training: 1) children as young as 2 years of age are capable of sorting by attributes, 2) children 3 years of age are capable of sorting at the level of basic objects at a ceiling level of accuracy, and 3) children's early word usage indicates the operation of more sophisticated strategies of equating objects and events for linguistic purposes than the earlier literature attributed to them.

How can such specific methods of measurement be operationalized to explore the relationship between cognition and language? It is necessary to identify and measure a specific concept that corresponds to a particular linguistic form. What linguistic domain is most suited to the delineation of specific conceptual underpinnings?

WHAT LINGUISTIC SKILL TO MEASURE?
THE CASE FOR ACQUISITION OF WORD MEANINGS

The acquisition of word meanings is an area of language development that lends itself to the study of the intersection between cognition and language. To be more precise, the acquisition of reference, that is, the process of naming, involves an intimate relationship between nonlinguistic conceptual categories and linguistic bundles of information.

There are two components involved in the child's ability to refer to objects, action, attributes, experiences, and so on: the thing to be named and the name. As Brown (1976, p. 139; 1978) points out, there are two possible directions of development: one considering the name as fixed and looking at the variation in referents, and the other keeping the referent as a constant and looking at the variation in names.

The first aspect of acquiring the meaning of a particular lexical item, that is, one name used for many perceptually different referents, entails a close association between the kinds of groupings measured on the concept tasks and the linguistic information encoded in particular kinds of words. For example, let's consider what is involved in learning a very simple word that is usually taught at the very beginning of training, such as "ball" (suggested by Holland, 1975, p. 521, and a traditional training item). The clinician begins with a particular ball (invariably medium-sized, red in color, spherical, and made of rubber). Holding the ball, the clinician says "ball" and expects the child to eventually do likewise, preferably with some evidence of reference to the object, ball. The child has to be able to recognize that, while the ball can have a different appearance under different perceptual conditions (lighting, angle of viewing, partial viewing, etc.), it is still the same ball and the same word, "ball," applies. If he has mastered this much, we could credit him with having *a* name for *an* object. However, the meaning of "ball" encompasses not just one ball, but instead many perceptually different balls—big balls, little balls, red balls, white balls, striped balls, hard balls, squishy balls, fuzzy balls, round balls, not-so-round balls (e.g., footballs), balls with holes in them (wiffle balls, bowling balls), balls with elastic strings attached to them (and usually attached to a wooden paddle), balls to play with (toys), balls to eat (melon balls, cheese balls), and balls that disappear (snowballs). Somehow the child has to learn that all of these perceptually different objects are equivalent in that they can be referred to with the same name. Even if the child learns only the objects that are most commonly and literally referred to as "ball," he must process a great many perceptual bits of information, decide which information is relevant for this particular category and bundle it all together as the referential meaning associated with "ball." We won't even consider more advanced bundling involved in learning multiple word meanings, as in "to go to a ball," and "to ball the tree," or metaphorical extensions like "the ball of your foot," or idioms such as "on the ball."

Normal children's earliest word meanings are certainly not limited to simple categories of real world perceptual information such as those encoded in the word "ball." Bowerman (1977b) provides examples of the rich variety of experiences encoded in her daughters' early productive use of such words as "off" and "on," "kick," "open," and "close," and "hi." A consideration of how children first use words reveals the great diversity in the objects, actions, experiences, spatial relationships, and so on that are grouped together for words like "off" (e.g., "Shut off the light," "Take off a sock," "Tear off a label," and "Get off the couch" all refer to events that may be perceptually quite different) or "open" (e.g., "Open a box," "Open a newspaper," "Open the door," "Open a tube of toothpaste," and "Open the window").

Since it is difficult to directly assess the internal set of defining properties that account for young children's first word meanings (the intension of a word), studies of how children acquire word meanings, such as Bowerman's (1976, 1977b), have generally relied on observations of how children use words to refer to real world objects, events, and relationships (the extension of a word). The kinds of errors children make when using words are particularly informative: errors indicating a pattern of reference for a particular word unlike that used by adults can be studied to discover possible categories of intensions unlike adult word meanings. Such putative intensions underlying word meanings in turn reveal how the child is capable of grouping nonlinguistic objects, events, and relationships, that is, his ability to form concepts that may or may not eventually get tied to a particular word meaning.

One particular kind of error of reference has generated much discussion—that of overextension, in which case the child uses a particular word to apply to a broader range of referents than an adult would. The opposite kind of error is that of underextension, i.e., referring to a narrower semantic range than that encompassed in adult meanings for a particular word. Another possible error is that of overlap, where the child's word usage overlaps with that of the adults', demonstrating both overextension and underextension, e.g., "muffin" for both blueberries and blueberry muffins but not for other kinds of muffins (Dale, 1976, p. 12). A further possibility is no overlap at all; that is, the child's meaning for a word is entirely idiosyncratic, with no components in common with adult meaning for that word.

These errors of extension are central issues for a number of questions about the relationship between the child's ability to form nonlinguistic conceptual equivalences and the representation of this knowledge in word meanings. Of the several questions that have been addressed in the literature, one is of particular interest at this point: how do children form nonlinguistic groupings for the purpose of representing that information in words?

Clark (1973) has proposed that perceptual likenesses account for how children equate objects for word meanings. She arrives at this hypothesis on the basis of two considerations: first, she assumes that children's first use of words is to express what they have already worked out nonlinguistically; second, children's use of words to refer to objects is controlled by perceptual similarities among the objects (as revealed by the kinds of errors of overextension reported in the diary literature). Since cognitive organization and semantic knowledge are regarded as inseparable at the early stages of language acquisition (Clark, 1977, p. 166), the child's use of words (according to perceptual similarities) is a direct reflection of his cognitive organization (equivalences according to perceptual attributes). According to Clark, the perceptual attributes controlling first word meanings are shape, then size, sound, movement, texture, and, to a much lesser extent, taste. (It is important for subsequent discussions to note that color is not used as a basis for overextension at this beginning stage of language acquisition.)

The evidence for how children equate objects and how this knowledge is expressed in word meanings is central to Clark's (1973) more general, theoretical explanation of how children acquire word meanings, the Semantic Feature Hypothesis. She starts from the premise that word meaning can be broken down into a number of smaller elements of meaning called "features." These features are not something a word "has" but instead represent what a child knows about how to use a word (Clark, 1975). This notion of features as elements in word meanings that are common to exemplars within a lexical grouping, e.g., "animate" as one defining feature of the word "dog," is consistent with the traditional concept formation literature, where concepts have usually been defined in terms of shared attributes common to all instances. The direction of acquisition proposed by Clark (1973) is the gradual acquisition of more defining semantic components until the child achieves an adultlike knowledge of the word; that is, children's first meanings for a word are based on only one or two of the more general semantic features, and they later add features that are more specific (an idea that has been challenged by evidence that the acquisition process is actually considerably more complex, e.g., Nelson and Bonvillian, 1978, pp. 542–543).

Nelson (1974) has formulated a different version of how children's early concepts are related to word meanings although she shares Clark's initial assumption that the child first works out nonlinguistic equivalences, then uses words to represent this knowledge. She bases her account on the Piagetian principle that the foundation for children's first conceptual groupings are the sensorimotor schemes, that things are similar if they can be acted upon in the same way. Nelson disagrees with Clark's (1973) claim that perception is the basis for classification. Instead, Nelson proposes that shared function, based on the child's action upon objects, determines how children equate objects for linguistic reference. Nelson notes that children's first words refer to objects capable of action or movement, such as people, animals, and foods, whereas names for static objects or places are not learned until later, even though the child has both kinds of words modeled for him. The role of perceptual attributes is limited to identifying or predicting category membership of a particular object when function cues are not available. By assigning different roles to shared function versus perceptual attributes (the former is "defining" whereas the latter only serves to identify instances of a concept), Nelson in effect subdivides a concept into two parts. One of these parts defines the "essence" of the concept and the other corresponds to the features that are used to determine if a particular object is a member of the category. (Some authors have taken issue with this subdivision, arguing that such a distinction is impossible to maintain, e.g., Papert (1977, p. 138) and Macnamara (1977, p. 144.) Nelson also differs with Clark in regard to the direction of acquisition. According to Nelson, the child begins with a "functional core concept" that contains all the known relational information. As the child attaches a word meaning to this functional core, he refines his initial concept by disregarding irrelevant functional information and adding abstract linguistic markers, such as "actor" and "action," and identifying attributes. The functional core defines the concept underlying a word; the other information is used to identify particular instances of a category. This idea that one feature, an object's function, is the defining feature for category membership is consistent with the traditional concept sorting tasks, where one attribute is common to all members of a class (cf. Bowerman, 1976, pp. 123–127; 1978b, pp. 121–124).

Clark (1973) and Nelson (1974) differ in their accounts of how children equate objects for the purpose of using words to stand for those objects (perceptual attributes versus function) and the pattern of development (a few initial general features with the later addition of more specific features versus an initial core containing all the relevant information that gets refined by selectively dropping some functional information and adding other attributes and linguistic features). The two positions also hold some assumptions in common. The first is that the child invents his own categories; his own cognitive functioning determines how he makes sense out of all the experiential information available in his world. The second assumption shared by both Clark (1973) and Nelson (1974) is that concepts, whether nonlinguistic or semantic in nature, are defined by attributes held in common by all instances.[3] These assumptions agree with those of the traditional sorting tasks that have purported to measure concept formation and organization.

A third version of how children go about clustering information for referential word meanings, quite unlike Clark's (1973) and Nelson's (1974), has emerged from investigations of the organization of semantic categories. (In fact, this new version differs so greatly from earlier accounts that Brown (1978) regards it as "a new paradigm of reference.")

The work of Eleanor Rosch Heider and her colleagues (Rosch and Mervis, 1975; Rosch et al., 1976) has played a central role in revealing that the assumptions of the traditional account of concept formation that Clark (1973) and Nelson (1974) brought to their analyses are inaccurate. Rosch and her co-workers have revised the traditional approach in three basic respects. First, Rosch turns upside down the traditional assumption that semantic categories are arbitrary, in the sense of "constructions" or "inventions" instead of "discoveries" (Bruner, Goodnow, and Austin, 1956, p. 232) by asserting that semantic categories are not entirely invented but instead reflect a world of separate things, where attributes are intercorrelated and do not occur with equal probabilities. There are basic objects[4] (categories at basic levels of abstraction) in the world determined by real world correlational structure. Such basic objects are maximally differentiated in terms of attributes, similar motor programs, and shapes. For example, the basic object level category of "dog" is more informative than "animal" (superordinate) or "collie" (subordinate) because "animal" referents have few attributes in common and "collie" referents share many attributes with "German shepherd." Basic objects are pre-

---

[3]See Barrett (1978) for a critique of this assumption shared by Clark and Nelson. Barrett argues that the acquisition of a word's meaning cannot be accounted for in terms of the criterial features which all of its referents have in common. Instead, the meaning of a particular word involves knowledge of both positive and negative examples of referents; meanings are characterized in terms of the contrasts that exist between positive and negative referential instances. However, Barrett presumes that the initial identification of the semantic field (the category of referent objects) is based upon an abstraction of the attributes held in common (p. 209), in agreement with Clark's and Nelson's assumptions.

[4]The notion of a "basic object level" has a precursor in Brown's (1958) suggestion that most objects have a "truest name," one that represents the referent's level of "usual utility." He regards Rosch's definition of a "basic object level" as an improvement "out of all recognition" of the idea of a truest name (Brown, 1976, p. 140).

dicted to be the first categories learned and named by children (Rosch et al., 1976).

The second respect in which Rosch differs from the traditional approach is in her claim that semantic categories are coded in terms of prototypes (also proposed by Anglin, 1977). A prototype is a kind of superexemplar consisting of an internal representation of a central tendency that most reflects "the redundancy structure of the category as a whole" (Rosch and Mervis, 1975, p. 602). Consistent with these first two points, Rosch firmly rejects the criterial attribute explanation of semantic concept formation and instead argues for multi-attribute processing of the correlational structures of bundles of attributes of real world objects (Rosch et al., 1976). It is not a matter of one particular attribute, be it perceptual information or function, accounting for how objects are regarded as equivalent for a particular word; it is a matter of how a number of attributes relate to each other in a particular package of information.

The third difference follows from Rosch's first point, that of a basic categorical organization inherent in the environment. With a common environmental organization available to all people, Rosch predicts universal principles of semantic organization, although the content of such categories should vary across cultures (Rosch, 1976, p. 18).

The implications of Rosch's work are apparent in Schlesinger's (in preparation) claim that the formation of concepts is constrained by the perceptual texture evident in the world (based on Rosch's finding that the perceptual world has structure, i.e., bundles of correlated attributes). According to Schlesinger, perceptual texture can suggest concepts; the concepts are fully formed when tied to a linguistic response. The nature of both nonlinguistic and linguistic experiences must be considered when accounting for the formation of concepts: "Texture and linguistic input must converge on the formation of a conceptual system" (Schlesinger, in preparation).

To conclude these considerations of what is involved when a child learns words, it is apparent that questions of how children acquire word meanings immediately lead to questions of how they form concepts. Several different explanations have recently been proposed to account for how conceptual knowledge gets mapped into words. While there is no evidence to conclusively demonstrate the superiority of one explanation over another, a growing number of empirical studies are looking at how young children use words to refer to objects, with results indicating partial support for various theoretical explanations (e.g., Gruendel, 1977).

But let's return to the strategy of first measuring concepts and then observing the acquisition of related word meanings. What do these different accounts of the acquisition of word meanings have to offer in the way of considerations for how to measure underlying concepts? The non-linguistic categorical equivalences suggested by Clark (1973) and Nelson (1974) could be measured in much the same fashion as nonlinguistic concepts have been measured in the traditional sorting tasks, i.e., matching a single attribute held in common by all members of the category. However, the work of Rosch and her colleagues (Rosch and Mervis, 1975; Rosch et al., 1976) demonstrates that such means of measuring nonlinguistic conceptual knowledge may not demonstrate what is involved in the organization of real world information underlying the meanings of object words. Semantic categories for object words are not organized in terms of single features or attributes held in common across instances, but instead reflect the intercorrelations of attributes found in the real world. The traditional format for sorting tasks would not provide an adequate measure of concepts underlying object words. Such tasks would have to be modified to reflect the multi-attribute nature of real world conceptual groupings.

There are additional problems to be considered when attempting to tie a measurement of nonlinguistic concepts to word meanings. These problems center around establishing a direct link between a particular conceptual grouping and a particular linguistic form (word meaning). Recall Brown's (1976, p. 139) differentiation of two aspects of development: one where the word is fixed and the referents vary, and the other where the words change and the referent is held constant. So far the discussion has addressed the former, how a number of different referents are lumped as equivalent within one word's meaning. The other aspect also has important implications for the measurement issue. As Brown has observed (1958), there is usually not just one name for each entity in the world (person, object, action, and so on) but instead each individual can be correctly named in many different ways. "The dime in my pocket is not only a *dime*. It is also *money*, a *metal object*, a *thing*, and, moving to subordinates, a *1952 dime*, in fact a *particular 1952 dime* with a unique pattern of scratches, discolorations, and smooth places" (p. 14).

The problem that confronts us is not only how to measure a non-linguistic concept that is represented in a lexical category, but also how to ensure that a particular word will be used to represent that particular category. This problem is a consequence of the training paradigm. We want to look at how nonlinguistic concepts influence how a child learns linguistic forms. The child will not have the linguistic knowledge in question at the beginning of training; he may or may not have the nonlinguistic knowledge—it will be the purpose of the conceptual measurement task to establish his conceptual knowledge. A particular linguistic form (word) would be selected for training. The key question is how can we know that the means for equating objects in the nonlinguistic groupings matches that used to equate information in the lexical category of the word? For example, when a child who does not know the word "dog" is asked to sort a group of toy animals to determine if he knows that perceptually different dogs can be grouped together to form a class of dogs, how can we be sure that this grouping corresponds to the lexical knowledge encoded in the word "dog"? He could conceivably group correctly on the basis of such lexical categories as "Rover," "puppy," "pet," "poodle," or "animal," depending in part on the stimuli provided as response options. How could we be sure that when we trained him to say "dog" that his response represented the adultlike meaning of "dog" and not something else? The linguistic form to be taught would have to have a relatively arbitrary pattern of use that corresponded directly to the criteria used for equating objects.

A further consideration is that of the age of the subjects. The issue involves the role of cognition at the earliest stages of word acquisition; therefore the subjects would be young, normal (or older, disordered) children. The measurement problem then becomes one of devising a nonlinguistic measurement procedure that young children can perform, that measures a nonlinguistic category that ties directly to a linguistic form (word) that young children do not already know but which can be taught to them.

What particular word meaning can fulfill these requirements? The psycholinguistic investigations of the acquisition of word meanings have been addressed almost exclusively to only one domain of referential word meanings, that of names of objects (Clark, 1973; Nelson, 1974; Rosch and Mervis, 1975; Rosch et al., 1976; Anglin, 1977). The problem of multiple names for one entity seems to rule out object words. However, other domains of word meaning may be less susceptible to more than one name for one entity. Where can we look for other candidates to serve as training content? Since the format of the concept measurement task is that of sorting objects, how about word meanings that are well suited to this means of measurement, for example, perceptual attributes? As it turns out, a careful consideration of one kind of perceptual attribute, color, reveals that it does have a very close relationship to lexical representation. Furthermore, the acquisition of color terms meets the other criteria for the linguistic form to be trained, i.e., relatively arbitrary reference, not learned at the earliest stages, but yet amenable to training. We will take a close look at the acquisition of color terms in the next chapter.

Chapter 3
COLOR TERMS
A Measurable Link Between
Cognition and Language

Almost every child learns the name of at least the most common color terms by the time he reaches school age (Mecham, 1958). And almost every adult seems to know just how the child learned to use those color terms—the adult says "What color is this?" in reference to a particular object, waits for the child to respond, supplies the proper color term if there is no answer or corrects the child's inaccurate response, and then repeats the pattern of interaction. It provides a good example of the Original Word Game (Brown, 1958, p. 194), in which the role of the child is that of hypothesis tester. He allegedly "forms hypotheses about the categorical nature of the things named" (p. 194). When he tries to name the new thing (in this case, the attribute of color), he is trying out a hypothesis. The feedback he receives allows him to confirm or revise his hypothesis. Most parents and teachers would accept this version of how children learn color terms. Indeed, how a child masters color terms is often regarded as so obvious as to be of little interest, except when the kindergarten teacher has to struggle to teach color words to the inevitable one child in the group who cannot perform correctly when asked to "find your *X color* crayon."

However, there is recent evidence that the acquisition of color terms is more subtle and complex than previously supposed. The commonly accepted account described above assumes that the hypothetical categories of referents that the child tests out are the product of his mental processing—that he imposes categorical structure on sensory experiences that are equally susceptible of different groupings. In the case of color terms, the child's problem, according to this account, is that of deciding where to draw the lines on a continuum of visual experiences to correspond to the lexical groupings of the various color terms.

Another assumption is that color terms follow the same pattern of acquisition as other words that have been studied, in which the child's initial semantic learning is that of reference, followed by semantic organization. After he works out what color term corresponds to what bundle of visual information, he can then go about learning how color terms relate to each other and other words as lexical items.

These two assumptions have been called into question by recent findings. Instead of the child's color categories reflecting his own arbitrary classification schemes, the lexical categories of color terms appear to be direct reflections of categories of sensory information evident in the real world. Instead of the child first learning how to tie a particular color term to a particular class of visual properties of objects, he learns how the color terms relate to each other within a semantic network, then maps out the referent relationship. The learning of color terms involves some special conditions of reference and semantic organization that bring about a particularly suitable situation for investigating the cognition/language relationship.

THE REFERENCE RELATIONSHIP BETWEEN COLOR TERMS AND COLOR PROPERTIES OF THE REAL WORLD

There is evidence that color-naming is directly linked to perceptual categorizing. Eleanor Rosch Heider (1971, 1972; Heider and Olivier, 1972; Rosch, 1973, 1975) has reported on a series of studies that indicate that there are perceptually salient colors, referred to as focal colors.[1] Young children attend to focal colors more readily than nonfocal colors (Heider, 1971) and recognize them as instances of their color category earlier than nonfocal colors (Mervis, Catlin, and Rosch, 1975). In experiments with adults, words for these focal colors were learned first and were remembered most readily, even for speakers of a language that lacked names for hues of colors (Heider, 1972). Heider proposes that these focal colors serve as natural prototypes or central instances for the organization of color categories, both as the child learns color terms ontogenetically and as languages historically add color terms.

An important corollary to Heider's findings is her conclusion that the perceptual domain of color is not arbitrarily categorized but instead reflects underlying perceptual/physiological predispositions to organize color around the prototypical focal colors. These focal areas are human universals (a hypothesis first proposed by Berlin and Kay, (1969). Heider concludes: "the color space would seem to be a prime example of the influence of underlying perceptual cognitive factors on the formation and reference of linguistic categories" (Heider, 1972, p. 20).

---

[1]"Focal points" of color is a term first used by Berlin and Kay (1969) to designate those areas of the color space most exemplary of basic color names in many different languages (for adults).

The notion of underlying physiological predilections for focal colors has been supported by studies of the neural organization in the visual system. Bornstein (1973) reported a direct match between Berlin and Kay's (1969) findings for focal colors and the sensitivity maxima of neural cells in the visual system specifically tuned to the coding of chromatic information. Another line of support is that of infants' preferences for colors. Four-month-old infants can not only discriminate among different colors, but they also prefer to look at color category centers, i.e., they look longer at colors in the center of the category than at color category boundaries (Bornstein, 1975).

The conclusion that color terms represent an intimate link between underlying conceptual development and linguistic acquisition is exemplified in an observation of a bilingual child reported by Burling (1959) and cited by Cromer (1974). He reported that the child learned simultaneously

> certain English and Garo words which expressed approximately the same meaning. It was as if once his understanding had reached the point of being able to grasp a concept, he was able to use the appropriate words in both languages. For example, when he suddenly grasped the meaning of color terms, he was able to use the English and Garo words simultaneously (p. 227).

What significance do these findings have for the problem of how to measure the nonlinguistic categorical equivalences that account for a particular word meaning? Rosch's point is that the real-world visual information relevant to color perception is organized into separate bundles of information that is centralized around focal colors. These focal colors in turn also serve as the center of the semantic groupings encoded by color terms. There is a one-to-one correspondence between underlying perceptual categories and word meaning.

Several predictions for how children would perform on sorting tasks follow from this conclusion. They would be able to match objects with the same focal colors, e.g., a prototypic red or green, more accurately and easily than objects with nonfocal colors, or objects with nonfocal colors to similar objects with focal colors. When the child is matching objects on the basis of focal colors, we can be reasonably sure that he is using the same perceptual information as would be involved if he were naming the color of the objects. This sensory information is readily identifiable; that is, a red-red can be specified in relatively objective terms. Rosch Heider (1972) used Munsell chips with assigned values. However, her findings indicate that most adults, and children, too, have no trouble identifying a red-red. Other perceptual attributes, for example, "big" or "rough," seem to be less definable in terms of physical properties.

An observation about how color terms are used is very important. Color words display a minimum susceptibility to the problem of naming discussed earlier, that of one referent taking many names. Color naming, especially for focal colors, is quite constrained. A red-red cannot be called "green," or even "pink" or "reddish-orange" or "light-red"—it is just "red." This arbitrariness of naming combined with the one-to-one mapping of perception and linguistic reference allows for confidence that the measure of nonlinguistic categorization ties directly to the acquisition of color terms.

Color has an additional property that makes it appropriate as an attribute for matching objects on a sorting task. Recall Rosch's conclusion (discussed earlier on p. 36) about how objects are equated for the purpose of semantic organization: it is not a matter of matching a single feature but instead a matter of processing multi-attribute bundles of information. If the sorting task is to be representative of real world semantic information processing, it must require multi-attribute processing. Color co-occurs in free variation with other attributes in real world objects, allowing for the construction of a sorting task in which color can be contrasted with other means of equating natural objects. Other attributes are more limited in their occurrence across objects and tend to systematically co-occur with other features, for example, "round" with the functions of "throwable" and "rollable," and "square" or "rectangle" with the functions of "construction" or "containment."

The reference relationship between color terms and color properties of the real world is such that it can be observed in a measurement of nonlinguistic concepts (a task requiring the sorting of objects by color) and a linguistic task (naming the colors of objects). What happens between the time that a child masters the nonlinguistic categories (assuming that it takes place before the use of words to express those same nonlinguistic categories) and the mastery of the linguistic category, the correct referential use of color terms? The training of the words will involve some assumptions about how children go about learning color words. A consideration of recent evidence about how children spontaneously acquire the meanings of color words adds some new information that has implications for training.

SPONTANEOUS ACQUISITION OF COLOR TERMS: SEMANTIC ORGANIZATION, THEN REFERENCE

The literature describing children's spontaneous acquisition of color terms has been limited. This gap in knowledge is quite striking when compared to the recent explosion of information about other kinds of linguistic knowledge acquired by children, especially considering the ubiquity of color-term learning. There have been incidental references to color terms in investigations more general in scope that addressed the acquisition of modifiers in children's earliest utterances (e.g., Nelson, 1976). Specific consideration of children's acquisition of color terms has been studied from the perspective of children's perceptual organization (e.g., Heider, 1971). The study of color terms in other languages has led to the predicted order of acquisition for children. Berlin and Kay (1969) concluded that the historical order of emergence of color terms into a particular language was black and white, red, yellow or green, blue, brown, and pink or orange or gray or purple. They predicted that children's acquisition of color terms, the ontological order of development, would be the same. Miller and Johnson-Laird (1976, pp. 350-355) have provided an enlightening discussion of conceptual and referential developments evident in children's early language acquisition that are relevant to the mastery of color-word meanings. But the actual evidence has been scanty. Recent experimental work by Bartlett (1977, 1978) and a diary study by Cruse (1977) have provided an empirical framework for describing how children go about learning color words.

Some additional characteristics of color terms need to be described before introducing Bartlett's work. A minimal set of color names has been defined as black, white, red, green, yellow, and blue (Miller and Johnson-Laird, 1976, p. 344). These six colors are referred to as the psychological primary colors. They form a perceptually salient contrastive set that names the entire color space and has "color" as its superordinate term. Each of these primary color terms can have its own hyponyms, referred to as secondary color terms, e.g., "pink" and "scarlet" are hyponyms for "red" (Miller and Johnson-Laird, 1976, p. 344).

Bartlett's work has addressed several aspects of the acquisition of color terms: how children group the various colors for the purpose of naming before they acquire a full color lexicon; how their groupings compare to adults'; the order of acquisition of various color terms; a comparison of individual versus group data (the preceding were explored in Bartlett, 1978); and semantic organization (how color terms relate to each other) and reference (the relationship between individual color terms and color properties of objects) (Bartlett, 1977). The matter of semantic organization and reference is of interest at this point.

The sample of subjects studied by Bartlett (1977, 1978) consisted of 33 middle class children between the ages of 2.4 and 4.0 at the time of first assessment (15 2-year-olds and 18 3-year-olds). The children were followed longitudinally, with four different testings at roughly 6-week intervals. The 11 basic color terms of English were assessed: red, green, yellow, blue, white, black, pink, orange, purple, brown, and gray. Each test battery included a number of color-naming and color-perception tasks. In addition, two sorting tasks were administered that are of special interest. The children's responses indicated differing levels of acquisition of color terms at the time of initial assessment. Eighteen subjects already used six or more color terms correctly, three used five color terms, and three used four correct color terms. There were only nine subjects with two or fewer color words, and of these only four subjects used no color words correctly. Those nine subjects with two or fewer color terms were designated "beginners" and the others as "advanced" color-namers.

Color terms did not first enter the subjects' lexicons as names for specific colors (as presumed in the work of Heider, 1971). Instead the children first learned color terms as a related set of lexical items, with a substantial amount of semantic organization[2] taking place before any referential mapping.[3] The relatedness of color terms was inferred from the children's performance on naming and sorting tasks. When children were asked, "What color is this?" almost all of them responded with a color term. Only occasionally did children make a certain kind of mistake, that of naming the object. They usually changed their response to a color term when the question was repeated.

Bartlett posited that her subjects apparently realized that color terms are related since they were used as responses to "What color is this?" She looked for further information to determine if the relationship was the result of learned routines with isolated selection restrictions, such as

---

[2]Bartlett defines semantic organization as "the relation of one word to another within a lexical domain" (1977, p. 1). In the case of color terms, the semantic organization described is that of the superordinate/hyponymic relation between the word "color" and the various color terms. That is, "Does the child know that words like 'red' or 'green' are examples of the word 'color'?" (1977, p. 1).

[3]Cruse's (1977) findings are consistent with those of Bartlett's. He observed that his son first used a single color term, "green," that was used to refer to any bright color, followed by the production of several color words within a month's time, all used incorrectly but all in response to "What color is the X?" Nelson and Bonvillian (1978, p. 525) also reported that they observed a similar pattern, i.e., the first use of "red" not as a specific label for red things only, but rather to indicate any part of the color domain.

Evidence that knowledge of how words relate to each other precedes the mapping of nonlinguistic information can be interpreted as corroboration of the argument that language acquisition involves specific linguistic knowledge in addition to the mapping of meaning into linguistic forms. That is to say, since knowledge of linguistic similarity is evident before knowledge of nonlinguistic similarities, something in addition to nonlinguistic meanings must be operating in the acquisition of color terms (Slobin, 1973; Cromer, 1974, 1976; Bowerman, 1978b).

knowing that "red" is what you say when someone else says "What color?" (Bartlett, 1977, p. 7) or, if, indeed, children saw color terms as semantically related to each other. When asked, "Do you know the name of any colors?" all but three children (of the three, only one was a beginning color-namer, i.e., less than three correct color terms) responded with color terms and only color terms. She concluded that the word "color" did define an area of the lexicon, with some kind of superordinate/hyponymic organization.

While the beginning color-namers did not indicate fully correct referential meaning, with a correct systematic mapping onto well-defined areas of the color space, it was possible that the subjects did have a general referential meaning for the dimension of color,[4] along with a referential meaning for the word "color" as well. Bartlett devised two ingenious sorting tasks to look at these two possible means of reference. For the word "color" children were presented with arrays of six objects, pairs of which could be grouped according to object category, e.g., a yellow bead and a yellow chair. The children were asked, "Which ones are the same color?" Bartlett (1977, p. 10) reports that most advanced color-namers organized these arrays in terms of the dimension of color, whereas most beginning color-namers did not. Such findings indicated that most advanced color-namers did operate with a general referential meaning for the word "color," and beginning color-namers did not.

Whether or not children's color terms were mapping onto the general dimension of color was assessed by means of a modified form of the sorting task, in which the colors of the original like-colored pairs were changed to other colors, such as tan or peach. Subjects were asked to "show me the two red (green, etc.) ones," where the color name was a term that the child had produced but that seemed to have no correct referent in his lexicon at that time. It was reasoned that if the child used "red," for example, to refer to the general dimension of color (where "red" was not used correctly to refer only to red objects), then he would be more likely to select identically colored pairs of objects than objects that were related in other ways. The results corresponded to those on the "same color" task: most of the advanced color-namers selected like-colored pairs for most choices, whereas the majority of the beginning color-namers' responses were not according to color.

Bartlett (1977, p. 14) concluded that a child needs to know very little about color or color naming in order to enter at least a few color terms into his vocabulary. He does not need to know the particular color to

[1]Bartlett defines the general dimension of color as "roughly correspond[ing] to what an adult would have for the dimensional word 'color' " (1977, p. 9).

which the term refers, or even have a notion of color as a separate, nameable dimension. A child can achieve some minimal use of color terms with surprisingly little knowledge about color.[5]

This early awareness of the superordinate/hyponymic relation in the case of color words is in contrast to evidence from other domains indicating that children first learn reference and only later learn how words are related to each other. Bowerman (1974, 1977a, 1978c) has reported that the two children she studied longitudinally used some words correctly for quite some time and only later began to make errors with those same words, errors of overregularization of word meanings that are analogous to the well-substantiated overregularizations of irregular morphological forms such as "camed," "breaked," and "foots." Examples of the overregularization of word meanings include errors involving the causative use of noncausative verbs and adjectives, e.g., "Mommy, can you stay this open?", nouns used as verbs, e.g., "Barrett my hair back" (as a request to fasten her hair back out of her face), and substitutions of "put," "take," "bring," and "give," for one another and related words, e.g., "I wanta put it off" (while taking coat off) (examples are from Tables 1, 2, and 3 in Bowerman, 1978c). Bowerman accounts for these later-appearing errors by proposing that her subjects' earlier-appearing correct use of the words was limited to relatively specific contexts and the word meanings were relatively discrete, whereas the later patterns of word use revealed that her children had arrived at a more abstract understanding about how the words relate to each other. Reference was worked out first, and knowledge of deeper underlying semantic similarities and regularities across words followed the period of correct referential use. Bowerman (1978b, 1978c) regards these errors of word usage as "progressive" in that they reveal more sophisticated strategies of linguistic processing than was evident in earlier errorless, that is, referentially correct, but restricted use of word meanings.

Kuczaj (1978) has offered a similar explanation of why the progressive inflection "-ing" is rarely overgeneralized to inappropriate forms. He posits that children first learn the progressive in a restricted fashion, limiting it to verbs that they have coded as "-ing"-able (as suggested by

---

[5]The idea that little or no referential knowledge is needed in order to know something about how color terms relate to each other is corroborated by how blind adults use color words. When asked to judge the similarity of pairs of color words, congenitally blind young adults (therefore completely lacking a referential mapping of color terms onto actual visual properties of objects) judged them in the same manner as did adults with normal vision (Marmor, 1978). When asked how they had learned about color terms, the blind adults stressed the tutorial significance of conversations about colored objects, or about how to dress to please the sighted public (p. 274).

Brown, 1973). Later on, children learn "some general basis for the application of the progressive" (Kuczaj, 1978, p. 170) that allows them to generalize to creative and appropriate uses. Again, reference is worked out first (referring to actions of temporary duration) and relationships with other words are learned later.

The acquisition of color words is different from other reported patterns of word acquisition in that some idea of how color terms relate to each other is mastered before the referential relationship of color terms to particular visual properties of objects is mapped out. What could account for this difference? A possible explanation can be found in the Original Word Game (Brown, 1958). The modeling of color words in the natural environment appears to be more frequently of a tutorial nature than for other words. Furthermore, the verbal prompt, "What color is this?" that is typically used includes the superordinate term "color." The superordinate-hyponymic relationship evident in the semantic structure of color terms is made explicit in the color word version of the Original Word Game. It is reasonable to expect that children learn that only a small set of words are possible responses to the question "What color is this?"

How can we apply what is known about patterns of normal acquisition of color terms to the question of how to train color words? Our initial assumption is that our training goal is fully correct, referential use of color words with as much of the semantic knowledge evident as would be present if the child had acquired color terms in less formal adult-directed circumstances. The two special characteristics of color-term learning discussed above both have implications for training. The early acquisition of semantic organization implies that it would be possible to train more than just limited or restricted, although correct, reference. The important role played by the Original Word Game suggests that the tutorial format of a training situation could be designed to closely parallel the tutorial interaction often observed in the spontaneous learning situation.

In short, the acquisition of color terms is a promising content area for starting to unravel the relationship between cognition and language within a training study because: 1) underlying perceptual categories and word meanings are directly linked (making it possible to measure nonlinguistic categories that are directly mapped into semantic categories), 2) correct reference is acquired within a semantic superstructure allowing for the study of word meanings acquired at an early age that are more than narrowly defined lexical entries, and 3) the spontaneous acquisition of color terms has a tutorial character that allows for the development of experimental procedures that directly mirror natural acquisition.

Chapter 4

THE INFLUENCE OF NONLINGUISTIC CONCEPTS UPON LINGUISTIC ACQUISITION
A Training Study

This chapter reports a training study designed to investigate the relationship between nonlinguistic concepts and the acquisition of word meanings. Before we move on to the study, however, let's review the rather convoluted maze of considerations that was necessary in order to build a rationale for the study and a format for operationalizing the questions.

The prediction that the acquisition of a particular cognitive skill precedes and is a prerequisite for particular linguistic skills has its theoretical basis in the strong form of the cognition hypothesis. While it has been suggested that this prediction be incorporated into training programs for children with language disorders, no studies have been reported that have directly investigated the relationship of preexisting nonlinguistic concepts and the acquisition of linguistic skills in a training context.

We must consider a number of issues when we try to operationalize methods to investigate the relationship between a particular concept and a particular linguistic form. The methods used in the Piagetian training studies to compare the acquisition of one nonlinguistic concept to another nonlinguistic concept are not directly applicable. There are special problems when nonlinguistic concepts are compared to verbal concepts. Not only must we find a way to measure nonlinguistic concepts but we also must have some confidence that a particular nonlinguistic concept is directly linked to a linguistic conceptual grouping. A viable strategy for finding such a link between cognition and language is to first determine a means of measuring nonlinguistic conceptual information, then find a corresponding linguistic form. The object-sorting tasks used in the psychological investigation of nonlinguistic conceptual organization are appropriate measures of nonlinguistic concepts. The language form that corresponds most readily to these sorting tasks is that of word meaning, that is, the information packed into semantic bundles is based on an equivalence across perceptually distinct experiences directly comparable to the equivalences across different objects assessed in object-sorting tasks. The acquisition of color terms is a lexical domain that demonstrates a particularly intimate relationship between concepts and linguistic form which renders it especially suitable as content for nonlinguistic assessment and language training.

The study reported here explored how to go about the specifics of operationalizing these various considerations, and, once the means of investigation were worked out, the effect of prior conceptual knowledge upon subsequent language learning within a training situation.

PURPOSES AND POSSIBLE OUTCOMES

The purposes of this study can be more formally stated as listed below. This chapter covers the first two of the three purposes:

1. To develop a means of assessing prelexical conceptual organization that corresponds to a specific linguistic acquisition, within the semantic domain of color terms.
2. To determine whether preschool children who match objects on the basis of color in a sorting task are more likely to benefit from training for productive uses of verbal color word terms than are preschool children who do not match by colors. Experimentally, the question is whether there are significant differences in the number of trials to criterion between two groups of children: color-concept-users and non–color-concept-users who receive identical training.
3. To explore the interaction between prelexical conceptual status, training, and subsequent conceptual status, with regard to these questions: Does verbal training affect concept performance, as measured by the sorting task? Is there a qualitative difference in the linguistic acquisition of concept-users versus non–concept-users?

Possible outcomes for the effect of prior nonlinguistic conceptual knowledge on linguistic acquisition (question 2) can be aligned with the various theoretical positions reviewed earlier:

a. Color-concept-users training in fewer trials than the non–color-concept users is most clearly predicted by the strong form of the cognition hypothesis (Sinclair, 1971; Sinclair-de Zwart, 1973; Macnamara, 1972).
b. No difference in the amount of training required for either group would be an ambiguous finding. The most obvious interpretation is

that it would represent no effect, that is, random variance of scores, which could be attributed to a true representation of real world relationships, i.e., no connection between prior nonlinguistic concepts and subsequent word learning, or to inadequate experimental design. Another possible interpretation of this finding is suggested by the homologue theoretical model (Bates et al., 1977a). Even if there were no difference in the linguistic performances between the two groups, it would not rule out a relationship between cognition and language at a deeper level. The particular tasks used to assess the relationship were just too superficial in nature, or perhaps cut across different domains, thereby making it impossible to detect "local homologies" (Bates et al., 1977b).

c. A finding of non–color-concept-users training in fewer trials than color-concept-users could also be interpreted in terms of the homologue model, i.e., the tasks did not tap underlying relationships.

Answers to the question of whether verbal training affects concept performance can also be predicated on a theoretical position. The interactionist position (Schlesinger, 1974; Bowerman, 1976, 1977b) suggests that sorting strategies should be affected by the introduction of word labels that explicitly refer to an attribute that can be used to equate the objects on the sorting task—non–color-sorters should switch to a color-sorting strategy after learning correct color reference. The cognition-tied-to-language hypothesis (Schlesinger, in preparation) implies that the non-linguistic color sorting strategy should be characterized by considerable variability and instability until color terms are learned, and relative stability after color terms are acquired.

The question of a possible qualitative difference in the linguistic learning of concept-users versus non–concept-users does not have specific predicted outcomes. However, it is possible that the conceptual knowledge involved in being a "color-sorter" may have an unforeseen influence upon aspects of acquisition not measured in the dependent variable of trials to criterion. The question of difference in performance in the two groups need not be limited to how quickly they learned color terms; it can also address in what fashion they learned them.

PROCEDURES

Nonlinguistic Concept Task

The development of a means of assessing nonverbal concepts required careful consideration of how young children categorize objects, since it would have to be appropriate for children who had not yet learned color terms. Preschool children often begin using color words correctly as early as 30 months of age (Mecham, 1958; Bartlett, 1977, 1978). The sorting tasks used by other researchers that were reviewed earlier served as initial guides for how to develop a sorting task. However, those tasks were designed to explore problems different from the present one, for example, to tap logical relationships among classes, to investigate the comparative salience of various levels of groupings, or to explore differences between children's and adults' performances. The differentiation of color-concept-users and non–color-concept-users for the purpose of training children younger than 3 years of age who do not know the color words requires a behavioral task that meets the following criteria:

1. Appropriate for children ages 2 to 3.6
2. Administered in minimum time, i.e., approximately 15 minutes, or less
3. Objective, observable behavioral criterion levels
4. "Meaningful" in the sense of representative of real world sorting behaviors, i.e., requiring multi-attribute processing
5. Available in a typical clinical setting

Given these criteria, each of the reported sorting tasks can be ruled out on the basis of one or more points. For example, Vygotsky's blocks require only single-attribute processing and are therefore not representative of real world sorting behaviors; the habituation procedures require instrumentation not available in a typical clinical setting; the oddity tasks require considerable time in order to present the number of combinations possible. However, it was possible to use features of the various sorting tasks in combination with new procedures designed to elicit information particular to the purpose of this study.

Purposes of Sorting Tasks   A series of sorting tasks was devised to meet the following specific purposes:

1. To differentiate color-concept-sorters from non–color-concept-sorters on the basis of the use of color as an attribute for equating objects
2. To establish that non–color-sorters were physically capable of sorting by color (i.e., to rule out color blindness)
3. To establish that subjects did not know color words in either a comprehension or a production task format

Description of Sorting Tasks   In order to meet the criteria of "meaningful" and available in a typical clinical setting the stimuli used were common and readily obtainable toys: small plastic colored animals and colored wooden blocks of the same size and shape.[1] The animals could be matched at the level of basic objects, i.e., dog to dog, chicken to chicken, cow to cow, sheep to sheep, and so on. However, the basic object match was confounded with shape (three-dimensional configuration), since all dogs, for example, were identical except for color.

The target colors were the primary colors of red, green, and yellow in clearly differentiated and ideal or prototypical hues. These particular colors were selected in view of Berlin and Kay's (1969) proposed universal sequence of linguistic evolution (the hypothesized historical development of color names in various languages) where red, green, and yellow are among the first. Great care was taken in selecting ideal hues, i.e., a red-red, a green-green, and a yellow-yellow, because of Rosch's finding that these are most salient for children and most easily learned (Rosch 1973, 1975).

The set of sorting tasks and criteria for scoring are defined on the score sheets in Appendix A. Five different tasks were presented. Task 1 was designed to elicit behaviors indicating how the child categorizes when several different criteria for sorting are available. Ten plastic animals were placed on the table in front of the child. The experimenter showed the child a toy animal as a standard and asked him to "Put all the other ones like this one in here" (referring to a large plastic box), or, when necessary, "Show me one like this one...put it in the box." No feedback as to accuracy or desirability of a choice was provided. The 10 animal response stimuli (including a figure of a man) were varied so that the child had five like-colored animals (two of which were identical matches (color plus animal) and three of which were same color but different animals), three same animals but different colors, and two foil stimuli that were not matchable on the basis of either color or animal. The available ways to match and their experimentally defined criteria were:

1. Color (use of same color on first four choices)
2. Animal (use of same animal on first four choices)
3. Identical (first two choices same color and same animal; scored as identical only if subsequent two choices not color)
4. Other (none of the previous criteria)

---

[1]Blocks were 1-inch wooden cubes available in a set of nine colors from Ideal School Supply Co., Oak Lawn, Ill. 60453, #6200.

Plastic colored animals were "Farm Set with Barn," #1175, available from Processed Plastic Co., Montgomery, Ill. 60538, purchased in a local variety store for $1.00. The animals were in red, yellow, green, and black. Three plastic men figures of comparable size and color intensity, also obtained at the local variety store, were added to the stimulus set, one red, one blue, and one white.

Three trials were run, using red, then green, and then yellow as the color of the standard stimulus.[2]

The second task, using the same format as the first with only four choice objects, was designed to eliminate the options of identical or animal match; that is, the only remaining options were "color" or "other." Of the four toy animals available as response options, none was an identical animal; two choices were like color. A color match was defined as the first two choices of the same color.

The third task elicited linguistic information, testing the child's comprehension of color terms through the command "Give me a *red* one."

The fourth task followed up with further linguistic information, testing production of color terms through the question "What color is this?" Six colors were included in this stimulus array, with white, blue, and black added to the red, yellow, and green. (These six colors correspond to Miller and Johnson-Laird's (1976) definition of a minimal set of color names.)

The fifth and final task was another sorting task, this time designed to rule out color blindness (i.e., the inability to differentiate among various colors). The stimuli were wooden blocks that were identical except for the single feature of color. The stimulus objects were 12 blocks, three each of red, green, yellow, and blue. The instructions were "Which (one) goes with this?" in reference to a standard held by the experimenter.

When this set of sorting tasks is compared with those of previous studies, several similarities and contrasts are evident. A procedure has been used in which the subject is free to select his responses in his own order of choice; this is commonly referred to as "free grouping." The options for equating objects in Task 1 combine features of both criterial attribute and multiple attribute sorting tasks in that both options are available. A color match would be on the basis of a single attribute with six discriminably different values. An animal match could be on the basis of either shape or basic object level. An identical match, of animal plus color, would be indicative of a conjunctive set.

An important feature of the series of sorting tasks is that they allow a look at a child's strategies for equating objects within a series of diminishing choice options, that is, his preference for criteria for grouping. A child who sorts by color on Task 1 indicates a preference for color as a means of equating multi-attribute objects when color is in competition with other possible criteria, i.e., animal or identical match. The child who does not

---

[2] A fourth trial for Tasks 1 and 2 was included in the pilot study with a random repeat of one of the colors as a control for a possible color / order effect. No such effect was apparent, and the fourth trial was dropped when the tasks were given to experimental subjects.

sort by color on Task 1 but does so on Task 2 may be indicating that color is available to him as a means of equating multi-attribute objects but is not preferred over other means. The child who sorts by color only on Task 3 indicates a very limited strategy for matching objects by color, available only when the "noise" of additional distracting attributes is eliminated.

Pilot Study   A pilot study was run to determine: 1) the feasibility of using the set of sorting tasks with young children, and 2) the usefulness of the tasks in differentiating between color-concept-users and non–color-concept-users. The pilot study indicated that the sorting tasks were appropriate for children ages 2:7 to 4:1 and elicited different strategies for grouping objects. A criterion for designating a color-concept-user was established: two or more color sorts summed across both Tasks 1 and 2, on two out of three occasions. A more detailed discussion of the pilot study is presented in Appendix B.

Training

The next phase of the study was that of training children who did or did not indicate nonverbal color categorization to correctly produce color terms.

Subjects   Ten children, ranging in age from 2:3 to 3:4, completed the training. All were enrolled in the day care center serving students of Haskell Indian Junior College.[3] All of the children were of Indian or mixed Indian heritage, with a variety of Indian tribes and geographic origins represented. English was spoken in all homes, and it was the only language spoken in the day care center. The Peabody Picture Vocabulary Test–Form B (Dunn, 1965) was given to each subject; all of their scores fell within normal limits. Audiometric screening indicated speech reception thresholds within normal range for all subjects.

None of the subjects responded correctly to color terms in either a comprehension or production format. All of the subjects were able to visually match colors on the block sorting task.

A mean length of utterance (MLU) measure was computed for each child for two reasons: 1) to determine that the child was capable of productive speech within a range of normal expectations, and 2) to investigate any possible predictive value of the MLU for subsequent training success. The MLUs were computed from a tape-recorded sample of each

---

[3]The day care center did not provide formal, structured preschool enrichment activities. To the best of the experimenter's knowledge, the children had not been exposed to systematic, directed repetitions of matching activities. These children were inexperienced with adult-introduced strategies for matching objects. Their naiveté allows for greater confidence in interpreting their sorting behaviors as representations of their own strategies, instead of some attempt to display knowledge previously introduced by an adult.

Table 1.   Description of subjects by groups: sex, age, and MLU

	Sex	Age	MLU
Color-concept-users			
Kathy	F	2:3	2.04
Melinda	F	2:11	3.78
Valerie	F	3:1	3.18
Steven	M	3:2	2.63
Non–color-concept-users			
David	M	2:6	2.1
Ronnie	M	2:6	2.02
Arlene	F	2:7	3.06
Helen	F	2:9	3.94
Rhonda	F	3:0	4.42
Sherry	F	3:4	4.48

subject's spontaneous utterances while responding to a set of pictured stimuli. The same pictures, in the same order of presentation, were used with each subject. The samples of spontaneous language were not collected until the completion of several weeks of training, in order to ensure familiarity with the examiner and a greater willingness to respond verbally (which was especially important in view of the initial shyness and hesitancy on the part of the youngest subjects). A minimum of 50 utterances was collected for each sample. Brown's (1973, p. 54) rules for computing MLU were followed in analyzing the samples. The MLU for each subject is reported in Table 1, along with group designation, sex, and age.

Design   Each subject was first designated as a color-concept-user or a non–color-concept-user on the basis of his performance on the nonverbal concept tasks. Training was then provided in a single-subject multiple baseline sequence. Red, green, and yellow were the training colors; blue, white, and black were the control colors. The nonverbal concept tasks were readministered mid-training and at the completion of training. The dependent variable for comparison of the two groups' performance was the number of trials to criterion for completion of the training.

Subjects were trained as they met criterion for being a color- or non–color-concept-user. Subjects were not paired as non–color-concept-user (NCC) and color-concept-user (CC) for concurrent training. The training phase continued over 8 months before all subjects were run. The amount of time required to train an individual subject varied from 2 weeks to 10 weeks.

Materials and Experimental Setting   Ten different objects were used as materials, five of which were used for training purposes and five as untrained probes. The training objects were toy watches, yarn hair ribbons,

Table 2.   Training and probe objects

Objects	Colors					
	Red	Green	Yellow	White	Blue	Black
Watch	T	T	T	CP	CP	CP
Ribbon	T	T	T	CP	CP	CP
Comb	T	T	T	CP	CP	CP
Spoon	T	T	T	CP	CP	CP
Plate	T	T	T	CP	CP	CP
Balloon	OP	OP	OP	CP	CP	CP
Barrette	OP	OP	OP	CP	CP	CP
Cups	OP	OP	OP	CP	CP	CP
Bowl	OP	OP	OP	CP	CP	CP
Pen	OP	OP	OP	CP	CP	CP

T, training; OP, untrained object probe for trained colors; CP, probe for untrained color (only a subset of these were actually used).

combs, spoons, and plates. Probe objects were balloons, barrettes, cups, bowls, and felt-tip marking pens. The 10 objects were represented in six colors: the three training colors of red, green, and yellow and the three control colors of white, black, and blue. All training objects were identical across the different colors. For example, the probe object of cup was exactly the same cup except that it varied by color, i.e., six otherwise identical cups which were red, green, yellow, white, blue, or black. The various object/color combinations are represented in Table 2.

All subjects were trained in the same location, a cul-de-sac at the end of a large hallway in the upstairs of an old house being used to house administrative offices at the day care center. Lighting was ample, with a large east window on one wall. The location was quiet, with few distractions or interruptions. The training situation consisted of a small table with the experimenter and the child seated directly opposite each other. Only those materials being used in a particular training sequence were placed on the table. Others were placed on the floor out of sight. There was an additional chair nearby for the use of reliability observers.

Training Sequence   The goal of training was a correct response to the question "What color is this?" for the colors red, green, and yellow in reference to either trained or untrained objects.

Training followed a multiple baseline sequence, training first red, then green, then red versus green discrimination, then yellow, then red versus green versus yellow discrimination. The multiple baseline sequence was chosen for three reasons:

1. Green and yellow could serve as controls for possible outside influences before their actual training.

2. An analysis of the number of trials to criterion for the different training steps would give an estimate of relative difficulty.
3. The probability of success in training would be greater if one discrimination was introduced at a time, rather than the multiple discriminations required by the concurrent training of red, green, and yellow.

Baseline   A baseline session consisting of the 10 different objects with the six different colors represented was run for each subject prior to training. It corresponded to the first trial of the untrained object and color probes for training red (see Probe Sheet, Appendix C). The actual stimulus objects were: red balloon, red barrette, red cup, red bowl, red pencil, black watch, blue ribbon, white comb, green spoon, and yellow plate. The criterion for initiating training was no correct response to any of the stimuli.[4]

Probes   The probes for untrained objects of the colors receiving training were presented at the beginning of each session and after reaching training criterion on the color being trained, i.e., 18/20 correct responses. Neutral social reinforcement was provided for these responses, such as "thank you," with no corrective feedback.

The probes for untrained colors were presented at the beginning of each session with one object selected to represent each color not trained to that point. For example, when training red, the untrained color probe items were: green spoon, yellow plate, black watch, blue ribbon, and white comb. Only neutral social reinforcement was provided for these probes.

Training Procedures   The child was seated at a table across from the experimenter. The training objects for the color(s) being trained were on the table. The experimenter elicited the child's full attention, then picked up or pointed to an object and asked "What color is this?" If the child's response was correct, the experimenter responded with immediate social reinforcement, first on a 1:1 ratio, later reducing to an intermittent schedule as the child's behavior indicated when that was appropriate. Food reinforcers were necessary at the earliest stage of training for the four youngest subjects, but were phased out as soon as possible. If the response was incorrect, the experimenter provided corrective feedback, such as "No, that's a green one," and immediately repeated the item. If

---

[4]Additional data were necessary for the child who used one color term, such as "red," as a rote response for all colors. The child was accepted as a subject if he failed the comprehension task and if the one color term was situationally variable, i.e., used on one occasion but not on others. The child was eliminated as a subject if he volunteered additional confirming data, such as spontaneously pointing to a red object and saying "That's red."

the response was unintelligible or if there was no response, it was not scored and the experimenter repeated the trial. A response was scored as correct if it was an intelligible approximation of the correct color term; accuracy of articulation was not required. Incorrect responses were intelligible words other than the correct color term. A trial was defined as the experimenter's presentation of the question "What color is this?" Time-out and verbal direction were used by the experimenter as needed to control extraneous or interfering behaviors.

The training procedures are obviously based on a behavioral philosophy of training, incorporating principles of controlled stimulus presentation and direct reinforcement, in contrast to Piagetian procedures allowing for learning based on "self-discovery." The behavioral procedures are justified on two counts: 1) they allow for the collection of data to demonstrate that learning was a consequence of training and not other environmental events, to compare the relative difficulty of different training steps (content), and to compare the individual subjects' patterns of performance, and 2) there is no evidence that the amounts of conceptual learning observed as a result of training differs for the two methods (Brainerd, 1977b, pp. 79–83).

Training was done on a daily basis, with one 15–30 minute individual session per day.

Training Steps   The training steps were as follows:

1. *Train red*
    Random order of presentation of five red training objects
    Criterion: 90% on two consecutive training blocks of 10 items (18 out of 20)
    4/5 correct on untrained object probes, across two sessions[5] (if fail probe after reaching criterion on training, repeat 9/10 correct with training items until reach criterion on probes)

2 . *Train green*
    Random order of presentation of five green training objects
    Criterion: Same as 1 above

3. *Discriminate red versus green*
    Random presentation of red and green training objects
    Criterion: 18/20 correct during training
    8/10 correct on untrained object probes across two sessions

---

[5]A session was ended following the first passing performance on untrained object probes, so that a new training step was not introduced until full criterion had been reached.

4. *Train yellow*
   Random presentation of five yellow training objects
   Criterion: Same as 1 above
5. *Discriminate red versus green versus yellow*
   Random presentation of red, green, and yellow training objects
   Criterion: 18/20 correct on training items
               12/15 correct on untrained object probes, across two sessions

Nonlinguistic Concept Tasks   The nonlinguistic concept tasks were given prior to training, when criterion was reached on red/green discrimination, and when criterion was reached on red/green/yellow discrimination (the conclusion of training).

Reliability   Reliability measures were obtained for both the nonlinguistic concept tasks and the training procedures. Observer reliability and other examiner reliability were the forms of reliability for the nonverbal concept tasks. Observer judgments were made live, in the room. The bases for these judgments were the stimulus objects selected by the child according to sequence, and the child's verbal responses to "What color is this?" Other examiner reliability was based upon the administration of the nonverbal concept task by another examiner on an occasion different from the experimenter's administration. Reliability was based upon a trial-by-trial comparison of the child's scored responses.

Observer reliability was also measured for the training procedures, with reliability judgments made live, in the room. Judgments were based upon both the experimenter's and child's behavior, with the experimenter's presentation of "What color is this?" defining a trial, and the child's verbal response defining the response. A trial-by-trial comparison was made with the observer's and experimenter's score sheets. Agreements were divided by total judgments, with the resulting percentage constituting the reliability measure.

RESULTS AND DISCUSSION

Two sets of results are presented in this section. The data collected on the sorting task, both before and during training, are discussed relative to how children categorized the objects, and how to interpret the findings as evidence for a prelexical concept, consistency of performance, reliability, and influence of training on sorting behaviors. The training data are reported and discussed in regard to differences between the two groups of children, reliability, potential predictors of performance, controls for external variables, and relative difficulty of training steps, and a comparison to patterns of normal acquisition is made.

Table 3.   Categorization of objects on the three trials of Task 1

	Color	Other	Animal	Identical	
Lower age	5	10	5	7	27
$N=9$					
(2:3 to 2:11)	(19%)	(37%)	(19%)	(26%)	
Upper age	4	15	6	17	42
$N=14$					
(3:0 to 4:1)	(10%)	(36%)	(14%)	(40%)	
	9	25	11	24	69
	(13%)	(36%)	(16%)	(35%)	

Nonlinguistic Concept Tasks   The nonlinguistic concept tasks were administered to all 11 of the subjects who started training[6] a minimum of two times, on two different occasions, in order to meet the two-out-of-three occasion criterion for designation as color-concept-user. For the eight subjects who were trained last, the tasks were given a minimum of four times, twice prior to training, once mid-training, and again at the conclusion of training. Several subjects received further testings post-training to follow qualitative differences between color-concept-users and non–color-concept-users, which is discussed in the next chapter.

Categorization of Objects   How did the children categorize the objects on the free-sorting tasks? The data from the training subjects were pooled with that of the pilot study subjects for a total *N* of 23, ages 2:3 to 4:1. The data consisted of the first administration of the sorting task for the training subjects, pooled with the once-only administration data from the pilot subjects. The subjects were roughly divided into chronological groupings, with an upper age group defined as 3:0 to 4:1 ($N=14$) and a lower age group defined as 2:3 to 2:11 ($N=9$). Their responses were categorized as matching by color, matching by animal, identical, or random match, according to the criteria on the score sheets in Appendix A.

The results, in terms of number of responses and percentage of total responses, are presented in Tables 3 and 4. The results for Task 1 and Task 2 are presented separately, because the response options were not the same for both tasks. Only color or random matches was possible on Task 2.

The results confirm that children as young as 2:3 to 2:11 are able to equate objects by various means, i.e., color, animal, identity, or other criteria (e.g., spatial arrangements, size). The data are consistent with Denney's (1972b) finding that many children in the 2- to 5-year-old age group do group according to one common perceptual attribute, in this case color or animal (shape).

---

[6]One subject had to be dropped from the program (see p. 67).

Table 4. Categorization of objects on the three trials of Task 2

	Color	Other	
Lower age N=9	10 (37%)	17 (63%)	27
Upper age N=14	19 (45%)	23 (55%)	42
	29 (42%)	40 (58%)	69

For Task 1 the percentage of sorts according to color (13%) was comparable to that for animal (16%). This equivalence of sorting preferences conflicts with findings reported by others. Suchman and Trabasso (1966) reported that their subjects in this age range preferred color. On the other hand, Denney (1972a, 1972b) reported that shape was the preferred dimension for free classification among 2- and 3-year-old children.

Thirty-five percent of the responses were identical matches, based upon a conjunction of animal and color. This result is compatible with Denney's (1972a, p. 1168) finding (with geometric stimuli) that two-dimensional groupings (form and size) were used more frequently than one-dimensional groupings at each age level (2, 3, and 4 years of age). However, the identical match category as defined here is confounded with the others. The criterion of "first two sorts if subsequent two not color" allows for the categories to be interrelated, in that a color match could also be an identical match category; an identical match could also be a match by animal or random. This interrelatedness reflects a hierarchical ordering on the part of the experimenter. The rationale was that the experimenter first needed to know if a child sorted by colors, even if the first two were identical match on the first two choices (only two stimuli were available that could be matched identically) and even if the child then switched to a sort-by-animal strategy or a random strategy. It is possible, with only two choices as criterion, that the child's identical choices were chance selections within an overall strategy of either animal or random matching.

The data were retabulated to eliminate the identical match category, creating the three independent categories of color, random, and animal matches. The results are presented in Table 5.

With such reclassification of the identical matches, in most cases the child's two subsequent choices indicated a match-by-animal strategy (animal sorts increased from 16% to 41% when the identical match was eliminated). The predominance of animal (shape) sorts shifted the evi-

Table 5.   Categorization of objects on Task 1, without identical match

	Color	Random	Animal	
Lower age	5	13	9	27
N = 9				
(2:3 to 2:11)	(19%)	(48%)	(33%)	
Upper age	4	19	19	42
N = 14				
(3:0 to 4:1)	(10%)	(45%)	(45%)	
	9	32	28	69
	(13%)	(46%)	(41%)	

dence heavily in the direction of Denney's (1972a, 1972b) finding of a preference for shape. It is not possible to determine if this change in sorting pattern (from identical to animal classification) reflected a shift in the child's strategy, from identical to animal, or if the first two identical choices were random choices within an initial sort-by-animal strategy.

The data from Task 1 suggest a slight developmental trend in the age range sampled, with the 2-year-olds more likely to sort by color than the 3-year-olds and the 3-year-olds more likely to sort by identical match or animal (depending upon the classification system used) than the 2-year-olds. This developmental trend is the same as that reported by Suchman and Trabasso (1966). However, color preference was not dominant even among the 2-year-olds.

Interpretation of "Prelexical Concept"   It is appropriate at this point to address the possible distinction between "having" a concept and selecting objects on a certain basis. "Having" a concept implies the presence of a well-formed strategy for equating objects, independent of the particular set of objects themselves, that allows for the testing of new items as possible instances of the concept across a variety of settings and objects. However, a child could correctly group objects without using such a sophisticated cognitive strategy. Instead he could select like objects out of an array of objects placed in front of him by recognizing the perceptual attributes and relationships of the particular set of objects. Such categorical groupings would reflect an immediate recognition of likeness and similarities that may not have been present prior to the presentation of objects, and may not generalize to other objects in other contexts.

It is not possible to determine on the basis of the present data whether the children who sorted by color on the sorting tasks did so at the level of "having" a concept (a well-formed strategy for equating objects that generalizes across settings) or if they sorted only according to the recognition of immediately available perceptual similarities. The evidence for the recognition level of grouping is present (i.e., equivalent groupings of objects according to color), but the evidence for "having" a concept is not, such as: 1) some indication of testing new instances according to a given attribute, for example, "Here's another red one" or "Here's another one the same color" (since none of the subjects knew color terms, such linguistic cues are not available), or 2) some indication of the children's perception of the correctness of their choice (since there was no feedback or "right" or "wrong" choices, it was unlikely that the children would spontaneously make such judgments), or 3) some signs of generalizing to novel contexts (data from other contexts were not collected).

This differentiation between "having" a concept and using a strategy based on immediate perceptual matching is similar to but not synonymous with Bates et al.'s (1977a) discussion of content-specific versus content-free knowing. Their distinction is based on Piaget's notions of figurative versus operative knowing. The figurative aspect refers to actions by which the child produces a "copy" of reality, where reality is literally represented using perception, imitation, and mental imagery. On the other hand, operative knowing refers to actions whose result is some transformation or change of reality, some active restructuring on the child's part (Ginsburg and Opper, 1969, p. 153). According to Piaget, language entails both aspects of knowing. (See Moore and Harris (1978) for a criticism of the Piagetian position on language acquisition that hinges on the interpretation of figurative and operative knowing in relation to language.) The point made by Bates et al. (1977a, p. 269) is that performance on a particular task, such as the sorting task, does not yield a measure of "pure cognition." However, the problem is that operative knowing cannot be measured without involving figurative content. Any particular measurement task devised would be vulnerable to the criticism that it didn't measure "pure cognition."

The idea presented here of a child "having a concept" does not imply that the child is being credited with "pure cognition" in the Piagetian sense of action-based operative transformations of reality. Instead, the notion to be pointed out is that a child could group objects either on the basis of a preexisting strategy for matching (that may be "figurative" or "operative" or both or neither), or simply on the basis of an on-the-spot recognition of perceptual similarities that could be a temporary strategy or serve as the start of a more stable strategy.

Given these interpretative problems, the designation "color-concept-user" is intended to describe a child who demonstrates either a well-formed strategy or a recognition of color similarities among a set of objects, while "non–color-concept-user" describes a child who has neither a prior strategy nor a present recognition. The sense of "concept prior to lexical acquisition," as determined by this set of sorting tasks, does not imply the existence of a fully attained concept prior to the testing, but rather a concept (categorical equivalence) that may be at a less sophisticated level of development.

Consistency of Performance   An important question is how consistent were the children's performances on the sorting task. The notion of "color-concept-user" implies some stability in the child's preferred strategy for equating objects. The literature on conceptual styles (e.g., Kogan, 1976, Chapter 5) does not provide specific information with regard to consistency of performance.[7] There simply is not much known about stability. Kogan (1976) emphasizes the relativity involved in conceptual functioning. . . . "for children as young as two years of age, alternative modes of conceptualizing may exist side by side in the child's cognitive repertoire, the particular mode chosen depending on the nature of the provided stimulus array and the general instructions to the task" (p. 114).

With the strong possibility of stability dependent upon the stimuli and the task, it was important to obtain measures of stability for the nonverbal sorting tasks used in this study. A critical question was how consistent was a child's performance on repeated administrations of the sorting tasks. The 11 training subjects' performances on the last two of the possible three pretraining administrations of the sorting task (for a two-out-of-three criterion) were analyzed in terms of agreement for the color-concept-user versus non–color-concept-user classification. The two test sessions were on different days (sometimes with a few days' interval) and, in some cases, were given by two different examiners. The agreement was 100% for all 11 subjects; that is, on both occasions their sorting behaviors revealed the same strategy across the six trials of Tasks 1 and 2, in terms of the color-concept-user versus non–color-concept-user distinction (criterion of two or more color sorts summed across both tasks for "color-concept-user"). Such consistency across repeated measures indicates the stability that is necessary if the term "color-concept-user" is to be interpreted as referring to a child who uses a strategy of equating objects by the attribute of color.

Another measure of stability was obtained, that of the possible effects of different examiners. Five children were given the nonverbal concept tasks by two different examiners on different occasions, in three

---

[7]Kogan (1976, p. 91) reports stability coefficients of conceptual style for the Sigel Object Categorization Task for children tested at age 3 years and then 1 year later. He reports only a modest stability for girls and none for boys. However, the time interval for stability in the present study is much less than 1 year.

cases on two different days, from 1 to 3 days apart. One examiner was the experimenter. The second examiner was a graduate student who received brief instructions, including one sample demonstration with a nonexperimental child. The second examiner gave the tasks in the same location. Only he and the child were present. The examiners elicited the same pattern of responses, that is, color-concept-user versus non–color-concept-user, for four of the five children. For the one child on whom there was not agreement, the pattern of responses was the same for five out of the six trials; he had two color sorts on one occasion and only one on the other, so the lack of agreement on one trial accounted for the lack of overall agreement as to CC versus NCC. Such high levels of agreement indicate that performance on the sorting tasks was not unique to the experimenter's presence.

Reliability   A further question addressed the reliability of the scoring procedures; that is, were the subjects' responses objectively scorable? Observer reliability was obtained. An adult observer watched the administration of the sorting tasks to four of the training subjects and scored the children's responses. In two cases the observer was an untrained classroom aide; in the other two cases the observer was a graduate student. Both observers received brief instructions regarding the score sheet and were allowed to examine the stimuli prior to actual observation and scoring. The observers sat in close proximity to the child and the examiner, but out of the range of vision for observing the examiner's scoring. The agreement for all four children for the six trials across the two tasks was 100%, confirming that the responses were discrete, readily observable, and such that they could be scored objectively.

Pre-, Mid-, and Posttraining Measures   The set of sorting tasks was readministered to nine of the training subjects following the completion of training; for seven of those subjects it was also administered during training, following criterion on red/green discrimination. All three color-concept-users for whom there were data indicated a consistent pattern of color-concept-responding, with no changes as a result of training. Four of the non–color-concept-users indicated the same consistency in sorting, maintaining an NCC strategy on all testings. Two of the NCC subjects changed their sorting strategies. One switched to a CC strategy at the completion of training. Interestingly, she was the NCC who completed training in the fewest number of trials. However, any possibility that this switch in sorting strategy accounted for her fast training was immediately weakened by two observations: the other NCC who trained in fewer trials did not switch to a CC sorting strategy, while the other NCC who did switch to a CC strategy required the second highest number of trials to complete training. This second NCC demonstrated an interesting relationship between her sorting strategies and certain linguistic behaviors. A discussion of her patterns of response is deferred until the next chapter when qualitative differences in the training performances between CCs and NCCs are discussed at length.

The general conclusion to be drawn is that the children were quite consistent in their preferred sorting strategy. This finding of consistency does not support the earlier predictions based on either the interactionist or cognition—first positions. It also runs counter to the commonly held (e.g., Miller and Yoder, 1974; Bloom and Lahey, 1978) clinical assumption that teaching word labels will introduce the corresponding underlying nonlinguistic concept. None of the NCC subjects switched to a CC strategy immediately following their mastery of color term reference to color properties of objects (a knowledge required for correct performance by mid-training; see later discussion of the difficulty of the training steps). Also, none of the CC-users indicated a difference in stability before learning color terms as compared to after training, when the concept could have been "anchored" by a word. While neither of these a priori predictions was upheld, there was evidence of another kind of phenomenon that bears on how mastery of the words and conceptual knowledge influenced each other. This evidence is presented in Chapter 5. At this point, it can be concluded that either the training procedures were not sufficiently powerful to overcome the subjects' sorting preferences or the training focused on specific linguistic abilities not directly utilized in the sorting task. The evidence presented later offers support for the latter interpretation.

Training

Eleven subjects started the training, with ten completing it (four color-concept-users and six non–color-concept-users). One subject, a color-concept-user, was dropped following a 10-day absence from training due to illness that required hospitalization. The absence followed the completion of criterion for red/green discrimination. When he returned, his responses for red/green discrimination had dropped to chance accuracy over several sessions. With trials to criterion as a dependent variable, it was regarded as misleading to repeat a segment of training with one subject, so he was dropped.

Group Data The results of training are depicted in Figure 1. (See Appendix D for individual subjects' training data.)

The mean number of trials for the six non–color-concept-users was 1,338.7, compared to a mean of 693.3 for the four color-concept-users, for a difference of 645.4. The exact probability of the difference between

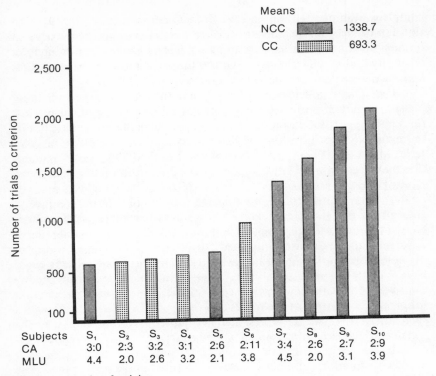

Figure 1.   Results of training.

the means was computed using the Randomization Test for Two Independent Samples (Siegel, 1956, pp. 152–156). The exact one-tailed probability of the occurrence of the observed scores was 0.0476. Therefore, the null hypothesis was rejected. The subjects designated as color-concept-users required significantly fewer trials to criterion than the subjects designated as non–color-concept-users.

The group data supported the prediction of the strong cognition hypothesis—conceptual status influenced ease of acquisition of color words. The comparison of the performance of the two groups also provides evidence of the validity of the sorting task. Since the two groups performed differently when learning color words, it is very likely that whatever the sorting tasks measured was directly related to the acquisition of color words.

Reliability   Reliability estimates were obtained for the training procedures, including probes, based upon a trial-by-trial comparison of the experimenter's recordings of the subject's behavior with that of a live adult observer in the room. Reliability estimates ranged from 91% to 100%, with a mean of 95.64%, pooled across seven randomly selected training sessions with different children at different steps in training. The reliability is sufficiently high to confirm the discreteness of training trials and the objectivity possible in scoring responses.

Individual Data   A look at the training performance of individual subjects provides information of particular interest for the questions addressed in the study. While the four subjects with the most trials to criterion were NCC, the one with the fewest trials to criterion was also an NCC, along with a second NCC who completed the training in a number of trials comparable to the CC. It is apparent that the variability in number of trials to criterion is much greater for the NCC subjects than for the CC. The results indicate that evidence of color concept acquisition prior to the training would predict greater ease in training color words, but the inverse is not necessarily so; that is, a lack of prior color concept acquisition does not always predict a longer training sequence. Insofar as the strong form of the cognition hypothesis predicts that cognitive knowledge is a prerequisite for linguistic acquisition, it does not account for how some NCC subjects trained as easily as the CC subjects. The findings can be illustrated in the form of a matrix:

	CC	NCC
Fewer trials	X (100%)	X (33⅓%)
More trials	0%	(66⅔%)

While CC versus NCC is the more accurate predictor for fewer or more trials, it did not account for one-third of the NCC subjects' performances. While this could be written off as a chance phenomenon, given such a small number of subjects, it is more productive to look for an explanation within the data available. Since prelexical conceptual organization did not account for the performance of all the NCC subjects, presumably other variables are involved.

Potential Predictors of Performance

Age   Among the variables that could be potential predictors of performance is chronological age. One could predict that older children would train faster. However, the Pearson correlation coefficient between age and number of training trials is 0.31 ($p = 0.19$), indicating a weak positive correlation; that is, the older children were somewhat more likely to require more training trials than the younger subjects. It is apparent that greater age did not predict greater success in training.

Linguistic Acquisition   Another potential predictor variable is linguistic ability. It could be predicted that subjects with more advanced linguistic skills would train faster than those with lower levels of linguistic competence. The mean length of utterance (MLU) was chosen as a performance measure that is a good simple index of linguistic development for the early stages of language acquisition (Brown, 1973, p. 185). The Pearson correlation coefficient between MLU and training trials is 0.18 ($p = 0.30$). The MLU values also do not predict training performance.

It would appear that level of linguistic ability, as measured by MLU, was not a predictor for relative ease of training. It is possible that the MLU did not measure the particular aspect of language ability that was critical for the training provided in the study. The MLU measures length of utterances, which is an indirect measure of grammatical complexity. The training addressed the acquisition of word meanings. There is no evidence available to directly link semantic sophistication with MLU; instead, there is some additional evidence that the two linguistic skills are at least somewhat independent. Nelson and Bonvillian (1978, p. 494) reported that children's word-learning competencies at age 2:6 did not predict the same children's utterance lengths at age 4:6. A specific measure of semantic acquisition, perhaps limited only to attributives, would perhaps have predictive value for training color terms, but no such measure is available.

Intellectual Functioning   General intellectual functioning is a potential predictor variable that has high intuitive appeal. Perhaps those children who trained faster were just "smarter," regardless of their CC/NCC status. No standardized IQ tests were administered to the subjects. The Peabody Picture Vocabulary Test–Form B (Dunn, 1965) was given primarily as a means of screening out subjects who had very limited language comprehension or possible subnormal intelligence. It also did not have predictive value. The Pearson correlation coefficient between the PPVT-B scores and the number of training trials was only -0.03 ($p = 0.46$). While considerable caution should be given to the interpretation of the PPVT-B scores, given the young ages of the subjects and their total unfamiliarity with such a test format, it is concluded that general intelligence, as inferred from a receptive vocabulary test, could not account for either the pattern of differences between the two groups or the performance of individual subjects.

Social/Emotional   Some potential social/emotional factors can also be ruled out. Subjects who required many trials were just as cooperative and attentive during training as were subjects who trained in few trials.

Performance of Identical Twins   The difficulty in accounting for the individual differences, in particular for the NCC users who required fewer trials, is illustrated by two of the subjects who were identical twins, therefore of the same age and presumably the same intelligence. Both boys sorted as NCC, yet one (David) completed training in 657 trials (commensurate with the CC subjects) whereas the other (Ronnie) required 1,573 trials (commensurate with the NCC subjects). Their MLUs were virtually identical, and Ronnie's PPVT-B score was a little higher than David's. There was one difference between the two boys. Ronnie had suffered a minor eye injury a few months prior to training that had required hospitalization. David was described as socially dominant over Ronnie, although neither of the boys was outwardly assertive during their individual training sessions. Both were relatively shy, in fact, a characteristic they held in common with the other NCC who completed training in few trials, thereby presumably ruling out social assertiveness as a factor.

To conclude, the most accurate predictor for training performance was whether or not a child sorted objects by color. Other subject variables—chronological age, mean length of utterance, PPVT-B score, and general social/emotional demeanor—were not predictive.

It is tempting to return to the homologue model (Bates et al., 1977a, 1977b) for an interpretation of these findings. Perhaps those NCC subjects who trained quickly really had some deeper conceptual knowledge of color equivalence that just was not tapped by the performance requirements or arbitrary criterion levels of the sorting tasks; perhaps they actually were more similar in conceptual knowledge to the CC subjects than the sorting tasks indicated. The problem is that there is no way of determining to which NCC subjects this interpretation should be applied. It could as justifiably be argued that the other NCC subjects, who did not train quickly, also had "real cognitive knowledge" not tapped by the sorting tasks, in which case the underlying conceptual information would not predict ease of acquisition. The measurement problems inherent in the homologue model limit its usefulness as a means of accounting for the specifics of the relationship between cognition and language.

Controls for External Variables

The next question is whether there were possible external variables influencing the subjects' performances. Of particular significance is the question of possible experimenter bias. Since it was not possible to provide additional trainers, the experimenter trained all the subjects. If the experimenter knew how each child had performed on the sorting tasks, it could be argued that his expectations for performance could have been subtly communicated to the subjects or could have influenced his judgments in regard to criterion behaviors. A control for experimenter bias was introduced for the last five subjects trained. The final, and deciding, presentation of the pretraining sorting task was administered by another examiner, as described earlier. The results were not known to the experimenter, who trained these five subjects blind. Of these five subjects, two turned out to be NCCs who required many trials, one a CC who required a few trials, one a NCC who required few trials, and the other was the subject who was subsequently dropped. Further indirect controls for experimenter bias were inherent in the design of the study. Not all of the subjects were run at the same time; instead, the training spread over a period of 8 months. Subjects were trained as they met criterion for being a color-concept-user, or non–color-concept-user. Subjects were not paired as CC versus NCC and trained concurrently. Therefore, it was not possible to estimate an expected number of trials for CC or NCC until almost all of the subjects were run. A further control was the objectivity inherent in the procedures and criterion levels of the training itself. In short, the possibility of experimenter bias accounting for the results is very unlikely.

Another question of external influence is whether the training accounted for the subjects' learning of color words. With color terms used often in the speech of adults to young children, particularly in a preschool context, it is reasonable to wonder if the subjects' acquisition of color words during the training period may have been attributable to spontaneous learning in informal circumstances. Several controls were implemented for this possible influence. There was no formal training of color words within the day care setting during the training period, although there were activities involving colors, such as painting and construction paper designs. Three controls were incorporated into the design of the training itself: the multiple baseline sequence of training red, then green, then yellow; the three control colors, white, blue, and black that received no training; and a control subject.

None of the subjects learned a training color before it was actually trained. The probes of untrained colors at the beginning of each training session (see Appendix C) indicated that green and yellow stayed at baseline levels for all the subjects until training was started on that particular color. The same was true for the untrained colors of white, blue, and black. At the conclusion of training, for all subjects the accuracy of naming white, blue, or black objects remained at baseline levels. A common error was to refer to white, blue, or black as red, green, or yellow. In other words, none of the subjects spontaneously acquired color terms other than those directly trained. Furthermore, one subject, an NCC, received

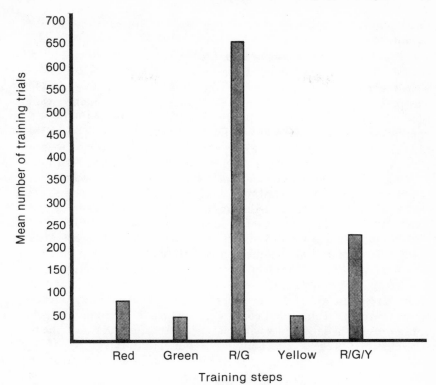

Figure 2.   Trials per training step (mean number of trials across all subjects).

no training during the same time period that two other subjects were trained. Her accuracy in color-naming remained at baseline levels throughout the time period. Therefore it is concluded that the training itself, not outside influences, accounted for the learning of color terms.

Difficulty of Training Steps

Group Data   An area of interest in regard to the training program is the relative difficulty of the various training steps. The subjects' performances were analyzed in terms of number of trials to criterion for each training step, pooled across all 10 subjects, with a group mean for each training step. The results are presented in Figure 2.

The red/green discrimination was the most difficult training step in terms of the mean number of trials across all subjects. It also was the most difficult training step for each individual subject. The group mean for the red training was 84.9 trials to criterion, for green, 52.7, for red/green discrimination, 658.5, for yellow, 51.4, and for red/green/yellow discrimination, 233.6.

Learning at Each Training Step   An explanation of the relative difficulty of the various training steps requires a detailed look at exactly what was required at each step. For the initial "red" training, the child was presented with five different red objects. The experimenter would randomly select one, hold it up, and say, "What color is this?" If the child responded incorrectly he was told, "No, that's red." The trial was immediately repeated. What does a child have to learn for such an apparently simple response? On a superficial level, he must learn to say "red" each time the experimenter asks him a question. Presumably, he might also learn that the word "red" is related to the word "color"; that the word "red" is absolute, in that another word even if it is another color term, will not suffice; that it refers to static visual properties of objects; and that the visual property (with discriminable differences in actual light wave values[8]) is the only feature common to the five training objects.

What was learned during the second step of training corresponded to the first, with the only additional requirement being that the child had to shift his response to "green" to a set of training objects that was identical to the first in all features but color. Only one child, Helen (a non–color-concept-user), had difficulty with this step, requiring 168 trials. She persisted in using "red" as a response to "What color is this?" even though she was provided with corrective feedback following each error. Her behavior indicated an argumentative stance, as if protesting the absoluteness of "green," and only "green," as correct whereas "red" had been acceptable earlier. It is possible that she just generally resisted change, or that she did not understand the absolute nature of color words (regarding her word "red" to be as appropriate as the experimenter's "green"), or that she had not associated the change in verbal response to the change in visual properties of the stimuli.

The third training step, that of red/green discrimination, was the most difficult for all subjects. It was so difficult for some that an arbitrary ceiling of 1,000 trials was set as a means of minimizing the frustration and boredom that can undermine training when there are repeated failure experiences. At the conclusion of 1,000 trials those subjects were moved into the fourth step of training without having met criterion on red/green discrimination. It was at this step of training that the child had to differentially associate the two previously learned color word responses with their

---

[8]Although every effort was made to keep the hue constant across objects, the different materials of which the objects were composed created some differences, e.g., the red of yarn ribbon is not exactly the same as the red of a shiny plastic cup or the red of a rubber balloon.

appropriate visual properties, if he had not already done so. He must have learned that a particular color, i.e., red or green, was a static property of a particular object, and that this was true of several objects (at a minimum, the 10 training objects and untrained probe objects); that this property corresponded to a verbal label; and that there were two different values of the property, with two different corresponding verbal labels. In other words, he had to map out a correct referential meaning for the words "red" and "green." It is important to note that the child did not have to know that a particular visual property, e.g., "greenness," was the only common feature of the training and probe objects. He could have performed correctly on the task by knowing "this one is green," "that one is green," "this one is red," "that one is red," without realizing "these are all red" and "these are all green."

The source of greatest difficulty was apparently the discriminative association required in responding "red" only to red objects and "green" only to green objects. This is inferred from the observation that almost all the subjects' errors consisted of incorrect labeling of red or green; that is, their responses were generally limited to "red" or "green" and their errors were incorrect reference to red or green objects.

The following training step, that of training yellow, was the easiest step for all subjects but one. It was essentially a repetition of the learning involved in the red and green training steps, simply requiring a switch to a different verbal response. For those subjects who met criterion on red/green discrimination, the training of yellow was presumably facilitated by their having learned that a given verbal label corresponded to a given static visual property. The one child who had trouble, requiring 214 trials, was Helen who earlier had had difficulty learning green and who subsequently did not reach criterion on red/green discrimination (she was trained to the ceiling of 1,000 trials and then moved to the next step). Her errors consisted of "red" or "green" responses, even when she was provided corrective feedback. Her strategy seemed consistent with the earlier one of "red" for "green," indicating either a reluctance to change, a refusal to accept the absoluteness of color terms, or a lack of association of verbal responses to visual properties (a lack of referential mapping). Her errors often indicated a pattern of consistent false responses, e.g., "red" for "green" and vice versa during red/green discrimination training, thereby indicating some accuracy in associating verbal responses to visual properties. By this time the experimenter was prone to interpret her errors as a reluctance to accept the absoluteness of color terms, although it was not possible to completely rule out the other two explanations.

The last training step, the discrimination of red, green, and yellow, was the second most difficult for all subjects but one (whose second most difficult step was the first). The learning at this red / green / yellow step appears to parallel that of the red / green discrimination, with the addition of the third color, yellow. The child had to remember the verbal responses "red" and "green" and the visual properties with which they were associated (in the case of those subjects who had reached criterion on red / green discrimination), and, in addition, had to add "yellow" and its visual properties. Those subjects who had not reached criterion on red / green discrimination had to learn to differentially associate all three word labels with the three different constant visual properties of the various objects. Once again, it is important to note that an awareness of the relationship among objects being that of a single common attribute was not necessary for success on this training step. The child could correctly respond on a "this one is red," "this one is green," "this one is yellow" basis.

Natural Acquisition Compared to Training

The preceding section discussed in detail what the children needed to learn in order to perform correctly on the various training steps. The question that reasonably follows such an account of learning via explicit training is: How does this correspond to how children acquire color terms spontaneously, without explicit training? Is there evidence for Brainerd's (1977b, p. 84) assertion that the learning that occurs in laboratory environments can be just as "natural" as the learning in the environment outside the laboratory?

The work of Bartlett (1977, 1978) and Cruse (1977) provides a detailed description of how children acquire color words in a natural environment to which we can compare the patterns of learning evident in training. One part of Bartlett's work, that investigating semantic organization and reference, was reviewed earlier (p. 43). She found that the children's first use of color terms revealed a knowledge of how color terms relate to each other and to the word "color," but not correct reference; reference was worked out later.

Semantic Organization and Reference How do Bartlett's findings concerning semantic organization and reference fit in with the interpretation of the training data presented above? Let us compare how children spontaneously sort out the relationship between color terms and colored objects in the world, and the requirements for learning color terms in the training situation. The data reported by Bartlett suggest that the natural acquisition process for color terms is as follows:

Level 1:   Produce several color terms none of which correctly refers to
           colored objects; such color terms are semantically related to the

word "color" in some kind of superordinate/hyponymic organization

Level 2:   Still incomplete mastery of color term mapping onto color spaces; for most children, the number of color terms available in the lexicon exceeds the number of terms with correct references; signs of a general referential meaning for the word "color" and the general dimension of color

Level 3:   Full mastery of color terms, with complete referential meaning and semantic organization

The learning required for successful performance in training was presented as:

1. Learn that several words, i.e, "red," "green," and "yellow," are related to the word "color" in that they are responses to "What color is this?"
2. Learn that these color terms are absolute, in that another word will not suffice
3. Learn that color terms refer to static visual properties of objects
4. Learn that there are discriminably different values of this visual property that are grouped into bundles of stimulus equivalence that correspond to different verbal labels

A comparison of the natural learning acquisition and the learning required for success in training indicates close parallels. The first step of training seems to correspond directly to the first level of color acquisition described by Bartlett, where children in training were paralleling the natural initial step of learning color terms as a response to "What color is this?" One difference in training was that in steps 1 and 2 the objects for reference were all appropriate for the color, whereas in the real world children must go through a trial-and-error system of matching color terms to colored objects. It is quite possible that the training subjects first learned isolated selection restrictions, such as "red" is what is said when someone else says "What color?" Since the color terms red, green, and yellow had to be used correctly to refer to 10 different objects at the conclusion of training, it is very unlikely that the subjects' final performances were governed by such isolated selection restrictions. It is reasonable to suppose that the subjects did acquire some awareness of the semantic relationship between "color" and color terms, although this was not directly assessed.

It is not clear from the data reported if and when Bartlett's subjects learned that color terms are absolute. Presumably those subjects who had mastered correct use of color terms had at some time acquired this knowledge. In Bartlett's testing there were no judgments of correctness in the use of color terms. In contrast, there was a definite judgment of accuracy in the training format (the experimenter's "yes" or "no" following each response), which required a child to realize that one, and only one, color term response was correct. This judgment of correctness made it possible to identify inefficient learning strategies such as those demonstrated by Helen, who seemed to resist the absoluteness of color terms. Bartlett's subjects may have persisted in similar inefficient strategies, such as using one favorite color term in reference to all colors.[9] The realization that color terms are absolute may not develop until relatively late in the acquisition of color terms, concurrently with correct referential mapping to color objects. That is, in the normal self-directed learning of color terms, the realization that the word "red" refers to red things may coincide with the realization that only the word "red" refers to red things.

Learning that color terms refer to static visual properties of objects corresponds to Bartlett's notion of a referential meaning for the general dimension of color. It is not clear from Bartlett's data how strong a prerequisite the referential meaning for the general dimension of color is for the learning of color terms. Most of the beginning color-namers did not respond according to the dimension of color on the sorting task, although some of these subjects had at least two color terms used correctly. It is difficult to account for correct use of even a few color terms without having a referential meaning for the general dimension of color. Bartlett (1978) hypothesizes that the child's earliest correct use of color terms reflects the concept that color can be named, using a few isolated or very local rules, each of which pairs one color with one name. Later a more general set of mapping rules is developed that determines which names go with which colors, and also how colors are organized with respect to each other.

Cruse's (1977) diary observations of his son's acquisition of color terms support the notion that learning that color terms refer to static visual properties of objects is a distinct step which precedes the correct referential use of color terms. He reported that when his son produced several color terms, but used none of them correctly, the child's behavior indicated that he had associated the color of certain objects with pictures and with the pictures' names. Specifically, the boy used a set of colored plastic beakers that had pictures embossed on the undersides, with each color corresponding to a different picture. The child correctly responded to "What's on this cup?" and "Show Daddy the cup with the cat/teddy

---

[9]Cruse (1977) did report such an initial learning strategy for his son who, as noted earlier, first used "green" to refer to any bright color.

bear," etc., when he could not see the bottom of the beaker. The only available clue was the color of the beaker (Cruse, 1977, p. 306). It is reasonable to assume that in order to accomplish this, the child would need to realize the constant visual properties of objects, i.e., that the beaker with the cat embossed on it would always be red, and not red one time and green, for example, at another. Such learning preceded the correct use of color terms.

The final step of learning for training corresponds to the third level of normal acquisition, that of full mastery of color terms. This step of training, requiring differential association of color properties of objects and their corresponding color terms, was very difficult for the training subjects compared to the earlier training steps. Once again, Bartlett (1977, p. 13) reports parallel findings in the normal acquisition process. She reported that "construction of a correct referential map was apparently quite difficult for all our subjects...by contrast, the semantic organization appears to occur very quickly."

One of Bartlett's observations differed from the children's responses observed in the training study. Part of Bartlett's evidence in support of the idea that children early on know the relationship between the word "color" and the various color terms was the observation that almost all of the children responded with a color term when asked "What color is this?" Only occasionally did they make an error, that of naming the object. The error was usually spontaneously corrected when the question was repeated.

Only one of the children (a color-concept-user) in the present study responded with a color term when asked "What color is this?" during the initial sorting tasks or on the initial training baseline, even though the question was often repeated in order to be absolutely certain that the subject did not have correct usage of color terms. Instead, the subjects generally named the objects, a few said "I don't know," and two repeated "this" or "color." Bartlett reports only one subject at this level of performance, and then only for the initial test session. These apparent subject differences seem due to Bartlett's subjects being more advanced in the acquisition of color terms (with 18 subjects having as many as six color terms used correctly at the first testing) than those of the present study, where every effort was made to ensure that none of the subjects performed correctly with color terms in either production or comprehension tasks.

Order of Acquisition Another question that Bartlett (1978) investigated with the same sample of subjects described earlier is that of the order of acquisition of various color terms. Since the order of acquisition in the training reported here was arbitrarily decided, it is interesting to see how well it parallels the order of acquisition that reflects the child's (instead of the experimenter's) decisions.

Bartlett's (1978) findings do not offer full support for the hypothesis (Berlin and Kay, 1969) that red, green, yellow, white, blue, and black would be the colors most likely to be learned first by young children. When Bartlett's data were pooled across subjects, the percentage of children with correct referents (defined as correct responses on both comprehension and production tasks) yielded color term rankings that corresponded well to the minimal set predicted by Miller and Johnson-Laird (1976), i.e., that black, white, red, green, yellow, and blue were used more correctly than other color terms. However, a further look at the data for individual orders of acquisition indicated considerable variability, with secondary colors, such as pink or orange, often acquired first by individual children. The individual orders of acquisition appeared to be quite idiosyncratic, and failed to coincide with Berlin and Kay's (1969) historical order of development. Only two of the beginning color-namers acquired six primaries prior to the other colors, and neither acquired them in the order predicted by the historical studies (Bartlett, 1978). However, Cruse (1977) reported the acquisition of color terms in the order predicted by Berlin and Kay for a child observed on a daily basis, substantiating that some children may reflect such an order. Furthermore, Cruse noted that secondary colors, such as pink, orange, and purple, were first used early on, but were unstable and became temporarily "unlearnt," whereas the primary colors were stable from initial learning onward.

Bartlett proposes that environmental factors, such as the set of contexts in which color terms are actually used, may account for these idiosyncratic individual orders of acquisition. Cruse's (1977) findings support this hypothesis. He reported that certain familiar objects were the first to be correctly labeled for color by his son, at a time when those same color names were still assigned randomly to general objects.

How does Bartlett's interpretation of the spontaneous order of acquisition compare with the training order of red, then green, then yellow? The training provided the child with a particular set of environmental contexts and in that very broad sense may be analogous to a nonlaboratory environment. However, judging from Bartlett's (1978) findings, if the training subjects had been left to their own devices, they perhaps would have learned color terms in a highly variable order. The fact that training resulted in a uniform order of acquisition adds further substantiation to the efficacy of the training procedures.

To conclude this section, the learning involved in the training program is quite consistent with what has recently been reported about the natural acquisition of color terms. There is no reason to believe that the training required some form of unique or atypical learning on the part of the subjects. The apparent differences between training and natural acquisition were the structured presentation of stimuli, the judgments of correctness of response, and the presentation of corrective feedback, all of which are usually present in the natural environment but to a less pronounced or systematic extent. These conclusions certainly will not come as a surprise to Brainerd.

SUMMARY AND CONCLUSIONS

The study reported in this chapter investigated the influence of nonlinguistic conceptual knowledge upon language acquisition within a training situation. Several procedural steps were required. First, a means of assessing prelexical conceptual organization that had direct links to subsequent linguistic learning was developed. Next, the measurement of nonlinguistic conceptual status was used to establish a baseline of conceptual knowledge demonstrated by a child prior to explicit training of the linguistic forms that represented the conceptual knowledge. Then the influence of prior conceptual learning upon subsequent linguistic learning was assessed by comparing the training performances of two groups of children: those who had already worked out the conceptual underpinnings of the linguistic form to be trained versus those who had not. The dependent variable was ease of acquisition (number of trials to criterion).

As a group, the children with prior conceptual knowledge learned the linguistic form more quickly, in fewer trials, than did those lacking such nonlinguistic information. Such a finding is consistent with the strong form of the cognition hypothesis, i.e., that language emerges as a way of expressing what the child already knows (Sinclair, 1971; Sinclair-de Zwart, 1973; Macnamara, 1972). However, a closer look at the individual data revealed that two subjects who did not demonstrate prior conceptual knowledge also learned the linguistic form readily in a number of trials comparable to the subjects with nonlinguistic information. So the relationship between cognition and language training is not as straightforward as the group findings would suggest. Instead, the results allow us to conclude that while conceptual knowledge does appear to facilitate language acquisition, the inverse is not true; that is, a lack of such knowledge does not necessarily hamper the child's linguistic acquisition. Such findings contradict the notion that cognition is a *prerequisite* (in the sense of prior to and necessary) for language acquisition, an assumption implicit in the strong form of the cognition hypothesis.

How well do other theoretical positions account for the findings? The problem is how to explain the relative ease of learning for the two non–concept-knowledge subjects. In the earlier discussion (pp. 69–71) it was established that other possible influences, such as age, linguistic acquisition (MLU), intellectual functioning (Peabody Picture Vocabulary Test–Form B), or social/emotional behaviors (cooperativeness, attentiveness) could not account for the results. If it was not a matter of subject differences, then perhaps it could be tied to the nonlinguistic concept task—perhaps the task did not measure the conceptual knowledge held in common by all subjects who performed well in training. Such an explanation would be consistent with the homologue theoretical model proposed by Bates et al, (1977a, 1977b). This possibility was discussed on p. 71, where it was pointed out that such an explanation is inadequate in that it is impossible to determine which subjects shared the conceptual knowledge without resorting to post hoc logic, i.e., the ones who trained well.

Perhaps the subjects without prior conceptual knowledge trained as quickly as those with such nonlinguistic information because the training itself served to introduce them to the nonlinguistic equivalences. Such an explanation is in line with the interactionist position, whose advocates argue that language can introduce concepts, that the influence between cognition and language can move in either direction, even at the earliest stages of language acquisition. However, this explanation also runs into difficulties. First, there was no evidence of changes in cognitive performance after the initiation of language training (see p. 67). Second, there is still the problem of predicting why some children without prior nonlinguistic information would be influenced by language training to develop a new concept while the other subjects did not.

A final possibility is that the factor that differentiates the subjects is not conceptual information but instead a particular linguistic processing facility. Supporters of the weak form of the cognition hypothesis (Slobin, 1973, Cromer, 1974, 1976a) point out that cognition alone does not account for how children learn to map meanings into language and that there is evidence of specific linguistic abilities involved in the mapping process. In order to learn the particular linguistic form trained in the study reported here, the subjects had to master at least part of the nonlinguistic equivalences (the nonlinguistic meaning) and the linguistic mapping of those equivalences into the use of a particular linguistic form. It was predicted that children who already knew the nonlinguistic equivalence groupings would have an advantage. However, it is possible that some children who did not have such nonlinguistic knowledge were able to compensate by means of facile linguistic acquisition abilities. Such putative specific linguistic skills evidentally would not be susceptible to indirect measurement by such procedures as computing the mean length of utterance, since the MLU did not predict training performance (see p. 70). However, as noted in the earlier discussion, the MLU does not measure semantic acquisition per se. A specific measure of semantic sophistication would perhaps have predictive value, that is, would serve as a measure of the particular linguistic processing skill involved in learning word meanings. But such a measurement is not available. We are once again left with the question of how do we know which of the children would be able to compensate for a lack of prior nonlinguistic knowledge; which children would have specific linguistic skills that would help them overcome the disadvantage of not having a prior notion of the nonlinguistic meaning?

The choice between competing theoretical explanations is thwarted by our inability to measure the kinds of linguistic or conceptual knowledge or processing that have been proposed to account for language acquisition, such as "local homologies" (Bates et al., 1977a, 1977b) and "certain specifically linguistic capabilities" (Cromer, 1976a, p. 326). While such putative mental processes are inherently difficult to assess directly, due to their covert nature and close interrelationships, we still need a better idea of how to define and describe them with the specificity required for measurement.

How does this study increase our understanding of the cognitive or linguistic skills involved in language acquisition? We can conclude that prior nonlinguistic categorization knowledge did not account for all of what is involved when children learn a corresponding linguistic form. Some other factor, as yet unspecified and unmeasured, is presumably involved. However, it is also true that cognitive knowledge did influence linguistic achievement. In fact, it accounted for a large share of the variance. Furthermore, a closer look at the nature of the cognition/language interaction obtained in this study reveals some rich subtleties in how cognition gets mapped into differing language performances, subtleties that suggest the possibility of different mappings of cognition under different language performance conditions. The evidence bearing on this matter is reported and discussed in the next chapter.

Chapter 5
INTERACTIONS AMONG COGNITIVE ORGANIZATION AND THE PRODUCTION AND COMPREHENSION OF WORDS

One of the purposes of the study reported in Chapter 4 was to explore possible qualitative differences in the linguistic learning of concept-users and non–concept-users to look for evidence of an interaction between cognition and language different from or in addition to that affecting ease of acquisition. No specific a priori predictions were formulated. It was presumed that any such qualitative differences would be subtle in nature, discernible by careful analysis of patterns of behaviors on the sorting tasks or training trials.

As it turned out, the evidence for qualitative differences was quite striking instead of subtle. Indeed, had the findings been less consistent they would have been overlooked, since they ran counter to a commonly held assumption about what is learned during language training. The assumption is that when a child is trained to correctly produce a word in a reference-making context, he also learns how to comprehend that word, probably sometime early on in the training. If the child has several words at his disposal and yet only uses one of them, for example, "dog," as a response each time he is shown an individual instance of the class of objects known as dogs, we assume that he "knows" the word meaning well enough to perform correctly on a comprehension task (when asked to "Show me the dog" he could choose a dog out of an array of objects).[1]

That was the assumption inherent in the design of the training procedures for this study. The goal of the training was the correct production of the color terms "red," "green," and "yellow." The correct produc-

---

[1]An assumption evident in Fraser, Bellugi and Brown's (1963) dismissal of the possibility of production preceding comprehension as "No reason why this should be so" (p. 126).

tion entailed correct literal referential mapping; that is, the child had to know that a color word corresponded to a particular visual property of objects. No comprehension training was provided; it was assumed that a separate training step was not necessary, that the knowledge involved in correct comprehension would automatically accompany the knowledge required for correct productive use of the color words, so that production training would spontaneously generalize to correct performance on comprehension tasks. That assumption turned out to be entirely false.

Some of the training subjects met the criterion levels of training that required correct production of the color words "red," "green," and "yellow," but did not learn correct comprehension. When asked, "What color is this?" in regard to various different objects, they consistently produced the correct color term, but at the same time were unable to identify the appropriate object when asked to "Show me the red (or green or yellow) one." Furthermore, these subjects had one feature in common: they all categorized objects in a pattern designated as "non–color-concept-user." There was no evidence of such a production/comprehension gap in the responses of subjects demonstrating a color-concept sorting strategy.

These results are presented and discussed in this chapter. Given the unusual nature of the findings, a rather detailed presentation of the individual data is first provided. Next, possible external factors, possible sources of other interpretations of the data, are considered. A period of comprehension training for two of the subjects who did not perform correctly on comprehension tasks at the end of training is reported, along with the subjects' performances on the control colors. Following this report of the various kinds of evidence, the related research is reviewed, research that reports correct production without correct comprehension of other linguistic forms in other circumstances. Finally, an explanation of the findings is posited. It is hypothesized that the discrepancy between production and comprehension in one group of subjects but not the other can be attributed to their differential ability to utilize color as a criterial attribute for equating real world objects.

FINDINGS

Individual Performances on Sorting Tasks

The difference in the performances of the two groups of subjects became apparent following training when the sorting task was readministered. The data of primary interest at the time of testing were the subjects' sorting behaviors (Tasks 1 and 2). Task 3, the comprehension task (see Score Sheet, Appendix A) was also given to eight subjects.[2] For the three color-concept-users for whom there were data, who finished training earlier than most of the non–color-concept-users, the comprehension task showed that they had correctly generalized to comprehension following the training. This was also true for the first NCC subject (Rhonda) for whom there was final sorting data. (She was actually the second NCC to complete training; the sorting tasks were not given at the completion of training for the first NCC subject trained.) Interestingly, Rhonda was the one who trained in the fewest trials and who switched to a CC sorting strategy at the completion of training. These findings were consistent with the experimenter's assumptions, so much so, in fact, that the experimenter almost stopped giving the task, since it was time consuming and seemed to offer no new or especially useful information. However, an NCC-user, Sherry, failed the comprehension task for red and green, but succeeded on yellow. Since this performance seemed so incongruous, it was regarded as idiosyncratic, reflecting either random subject or task error. No further information was sought regarding this subject's comprehension. When another subject, also an NCC-user (one of the twins, David) failed the comprehension task, further information was obtained. Two more NCC subjects subsequently indicated failure to comprehend, for a total of four NCC-users who demonstrated comprehension difficulties following training. In contrast, the CC-users, for whom there were data, all succeeded on the comprehension task.

Additional data were obtained for three of the NCC-users, a girl named Arlene and the identical twins, David and Ronnie. Since each presented a somewhat different picture, they are discussed below individually.

Arlene, an NCC subject who required 1,884 trials to reach criterion on the training, presented a transitional pattern of behavior. When the sorting task was administered in the middle of training, Arlene had switched to a CC sorting strategy (one color sort on Task 1 and one color sort on Task 2) but failed all the comprehension items (even though red and green had been trained). At the end of training, which was 20 days after the time of mid-training assessment, the sorting task revealed an NCC sorting strategy, although Arlene was only one response from a CC

---

[2]The sorting task was not readministered to one color-concept-user who was the first subject trained, so final sorting data are only available for nine subjects; Task 3, the comprehension task, was inadvertently omitted for an NCC subject who did receive the other sorting tasks; both omissions were early in the study, before the importance of the final comprehension tasks was apparent.

status, i.e., she had one color sort on Task 2 and would have had a color sort on Task 1 (for CC criterion) if she had reversed the order of her fourth and fifth choices on trial 1 of Task 1. Her comprehension performance was consistently incorrect for red and green and consistently correct for yellow, but she also chose yellow incorrectly for red and green, making it difficult to unequivocally judge if she knew yellow. Five days later she was again tested for production and comprehension. The stimulus items were the untrained object probes for the red/green/yellow step of training (see Appendix C). Production remained above criterion levels; comprehension had improved to 5 errors out of 15 items (two on red and three on green). She sorted by color on the sorting task administered at that time (color sorts on two trials of Task 1, one trial of Task 2). Two days later, she indicated fully correct comprehension and again sorted by color (color sorts on two trials of Task 1 and two trials of Task 2). It would appear that Arlene was at a transition stage at the completion of training, solidifying a CC-sorting strategy while concurrently mastering the comprehension task.

The twins, David and Ronnie, indicated stable behavioral patterns over a much longer period of time. This conveniently allowed for the collection of much related evidence, which is presented in detail in the following discussion.[3] David was an NCC-user who required only 657 trials to reach criterion on training. His preference for an NCC sorting strategy was consistent, evident at mid-training, at the completion of training, and through seven posttraining assessments encompassing 11 weeks (until he finally mastered comprehension).

Ronnie was an NCC-user who required 1,573 trials to reach criterion on training. He also indicated a consistent preference for NCC sorting on his pre-, mid-, and posttraining assessments. However, he switched to a CC sorting strategy during a time when he was receiving comprehension training. This CC sorting strategy was evident in three different testings during a period of 3 weeks. Then for three subsequent testings he returned to an NCC sorting strategy. Eleven weeks elapsed between the completion of training and the time Ronnie indicated full comprehension of red, green, and yellow.[4]

The twins' ability to correctly produce color terms while failing comprehension was most striking in the comprehension, then production, format. When asked to "Give me the red one," a typical response was a random selection of object. Immediately following the incorrect choice, the

---

[3]Since the long time frame was certainly not anticipated, the additional evidence is not as systematic as would be desirable.

[4]Although the time interval between completion of the production training and mastery of comprehension was the same length for both boys (11 weeks), the two time periods did not coincide. David, who trained in fewer trials, preceded Ronnie by several weeks.

experimenter would ask "What color is this?" and invariably David or Ronnie would glance at the object, and then promptly and correctly say "red" (or "green" or "yellow"), apparently not forming any connection at all between the two modes of performance. This pattern of responses is documented on film (Ruder and Rice, 1977).

Possible External Factors   An immediate question is how much of this production/comprehension discrepancy is real and how much could be accounted for by external factors. One obvious possible factor would be experimenter bias in recording the behaviors. At the completion of training, observer reliability was obtained for both the sorting task and for the production/comprehension probes (using as stimulus items the untrained object probes for the red/green/yellow step of training; see Appendix C). The observer was another graduate student who sat at the table during the presentation of the stimulus items, out of view of the experimenter's score sheet. Reliability was computed from a trial-by-trial comparison, using agreements divided by agreements plus disagreements × 100. Reliability for the sorting tasks was 100% for both boys; for the production/comprehension probes it was 98% for Ronnie, 100% for David. Both videotapes and movie films were subsequently obtained during the period between the completion of training and mastery of comprehension. The same pattern of differential performance on production and comprehension tasks was evident throughout. In short, the possibility of experimenter bias in observing and recording the behaviors can be ruled out.

What about task variables? Perhaps the twins' failure was a function of the linguistic composition of the comprehension verbal stimuli, i.e., "Give me a red/green/yellow one." Perhaps they did not understand the task, did not know how to play "the comprehension game." However, when they were asked to "Give me the cup," they readily responded correctly. Perhaps they could not differentiate adjectives in the prenominal position. Yet both the twins and Arlene could correctly respond to such commands as "Give me the wet/dirty one," or "Give me the big/little one," which require comprehension of modifiers in the prenominal position describing transient states or changes in size.

A change in the verbal stimulus for comprehension of color terms yielded interesting findings. When the twins were asked, "Which one is red?" occasionally followed by the prompt "Put your finger on red," their comprehension performance improved markedly, to 11/15 correct for Ronnie and 12/15 correct for David. When the stimulus was shortened to only "red" combined with an outstretched hand to indicate the requested response, David was correct on 14/15 trials, whereas Ronnie was correct only once. However, the "red" stimulus was the last of several variations of stimuli presented during that session (held on the same date for both boys, two days after the completion of training for Ronnie; 21 days after completion of training for David), and the experimenter recorded that Ronnie was showing many signs of fatigue. Unfortunately, these last two variations in stimulus presentation were not systematically presented in subsequent sessions. However, during the movie filming, the experimenter presented "red" as a request to Ronnie for a number of trials on different occasions. His accuracy was not above chance levels, although there was more informal evidence of search behavior. While the evidence about the change in verbal stimulus is inconclusive, it does seem possible to rule out inability to understand the general format of the comprehension task, and a general inability to segment or understand prenominal adjectives.

Another task artifact that conceivably could have controlled responses was that of position preference. Both boys demonstrated a weak position bias in that they would sometimes adopt a left-to-right or right-to-left sequence of responding for the comprehension tasks. However, both boys were variable in this regard, seeming to use it occasionally and then going on to an apparently random selection sequence. It seemed to reflect a momentary interest in imposing an orderliness or system onto an otherwise meaningless task. Given the many measures of comprehension collected from both boys over the 10- or 11-week period, with random placement of stimulus objects and random presentation of color term stimuli, such considerations as position preference or other response biases based upon some aspect of the stimulus situation simply do not account for the data.

Another possibility is that the production responses were somehow rotely learned responses to idiosyncratic training objects (comparable to a child's first learning color terms correctly in reference to a few favorite objects). Two different observations provide counter-evidence to this notion: 1) the training objects were alike except for color; thus, the only way to differentiate the spoons, for example, was by color, and there was no possibility of rotely matching color to a unique object; and 2) criterion for training included generalization to five untrained objects, for a total of 10 different objects named correctly for each of the three colors. With such stimuli and with a generalization criterion, it is unlikely that the correct production represents a narrow rotely learned response, although systematic evidence was not collected to ascertain how far correct color term production generalized to totally unfamiliar objects. Some anecdotal evidence was obtained for David, however; his teacher reported that he was spontaneously naming red, green, and yellow during class activities, at a time 7 weeks after the completion of production training, concurrent with failure in comprehension training.

The twins, David and Ronnie, and Arlene were among the youngest subjects (with ages of 2:6 and 2:7, respectively) and also had low MLUs (2.1, 2.0, and 3.1, respectively). This raises the possibility that the production/comprehension discrepancy is somehow a function of level of development. However, disconfirming evidence came from Kathy, who despite a comparable age (2:3) and MLU (2.0) performed correctly on the comprehension tasks, and from Sherry, who despite greater age (3:4) and notably higher MLU (4.5) performed incorrectly on the comprehension tasks. The only common denominator among those subjects who failed the comprehension tasks at the completion of training was their preference for non–color-concept sorting strategies.

Comprehension Training

A period of comprehension training was provided for David and Ronnie. The purpose of comprehension training was to explore the stability of their failures within the comprehension format, and the modifiability of errors via immediate corrective feedback. The procedures were as follows:

1. *Step 1*
   Stimuli: Three like training objects that differed in color, e.g., red spoon, green spoon, and yellow spoon
   Verbal direction: "Show (or give) me the _____ one"
   Response: Selection of appropriate object
   Criterion: 18/20 correct
2. *Step 2*
   Stimuli: Three unlike training objects of the three different colors, e.g., red spoon, green plate, yellow watch
   Verbal direction: Same as 1 above
   Response: Same
   Criterion: Same

Corrective feedback was provided immediately following each incorrect response, such as "No, that's not green...that's red." Social praise was provided for correct responses, along with intermittent reinforcement of food (sugar-coated cereal). The corrective feedback was later expanded to asking the child, after an incorrect response, "What color is this?" whereupon the child would correctly name the color and the experimenter would follow with "I don't want the _____ one; give me the _____ one."

The plan was for comprehension training to be offered on a daily individual basis, comparable to production training. However, it did not work out as planned. The training was started in May and ran through June, which turned out to be a time of transition in schedules for the day care center and the family, with some absences due to scheduling adjustments. Also, it was becoming apparent that the twins' behaviors were both stable and striking enough to warrant filming, which accounted for further interruptions and delays in comprehension training.

All in all, David received 10 training sessions and Ronnie nine, over a 3½-week period. The boys' performances were comparable and both notably unsuccessful, even with such selective stimuli presentation and ample corrective feedback. By the final training sessions, both boys' accuracy was only a little above chance. Both were beginning to show some signs of search behavior, although this was not yet stable. The first six sessions for both boys were characterized by entirely random responses and numerous indications of boredom. They apparently regarded the task as meaningless, which provided more evidence that their failure on the comprehension tasks was not just a situational aberration but instead represented a real lack of competence. Furthermore, the behaviors were so stable that they were scarcely influenced by corrective feedback, even over 10 sessions and 3 weeks' time interval.

It could be argued that the boys' lack of response to comprehension training is support for the strong form of the cognition hypothesis, i.e., that they did not have the necessary conceptual knowledge to benefit from the training. However, that explanation does not account for how they mastered the production tasks. An alternative interpretation of why they failed the comprehension training is presented later in this discussion.

The comprehension training was suspended during the time of movie filming. The boys' performances were evaluated by means of periodic unreinforced probes of production/comprehension and administrations of the sorting task, approximately every 10 days. David reached criterion on the comprehension tasks (12/15 correct on the probes, or better) 1 month after the last comprehension training session; Ronnie met criterion 7 weeks after the last comprehension training session. There was no apparent change in their classroom activities or at home (according to teacher and parent reports) that directly related to the mastery of comprehension.

Performance on the sorting tasks indicated consistent NCC strategies for David across a total of 13 task administrations, whereas Ronnie switched to a CC strategy toward the end of comprehension training and maintained it during two more testings over the next 2 weeks. He then switched back to an NCC strategy on the testing 2 weeks after the final comprehension training sessions and maintained this on two subsequent testings. Ronnie also received a total of 13 administrations of the sorting task.

Performance on Control Colors

During this time of preoccupation with comprehension training, filming, and probing of production/comprehension, an informative source of evidence was overlooked, i.e., the production and comprehension of the control colors, white, blue, and black. At the conclusion of training, none of these color terms was correctly produced by any of the training subjects, including the twins. The comprehension of these three colors was not assessed until much later—5 weeks after the final comprehension training session. At that time, both boys performed correctly on the comprehension task for white, blue, and black, while Ronnie still could not name any of the three colors correctly on the initial production testing and David only had an inconsistent "blue." An additional interesting observation was that the boys first failed the production items, then passed the comprehension items. When the production items were repeated, they improved their production accuracy with minimal feedback from the examiner, to the point where David was able to correctly produce all three colors (in a limited number of trials), and Ronnie picked up blue and black. Subsequent testings indicated that blue and black were stable for both boys.

At the time of testing for white, blue, and black, David had passed criterion for comprehension of red, green, and yellow; Ronnie had not. However, on the session of the white, blue, and black testing, Ronnie had initially been probed on red, green, and yellow, where he produced them correctly and failed comprehension (only 2/15 correct). Following the presentations of white, blue, and black, the red, green and yellow comprehension probes were repeated with definite signs of search and improved accuracy (9/15 correct). At the next testing, 1 week later, the red, green, and yellow comprehension probes were 100% correct, and stayed above criterion in subsequent testings. It would appear that the experience with white, blue, and black interacted with red, green, and yellow to improve Ronnie's comprehension performance. An anecdotal note on the data sheets may provide a clue. Ronnie spontaneously noted that several objects were alike in their whiteness. This was the first time the experimenter had observed Ronnie verbally equate objects by color.

Ronnie's performance on white, blue, and black confirmed that the failure to comprehend red, green, and yellow was not due to a lack of understanding of the task, lack of prenominal adjective processing, or other artifacts of the task itself. It is difficult to assess the possible facilitative effects of the prior comprehension training on red, green, and yellow. However, Ronnie's data (he first failed red, green, and yellow comprehension and then immediately passed white, blue, and black comprehension tasks) seem to indicate that whatever training effects there were must have been weak in that the target colors were not affected but nontrained colors were. The frustrating missing piece of information is the time at which the boys learned to comprehend blue, white, and black.

RELATED RESEARCH

The discrepancy between production and comprehension in David's and Ronnie's responses to color terms is not a unique phenomenon, although the stability may well be. The relationship between production and comprehension that they demonstrated is consistent with evidence from two other sources: studies of normal acquisition, and research in the training of language.

Before addressing the studies of normal language acquisition, it is helpful to have in mind a notion of what differentiates the production and comprehension modes of responding. Huttenlocher (1974) provides a succinct description of the difference between receptive and productive language: reception involves the "recognition of words and recall of the objects, acts and relations for which they stand," whereas production involves the "recognition of objects, acts, and relations and recall of the words that stand for them" (p. 335).

Production and Comprehension in Normal Acquisition

Chapman (1978) notes an apparent paradox in current generalizations about children's comprehension skills. On the one hand, it has been traditionally assumed that comprehension precedes production. This assumption is supported by observations of very young children's apparent ability to comprehend while their production is very limited. On the other hand, recent experimental evidence indicates that the relationship becomes more complex when the child is able to readily produce verbal language.

There is both indirect and direct evidence of greater accuracy in production than comprehension tasks. The indirect evidence consists of a number of studies that have indicated inaccurate comprehension of various sentence structures and word meanings at a time when the subjects could be assumed to be using the particular forms correctly in their spontaneous utterances. (See Cromer, 1976b; and Chapman, 1978, for reviews; also, see Clark and Garnica, 1974, and Richards, 1976, for a specific example of different ages of acquisition for the deictic terms *come/ go* and *bring/take* for a production task (earlier age of mastery) versus a comprehension task (later age of mastery).) Direct experimental evidence is available in two linguistic areas: word order and word meanings. The findings have been accompanied by various explanations of how children could appear to know something productively that they didn't demonstrate in comprehension tasks.

Chapman and Miller (1975) and de Villiers and de Villiers (1973) found that children who can produce sentences with appropriate agent-action-object word order fail to use word order as a cue to agent and object-of-action in the sentences of others. Chapman accounts for these findings by the influence of contextual cues. The young child uses situational cues and his knowledge of probable meanings to give the appearance of comprehending a string of words long before he can do so on the basis of its structural cues alone, thereby giving the misleading impression of accurate comprehension at the earliest stages of linguistic learning (cf. Cromer, 1976b, p. 315, for a summary of the comprehension strategies proposed by various authors to account for children's interpretations of sentences and words). Chapman (1978) hypothesizes that the developmental order of comprehension and production for a given grammatical structure is: first, comprehension in context, next, production in context, followed by production out of context, and, finally, comprehension out of context concurrent with rule-governed production.

De Villiers and de Villiers (1973, pp. 338–339) suggest the child's understanding of semantic constraints accounts for correct production, that is, knowing which words are likely to go with which actions. But, when such constraints are not available (as in word order comprehension tasks), the apparent competence with word order is no longer evident. Bowerman (1978b, 1978c) presents a different perspective. She implies that the comprehension tasks do not tap the child's real competence with word order. She attributes incorrect performance on comprehension tasks by children who produce appropriately ordered sentences to the use of processing shortcuts, such as semantic interpretations, which override actual syntactic knowledge.

Since the completion of this study, there has been a report of similar findings of production preceding comprehension in young children's acquisition of the names of objects. Nelson and Bonvillian (1978) investigated how 25 children ages 21 to 28 months acquired the names of unfamiliar or novel objects. When they compared production and comprehension performances for individual children, they found that, while some children learned in a comprehension first then production sequence, a number of the children showed a marked "production bias," i.e., a greater proportion of object names produced only than comprehended only, or produced and comprehended correctly (pp. 535–536).

While the results of Nelson and Bonvillian (1978) are consistent with the color term training reported earlier, there are several important methodological differences between their study and the one reported here: the word meanings to be learned, the nature of the training, the criteria for production and comprehension, and the notion of "conceptual growth." The 18 training words were nine unfamiliar English nouns, e.g., "compass," and nine novel nouns, e.g., "fiffin," with corresponding real world objects or specially constructed novel objects. The number of exemplars presented for each object varied from four to seven. The words were trained by the child's mother in 10 laboratory sessions spaced over a 5-month period. The mother determined the interaction patterns; the experimenter told her when to introduce a particular training object, which the mother verbally labeled for the child, and a particular generalization item, which was not labeled. For the purpose of comparing production and comprehension, production was defined as "any production of concept name for appropriate exemplar" and comprehension was defined as "at least 50% correct choices (where chance success = 14%)" (p. 535). As Nelson and Bonvillian note (1978, p. 537), these criteria are fairly low—recall the criteria for correct production during the color term training reported here were correct responses on 18/20 training trials and 12/15 correct on untrained probes; for comprehension, correct responses on two out of three trials per color. However, Nelson and Bonvillian argue that the relative tendencies toward production or comprehension within the sample are not appreciably altered when the criteria are shifted (p. 537). One more difference between the studies is the use of the term "concept." In the color term study, "concept" referred to nonlinguistic categorical knowledge. In Nelson and Bonvillian's study, "concept" refers to "noun concepts," that is, the word meanings. They did measure other nonlinguistic cognitive skills, such as sensorimotor knowledge, but not the nonverbal categorical knowledge directly linked to the word meanings.

How did Nelson and Bonvillian account for findings different from studies that show comprehension appearing first in young children's language competence? They suggest that the novelty of the training items allowed for observation of children's language learning very early in the process, whereas studies using familiar names may have observed the child when he had already learned the items on a comprehension basis. A second reason they propose is the age of their subjects, that is, old enough to have achieved a production proficiency that allows a wider range of possible comprehension/production relations than is the case when observing children who have not yet begun to produce much language (p. 538).

There is also some evidence, albeit quite limited, indicating production/comprehension discrepancies in the acquisition of color terms within the natural environment. Bartlett (1977) administered production and comprehension tasks similar in format to those used in the present study. She reported different production/comprehension relationships for advanced color-namers (subjects with four or more correct color terms) than for beginning color-namers (subjects with less than three terms). Comprehension far exceeded production for the group of advanced color-namers. In contrast, for the group of beginning color-namers comprehension was never much better than production and never rose above chance. The fact that some of the beginning color-namers correctly named as many as two colors suggests that perhaps some of them were able to produce but not comprehend a given color term.

It is not possible to determine if this was the case from the data given in Bartlett's 1977 report of her study, but Bartlett has supplied this experimenter with the individual data for the nine beginning color-namers' performances on the initial production and comprehension tasks (Bartlett, personal communication). Two of the nine subjects did produce color terms correctly that were incorrect in the comprehension task. One subject named "red" and "yellow" correctly while failing all comprehension items; the other subject named "blue" correctly while failing all comprehension items. While such evidence is encouraging in its similarity to the findings of the study being reported here, it must be viewed cautiously and within the context of the experimental situation. Since it was not the purpose of Bartlett's study to compare response accuracy in production and comprehension tasks, those children who did indicate such differential responding presumably were not assessed beyond the initial one-trial presentations to check for stability of their correct naming of colors or for the possible effects of chance or irrelevant factors, such as stimulus salience or preference, in the comprehension tasks. On the basis of such preliminary evidence, one can speculate that perhaps some children, maybe a small percentage, are able to first perform correctly when asked, "What color is this?" and only later perform correctly when asked, "Show me the red one."

Production and Comprehension in Formal Training Circumstances

The second source of evidence indicating differences in production and comprehension is research in training language. The general format of the studies is to train either comprehension or production, and then test to determine if appropriate correct responses generalize to the other modality. Failure to generalize is interpreted as evidence of functional independence, i.e., separate response classes.

In one of the first studies reported on this topic, Guess (1969) trained two retarded adolescents on the plural morphemes /s/ and /z/. Reception was trained first, with probes to check generalization to production. Next production was trained. In Condition III, reversed reception was trained, i.e., "dogs" for a single dog, "dog" for a pair of dogs, with probes for production. The subjects did not generalize from receptive training to production in the first condition and they also did not generalize the reversed receptive plural training to production.

Guess and Baer (1973) followed this study with a further look at the production/comprehension relationship. Four retarded subjects were trained on reception and production concurrently, using two different classes of plurals (-s and -es). Probes were presented in the response modality not being trained in baseline. Three of the four subjects did not generalize clearly from receptive training with one class of plurals to correct productive use of that class, nor did they generalize from productive training of the other class of plurals to correct receptive response to that class. Guess and Baer (1973) concluded that generalization between production and comprehension is not an automatic outcome of language training for retarded subjects. They called for further research to clarify the relationship.

The relationship between comprehension and production was addressed in a recent study by Wetherby (1977). Normal preschool children were trained two-word nonsense labels corresponding to color and shape terms for geometric shapes that varied in color and shape. Some items were trained receptively, some productively, with various probes to check generalization across modalities. Generalization was found from production to reception but not from reception to production.

To summarize, the studies of language training described above corroborate the observation derived from studies of normal language acquisition: the relationship between production and comprehension is not a simple matter of 1) first one, then the other, or of even 2) if one, then the other. Within the training literature there is considerable evidence across different kinds of linguistic tasks of a lack of spontaneous generalization from comprehension to production (Guess, 1969; Guess and Baer, 1973; Wetherby, 1977). There is also some evidence, within the limited linguistic domain of plural morphemes and the limited subject population of the mentally retarded, indicating a lack of generalization from production training to comprehension (Guess and Baer, 1973).

EXPLANATION OF FINDINGS

How do these related findings and observations assist in the interpretation of the evidence from the present study? A rather obvious correspondence is that differential performance in the production and comprehension of color terms is directly comparable to production appearing to precede comprehension for word order and word meanings (de Villiers and de Villiers, 1973; Chapman and Miller, 1975; Nelson and Bonvillian, 1978) and comparable to production without generalization to comprehension for plural morphemes (Guess and Baer, 1973). While such agreement with findings in other domains supports the validity of the present findings, it does not explain them. In particular, *how* were the NCC subjects able to perform correctly on production but not comprehension tasks, and *why* was the production/comprehension difference evident only in the subjects who preferred an NCC sorting strategy?

The explanations offered to account for the findings of the studies reviewed above cannot be extended to the present study. The "processing shortcuts" or situational context explanations of the production/comprehension difference is not applicable for two reasons: 1) no "processing shortcuts" were apparent that could account for failure on the comprehension task, and 2) any such possible contextual supports or processing shortcuts were presumably as available to one group of subjects as to the other. The idea that production appearing first may somehow be a function of the novelty of the items to be learned is also not supported. During the training trials alone the children certainly became familiar enough with the color terms to learn to comprehend them spontaneously if familiarity were the determining factor, nor does it account for group differences. The designation of production and comprehension as different response classes, Guess and Baer's (1973) explanation for their findings, also does not account for why there were different response classes for one group of children and not the other.

In order to account for the findings of the present study, it is necessary to take a very close look at what color-concept-users may have known that non–color-concept-users did not know, a knowledge which may have facilitated spontaneous transfer to comprehension for the former but not the latter. The first question is what did the children need to know in order to sort by color? They needed to be able to discriminate color values, i.e., red versus green versus blue, and so forth. Subject screening criteria for the study ensured that both CC and NCC subjects could discriminate colors: they all were able to correctly match colored blocks. A further bit of knowledge needed for sorting by color is the fact that the attribute of color can be used to equate multi-attribute objects. That is, colors are attributes that not only can be used to discriminate among various objects, but they also can be the basis for grouping objects as equivalent.

The child who selects objects of the same color when asked to "Find one like this one" is presumably regarding color as a means of equating the objects for "likeness," that is, creating a class. In this instance, color is regarded as a criterial attribute, defined by Bruner, Goodnow, and Austin (1956) as "any attribute which when changed in value alters the likelihood of an object being categorized in a certain way. . . for the person doing the categorizing" (p. 31). The performances of the CC subjects on the sorting tasks indicated that they were capable of using color as a criterial attribute for class membership.

On the other hand, children can recognize color as an attribute (and use this information to match colored blocks correctly) but still not recognize that it can be a means of equating objects for "likeness." As Schlesinger (in preparation) has put it, "perception of similarity in itself does not constitute categorization." In this case, color is noncriterial for the categorization of objects. It is "noisy", i.e., a nondefining attribute that varies from instance to instance (Bruner, Goodnow, and Austin, 1956, p. 48). An example of an attribute of objects that is commonly "noisy" is a scratch on the surface. In a given set of objects, all of them may be scratched; the scratches are readily recognizable; the objects could be matched according to the presence of scratches, or perhaps scratch length or location. But the existence of scratches is seldom regarded as criterial for class membership, i.e., as a means of equating objects for "likeness." The sorting strategies of the NCC subjects indicated that color was analogous to surface scratches in that it was "noisy" and noncriterial.

From an adult's perspective, color seems to be such an obvious means of equating objects that it seems a little implausible that children who can match colored blocks would not also match multi-attribute objects by color. However, this readiness to match by color may be influenced by social learning. Miller and Johnson-Laird (1976, p. 349) report that there is some evidence of cultural influence upon our readiness to categorize by colors, in that color is not as completely abstracted from objects in some other cultures as it has been in ours. For example, a native group in the Philippines uses their words for red and green to signify dessicated and succulent in reference to newly cut bamboo (Conklin, 1955). An instance of cultural influence upon children's ability to abstract colors is the apparent impact of the introduction of color crayons. Miller and Johnson-Laird (1976, p. 351) observe that prior to the advent of colored wax crayons in homes and schools the age of acquisition of color terms was much later than it is now. Much of our readiness to equate objects by color may well be rooted in the technology that surrounds us in our society, but which is not yet assimilated by the very young child.

The next question is this: What did the subjects need to know for success in training, which was defined as the correct production of color terms? This topic was discussed in detail earlier (see pp. 74–76). The relevant point to reiterate here is that the subjects did not have to know that a particular visual property, e.g., "greenness," was the only common feature of the training and probe objects. They could perform correctly by knowing "this one is green," "that one is green," "this one is red," "that one is red," without realizing that "these are all red" and "these are all green," just as one can know "this one is scratched" and "that one is scratched" without realizing that "these are all alike in that they are all scratched."

To return to the question of what the one group of children knew that the other did not, color-concept-users knew that color could be used as a criterial attribute for equating objects and non–color-concept-users did not demonstrate this knowledge, even though they successfully completed the production training. The remaining question is whether the NCC-users' failure to comprehend, while at the same time responding correctly on the production tasks, could be related to their lack of knowledge of color as a criterial attribute. A close look at exactly what was required for correct performance on the production and comprehension tasks can help answer the question. Huttenlocher's (1974) descriptive framework is used as a means of delineating the different requirements for the two tasks.

What did the subjects need to know in order to respond correctly to the question "What color is this?" within the training situation? They needed to recognize the constant visual property of the particular stimulus object and then recall which color term is associated with that visual property. In addition, the word "color" in the stimulus question provides an initial cue, requiring an initial recall of the relationship between "color" and a particular family of words (Bartlett, 1977, 1978). When by the end of training the child was shown a yellow object and asked, "What color is this?" he needed to know that "color" called for a color term (one of the three that he had learned). He had to be able to recognize the color of this particular object, and then be able to recall which one of the three color terms corresponded to this color.

What information was necessary to make correct responses to the comprehension task requests, "Give me the red/green/yellow one?" The more general necessary information, such as understanding "Give me..." and prenominal adjectives, was discussed earlier: it was established that all the children had this knowledge. When asked to "Give me the red one" a child had to recognize the word "red" and hold it in memory as he tried to recall the relation for which it stands, i.e., the complex interrelationship between the color term "red" and the color properties of objects delineated by Bartlett (1977, 1978).

To recapitulate, the color-concept subjects performed correctly on both production and comprehension tasks. They were able to both recognize (on production tasks) and recall (on comprehension tasks) the relationship between the color terms and color properties of objects. They also knew that color could be used as a criterial attribute for equating objects. The non–color-concept subjects only performed correctly on the production tasks, indicating the ability to recognize the relationship but not recall it. They did not demonstrate knowledge of color as a criterial attribute.

The differences between the groups in terms of sorting behaviors and task performances seem to reduce to the ability to recall the relationship between color terms and color properties of objects and the ability to use color as a criterial attribute for equating objects. Perhaps these two pieces of information are functionally linked; perhaps it is necessary to code the relationship between color terms and color properties of objects as that of criterial attribute for categorical equivalence in order to be recalled when asked to "Give me the red one." What is recalled is dependent upon whatever original information is stored. When the original information to be stored is "these objects are all the same color, red," or some such indication of color as a criterial attribute for equating objects, that information can serve to represent the relationship between color terms and properties of objects for the purpose of recall. Perhaps it is *necessary* for recall that the original information be stored as criterial attribute. If this interpretation is correct, the particular production and comprehension tasks presented in this study would have tapped into different levels of conceptual organization with production tasks not requiring categorical equivalence of color and comprehension tasks requiring such conceptual information.[5]

---

[5]It is apparent that this interpretation of the relationship between production and comprehension is based upon some assumptions about how young children remember and retrieve information. While it is beyond the scope of this book to review the relevant memory literature, two points need to be made: 1) to the best of this writer's knowledge, there are no reported studies directly applicable to the explanation presented here, i.e., no reported studies of young children's ability to recognize versus recall sets of multi-attribute objects equated on the basis of color, and 2) such an account is not inconsistent with what is known about children's memory (e.g., see Mandler (in press) for an overview).

It is interesting to note that Huttenlocher (1974) also used her model of differences between production and comprehension of language to account for asymmetries in performance, but in her case the observed asymmetries were the opposite of the ones reported here; that is, her very young subjects could comprehend more linguistic forms than they could produce. She used the recall/recognition model to account for why the children did not produce words that they seemed to understand. The lack of production was attributed to difficulties retrieving words, i.e., "that it is easier to retrieve object-information on the basis of a word than it is to retrieve word-information on the basis of an encounter with an object" (Huttenlocher, 1974, p. 366).

However, in this case the argument is the opposite, i.e., that it is easier to recall the word than it is the relationship. This difference from Huttenlocher's argument could be related to differences in subjects, or the experimental context, or the content of the word meanings. The subjects in the study reported here were older and more linguistically advanced than Huttenlocher's, therefore presumably operating with more advanced mental representation than the simple object-action schemata available in the 10 to 18 month age range of Huttenlocher's subjects. The training context of the present study made it easier for the subjects to recall the color terms than would be the case in spontaneous, unstructured situations. (The subjects could have readily learned to associate the three color terms with the experimenter and the tasks.) The object-information involved in the knowledge that color can be a means of equating objects is evidently more difficult to acquire than the object-information involved in knowing that a particular object is a distinct entity with a particular name, or the mental representation involved in relating actions and objects. Children indicate a knowledge of equivalences among objects by other features and properties some time before they recognize that objects can be regarded as equivalent when they are the same color. Considering the factors of subjects, experimental context, and the semantic content, the children in this study may have had some additional help in recall of the words as a function of the training context, but they also were dealing with a word meaning that is based upon a relationship among objects that can be relatively difficult for a young child to learn. Those children who did not have the nonlinguistic knowledge prior to training were able to recognize the relationship within a structured context but not recall the relationship. It appears that Huttenlocher's model is useful in accounting for the asymmetry between production and comprehension in either direction.

Given this explanation, why are the findings so unusual? Why isn't such a production/comprehension discrepancy generally observed in the use of color terms? As Bartlett's (1977) observations (discussed earlier on p. 97) indicate, it might not be so unusual in the very early stages of color-naming. In the present case the provision of a specific training program may well have had the effect of artificially distinguishing two aspects of the meaning of color terms which usually develop in a closely related manner. The use of color terms to describe static visual properties of a particular object, such as a favored toy, may well develop first, but the next step—realizing that a given color is an attribute that is common to a number of objects and can therefore be used as a means of equating them—seems to be a small step that may be taken practically simultaneously for many children. On the other hand, there may be some individual variation in the time interval between the two steps. In this case, the effect of training could more accurately be described as an artificially induced exaggeration of a normally occurring minor discrepancy in comprehension and production.

Supportive Evidence

It is hypothesized that the differential performance of CC-users and NCC-users on comprehension tasks is accounted for by the knowledge (or lack of it) that color can be used as a criterial attribute for equating objects. What evidence is there to support this hypothesis? Evidence from the subjects' behaviors is presented first. Of course, the critical evidence is that the CC-users passed the comprehension test whereas the NCC-users did not. Furthermore, the one NCC subject, Rhonda, who trained quickly and who also had switched to a CC sorting strategy at the end of training was the only NCC subject who demonstrated complete mastery of the comprehension tasks at the end of training.

A number of behaviors of the twins can be interpreted as supportive evidence. Their inability to benefit immediately from corrective feedback provided during comprehension training is one example. If their inability to comprehend was a function of their unawareness that color can be used as a criterial attribute for categorizing, the format of the comprehension training was not directly related to the deficit. Instead, specific training on equating objects by color would have been appropriate. (This type of training was not provided because of the confounding effects upon the sorting task.)

David's and Ronnie's performances on the blue, white, and black testing can be explained by reference to the notion of color as a criterial attribute. David had already met criterion on comprehension of red, green, and yellow, and correctly comprehended white, blue, and black, as would be expected, even though he did not correctly produce those color terms.

Ronnie, in contrast, had not yet mastered comprehension of red, green, and yellow but, like David, understood white, blue, and black. While this difference between the colors would not be predicted by the hypothesis, there were signs that an awareness of color as a criterial attribute for categorizing was just then emerging for Ronnie. His spontaneous comments about the similarity of whiteness across objects were a clue (noted earlier on p. 93); immediately following these he improved on and subsequently mastered red, green, and yellow comprehension tasks. A key piece of information needed to evaluate these performances on the control colors is the time at which the boys learned to comprehend white, blue, and black. Unfortunately, this information is missing. If it had been much earlier than red, green, and yellow comprehension, that would not be consistent with the hypothesis that their lack of red, green, and yellow comprehension was a consequence of their failure to recognize that color can be used as a criterial attribute.

Arlene's performance on comprehension tasks at the conclusion of training was similar to Ronnie's performance on white, blue, and black, in that it seemed to reflect a transition period. At the completion of training she used an NCC sorting strategy (but almost a CC) in conjunction with correct comprehension of yellow but not of red and green. Five days later she switched to a CC sorting strategy, with a parallel improvement in comprehension (10/15 correct). Two days later the comprehension was 100%, with another CC sorting pattern. Her improvement in comprehension directly paralleled the use of CC sorting strategies. This supports the hypothesis that comprehension of color terms is tied to mastery of the use of color as a criterial attribute.

There were anecdotal observations on the other subjects' spontaneous comments or interesting incidental behaviors during the training sessions that are consistent with the hypothesis offered to account for the differential performance of the two groups of children on comprehension tasks. One particularly interesting observation is from a subject named Helen (an NCC-user who required 2,021 trials to meet training criterion). Helen was at the "yellow" step of training and was persisting in using "red" as a response for probe items even though she had met training criterion (18/20 correct) twice and had earlier mastered similar training steps for "red" and "green." In exasperation when Helen started to respond "red" again on the third presentation of the probe items the experimenter asked her, "What about yellow?" Helen replied, "It's down there," pointing to the training objects that had been placed on the floor. She apparently was having trouble generalizing "yellow" to the probe items, being unable to realize the similarity in yellowness between the probes and the training colors. Such difficulties with the probe items were much more striking for NCC subjects that for CC subjects.

A related remark was made by Sherry, an NCC-user who required 1,884 trials to reach criterion, when she was experiencing repeated failures on the untrained object probes for the red/green level of training. She looked at the untrained object probes (including five red and five green objects) and declared, "Those are all red." Since she could correctly match red and green blocks before training started, this error could not have stemmed from inability to discriminate between the two colors. Alternative explanations are that "red" was a general term referring to "coloredness," or that red and green colors were both included in the lexical item "red," or that she didn't understand "allness" in the sense of the same color across objects. The first explanation is regarded as improbable in view of Bartlett's (1977) finding that beginning color-namers do not indicate awareness of color as a general dimension. Instead, it is likely that a combination of the latter two explanations accounts for the error—that she included both red and green in the lexical category of "red," and also had not differentiated red and green for the purpose of equating objects.

A last observation is that it was not until training was near completion that some of the children spontaneously began to ask, "What color is this?" with reference to training or other objects. Valerie, a CC-user, spontaneously asked the experimenter, "What color is this?" in regard to some clothing one week after she had finished training. Steven and Melinda, both CC-users, asked during the red/green/yellow step. Arlene, an NCC-user, asked during the red/green/yellow step which followed a switch to CC strategy in the middle of training. The experimenter noted these questions because they were neither rote nor direct imitations but instead appeared to be clear instances of information seeking. Such question asking seemed to indicate that the children regarded color as a meaningful way of describing and classifying objects. However, the asking of such questions was not a uniform clue to the ability to classify by color, since some CC subjects, with correct comprehension, never asked questions. On the other hand, there were no observed instances of NCC subjects asking such questions.

It has been observed (Miller and Johnson-Laird, 1976; Cruse, 1977) that children do not learn color terms until long after they are able to differentiate colors, match colored objects, and show a preference for color in matching geometric forms (e.g., Suchman and Trabasso, 1966; Denney, 1972a, 1972b). Perhaps this lag in the acquisition of color terms may be accounted for by postulating that there is an additional step of learning required before the child can correctly use color terms. This additional step consists of acquiring the knowledge that color can be used as an attribute for categorizing multi-attribute, real world objects. This categorization knowledge may well be a complex achievement that requires additional time and experience with real world objects beyond the mastery of simple matching skills.

The manner in which children generalize their earliest words is also interpretable in terms of the hypothesis that the correct use of color terms requires mastery of color as a criterial attribute. In an earlier discussion (pp. 32–33), it was reported that when children are at the earliest stages of learning the meanings of words, they often overextend a particular word, i.e., use the term to apply to a broader range of referents than an adult would. For example, they may refer to all four-legged animals as "doggie." These overextensions are generally interpreted as evidence that the child is attempting to categorize objects as equivalent for the purposes of word use.

Recall Clark's (1973) observation that color is not used as a basis for extension of a word to new objects. This finding has been accepted and confirmed by additional evidence (Bowerman, 1976, 1978a; Anglin, 1977, pp. 183–184). This notable neglect of color as an attribute that could be used as a basis for generalizing a word to new objects may stem from children's unawareness, until later in their development, that color can be a means of equating objects. Bowerman (1978a) has argued that children analyze the attributes of referents in order to determine if a novel referent is similar to the known and prototypic referent of a particular word. If a novel referent is seen as sharing one or more defining attributes or features with a known referent, the child may extend the word to the novel referent. Color could be a basis for word generalization only if the children realized that objects can be similar on the basis of color. Since children do overextend word meanings on the basis of perceptual attributes other than color, such as shape, it is reasonable to infer that they do not do so on the basis of color because they do not realize its usefulness as a means of equating objects.

Counter-evidence

The preceding evidence and observations were supportive of the hypothesis. There is, however, some evidence that is inconsistent with the notion that comprehension of color terms is tied to mastery of the use of color as a criterial attribute: that is the lack of correspondence between David's and Ronnie's sorting strategies and their comprehension performance. If they did not comprehend because they did not regard color as a possible criterial attribute, then presumably their mastery of comprehension indicated that they had achieved a recognition of color as a possible criterial attribute. But such knowledge was not reflected in their sorting strategies, even after they were able to comprehend. They persisted in the NCC strategies even when color was the only available means of equating the objects (Task 2 of the sorting tasks).

Ronnie did change to a CC sorting strategy during and immediately after comprehension training, but this was not reflected in an immediate improvement in comprehension performance, in contrast to Arlene's comprehension which improved considerably following her switch to a CC sorting strategy, as discussed on pp. 87–88. In the three subsequent testings, with no concurrent comprehension training, Ronnie returned to an NCC strategy for sorting objects. It could be argued that he was just beginning to form the notion of color as a criterial attribute toward the end of the period of comprehension training and then "lost it" when training was suspended. This seems to be a plausible but weak explanation—weak in that there was no concomitant improvement in Ronnie's comprehension and that comprehension training apparently did not affect David's sorting strategies.

There is another observation that may account for the apparent discrepancy. The last several administrations of the sorting task were characterized by many indices of boredom on the part of both boys. It is quite possible that the validity of the sorting tasks was greatly reduced after as many as 13 administrations. The boys could have either adopted the same strategy by rote (which could account for some of David's persistence in the NCC strategy even as he may have been learning color as a criterial attribute) or could have adopted a purely random, meaningless strategy (which seemed to be apparent in Ronnie's last testings).

The evidence available from this study in support of the criterial attribute explanation for the production/comprehension discrepancy is far from conclusive. However, the consistency across observations warrants a further, specific look at such an explanation.

SUMMARY AND CONCLUSIONS

At the conclusion of training in which the subjects learned to correctly produce color terms in reference to various colored objects, four children failed comprehension tasks for the same words that they correctly produced. That is to say, when asked, "What color is this?" in reference to a particular object, they readily provided a correct answer; however, when asked to "Give me the _____ one," requiring the use of the same color term as in the first question, they did not answer correctly. Those subjects demonstrating such a gap in production and comprehension all had one characteristic in common: they were all in the group of subjects defined as lacking the nonlinguistic conceptual knowledge tied to the word meanings being trained. In contrast, those subjects demonstrating such conceptual knowledge prior to training responded correctly to both production and comprehension tasks, even though comprehension tasks were never explicitly trained.

A careful search for possible experimental or procedural artifacts that could account for the findings did not uncover any spuriousness about the pattern of responses. In fact, two of the subjects demonstrated such a production/comprehension gap for a full 11 weeks (that was not concurrent for the two of them). A period of explicit comprehension training was even provided during part of this 11-week period, and the unusual pattern of responses still persisted.

While contrary to the general expectations for performances on production and comprehension tasks, the findings are consistent with evidence of correct production without comprehension on tasks assessing word order (de Villiers and de Villiers, 1973; Chapman and Miller, 1975) and word meanings (Nelson and Bonvillian, 1978). Other parallel findings were reported in a training study (Guess and Baer, 1973) in which retarded subjects who had been trained to correctly produce a plural morpheme did not correctly comprehend the same form.

The explanations proposed to account for production without comprehension in word order and object-naming tasks did not pertain to the findings of this study; there was no evidence of processing shortcuts or contextual cues available to the subjects, nor any reason why they should only be available to part of the subjects. The interpretation of the mentally retarded subjects' lack of generalization from correct production of plural morphemes to correct comprehension also did not apply to these findings; there is no explanation of why there would be different response classes for one group of children and not the other. The idea that children sometimes first learn to produce object words because the objects are unfamiliar is not pertinent; the color words were quite familiar and equally so for both groups.

A consideration of what the one group of children knew that the other group did not, a knowledge that would account for spontaneous mastery of comprehension tasks for one group and not the other, led to a new explication of how correct production could coexist with incorrect comprehension. The explanation was cast within Huttenlocher's model of what differentiates the production and comprehension modes of responding. According to Huttenlocher (1974), reception involves the "recognition of words and recall of the objects, acts, and relations for which they stand," whereas production involves the "recognition of objects, acts, and relations and recall of the words that stand for them" (p. 335).

The concept-knowledge group of subjects knew that color could serve as a criterial attribute for regarding objects as equivalent. They learned to produce color terms in reference to colored objects more quickly than the subjects without such knowledge, and they spontaneously mastered correct comprehension. In other words, they could recognize either the words or the relationship among like-colored objects and they could recall either the words or the object relationships.

On the other hand, the group without prior nonlinguistic knowledge, by definition, did not demonstrate an awareness that color could be used to equate objects. They learned to correctly produce color terms in reference to colored objects, albeit in a more extended period of training, but they did not simultaneously demonstrate correct performance on comprehension tasks. To put it another way, they were able to perform successfully when the task required recognition of the relationship among objects and recall of the word, but not when the task required recognition of the word and recall of the object relationship.

An important question is how could the subjects "know" the word in production, that is, use it correctly to refer to various objects, and yet not "know" it in comprehension? The answer to this question requires a careful consideration of what knowledge was necessary in order to perform correctly on the training task. It happened that the children could correctly refer to colored objects on the basis of "recognize the object-color relationship of the object immediately present" and "recall the word." The child only needed to know "this object is red"; he never needed to know "this object is red and that object is red and they are alike in their redness."

The subjects could manage the production tasks without knowing that color could be a criterial attribute for equating objects. However, this knowledge appears to be very important for correct performance on the comprehension tasks. When asked to "Give me the red one," the child had to recognize the word "red" and recall the relationship for which it stands. The subjects who did not use color as a means of equating objects were unable to perform correctly on the comprehension tasks. It was posited that the comprehension failure was tied to the lack of conceptual knowledge (how to form groups of objects alike in their coloredness) or, more precisely, to the inability to recall the relationship. If the children did not know the relationship among the objects, they could not recall it. It is hypothesized that under this particular set of training circumstances, the coexistence of correct production with incorrect comprehension is accounted for by the underlying cognitive organization.

There was evidence from the subjects' behaviors to support the hypothesis. The major finding consistent with the notion that nonlinguistic knowledge (strategies for grouping objects) is linked to the production/comprehension gap is that children with such knowledge could both produce and comprehend color terms, whereas children without such knowledge failed the comprehension tasks. Another important finding that is consistent with this explanation is that explicit training on the comprehension tasks (without training on nonlinguistic grouping strategies) was a failure. The two subjects for whom comprehension training was provided received plenty of corrective feedback and linguistic information about their performances on the comprehension task, with a notable lack of effectiveness in improving the accuracy of their linguistic responses. Such a result would be expected if the problem was based on their nonlinguistic learning—the comprehension training did not provide the appropriate information.

There are some oddities about the relationship between nonlinguistic knowledge of colors and the acquisition of color terms that are consistent with the assumption of a link between knowing that color can be a means of equating multi-attribute objects and learning the names of colors. For example, children do not learn color terms until long after they are able to differentiate colors, match colored objects, and show a preference for color in matching geometric forms. This time lag could be the time required for the child to learn that color can serve as a means of grouping multi-attribute objects in the real world for the purposes of naming. It is also curious that children do not overgeneralize their earliest words on the basis of color, even though they do so on the basis of other perceptual attributes. Insofar as children's overgeneralizations are based on their ability to process and match features or attributes of objects, they would not use color as a dimension for overextending words if they did not realize that color could be a means of equating objects.

In the literature addressing how cognition relates to language, there has been a tendency to treat the two factors as if they were each homogeneous entities. However, there have been some subdivisions. Cromer (1974, 1976a) and Slobin (1973) divided language into grammar versus meaning, with cognition accounting for the latter but not the former. Bates et al. (1977b) divided cognition and language into "local homologies" or local task-specific areas of interlocking relationships instead of one more general relationship. The relationship between cognition and language that has been described here suggests a further subdivision of language according to performance mode, i.e., production versus comprehension. Different means of eliciting the same linguistic form may tap different levels of cognitive organization. Put another way, it is not safe to assume that the same kinds of cognitive knowledge underlie the use of a particular linguistic form in production versus comprehension. A corollary of this observation is that a child's linguistic productions may give a misleading impression of what the child "knows" semantically or cognitively.

The question of what the child's utterances reveal about his knowledge of word meaning is a matter of current debate among those investigators who are looking at children's word acquisition at the earliest stages. The central issue is how to interpret the different patterns of reference evident in children's productions versus their comprehension of the same words. The general assumption has been that children's first words map their underlying conceptual knowledge; therefore, their knowledge of word meanings directly reflects their cognitive understandings. But how can we know the meaning of a word and its underlying cognitive information for a child when he uses it differently in production compared to comprehension?

The focus of current explanations is to account for the broader range of reference evident in children's spontaneous productions than in comprehension, their productive overextension of a word. For example, Gruendel (1977, p. 1574) reported that one of her subjects used "car" to refer to many vehicles when he produced the word, but when presented with a comprehension task he only selected cars; she has several such examples of overextension of a word in production coexisting with correct reference in comprehension for both of her subjects. (But also bear in mind that Anglin (1977) found overextension in both comprehension and production for children only somewhat older—however, the overextension was more likely in production and underextension more evident in comprehension.)

Attention has centered on the child's intentions for the utterance—the discrepancy is interpretable if the child does not mean for his productions to be taken for literal reference. Clark (1977a, 1977b) argues that children's overextensions are reflections of communicative need. If they have no appropriate word in their repertoire, or if they cannot retrieve the right word, they may knowingly overextend a word in order to communicate.[6] A similar explanation is proposed by Nelson (1977a, 1977b), who

---

[6]This explanation of overextension was not supported by one of the findings reported by Nelson and Bonvillian (1978, p. 515). The children who were most successful learning the concept names (and presumably had more of the appropriate words available to use) were also those who used the largest number of extensions of nonexperimental words to label the object for which they had already learned new names.

suggests that the child intends an analogy instead of direct reference in cases of overextension, i.e., "it's like but it isn't really." Nelson ties this analogous intent to the child's cognitive development; she characterizes the child as knowingly using words to discern similarities for categorization purposes.

But such explanations have limitations. As Bowerman (1978b, p. 125; 1977b, pp. 2–3) has observed, the reasoning involved in these interpretations does not account for how the child first learned a given category and linked it to a particular word. And the proposed hypotheses do not explain how the child knows that one word is "like" another in reference to a particular object, relationship, or experience. Another drawback to the analogy explanation is that it raises the issue of how to tell which of a child's utterances are referential and which are not.

There is a growing awareness that the relationships between comprehension and underlying cognition, and production and cognitive knowledge at the earliest stages of word learning may be different. For example, Gruendel (1977) speculated that "it is as if in comprehension the word functions to denote a concept or class instance, while in production it may also serve as a category term whose referents legitimately cross class boundaries" (p. 1575). Nelson (1978, p. 966) has suggested that the closest match between underlying concepts and word meanings will be evident in the child's comprehension meaning for a word. This suggestion agrees well with the findings of the study reported here. If only the training subjects' production patterns were considered, their knowledge of relevant nonlinguistic categorizational principles would have been overestimated. On the other hand, the children's comprehension performances did correspond to their strategies for equating objects.

However, the direction of the production/comprehension gap in young children at the earliest stages of word acquisition is the opposite of the one reported in this study. Comprehension of word meanings appears to be more accurate than production for the very young children, instead of the pattern of accurate production coexisting with a lack of comprehension evident in the behaviors of the training subjects, and also reported for children's use of agent-action-object strings (de Villiers and de Villiers, 1973; Chapman and Miller, 1975).

How can this apparent reversal of the comprehension/performance accuracy be reconciled with the interpretation proposed here for the child's apparent ability to produce color words (with correct reference) while at the same time failing to comprehend the same words? As discussed earlier, there were several factors that may have contributed to the training subjects' ability to recall the word while they were apparently unable to recall the relationship: the age of the subjects (older than the very first stages of language acquisition), the experimental context (intensive modeling of the color terms and a restricted set of responses from the child), and the semantic content (the equivalence of colored objects, a conceptual knowledge that seems to be acquired relatively late). Just how general is this interpretation? Is it more probable that production might precede comprehension when the nonlinguistic relationship to be encoded is more difficult to recall than the word?

Let's look at how this reasoning corresponds to some of what is known about the production/comprehension relationship as normal children acquire language. Young children first show evidence of comprehending the meanings of certain words before their production of those same words (Huttenlocher, 1974; Goldin-Meadow, Seligman, and Gelman, 1976). Huttenlocher (1974) noted that the words that children comprehended designated individual objects, classes of objects, and perceptible acts. These referents were not only easy to point out, but they also "involved aspects of the child's experience that were distinctive and salient to him at the time the words were learned (p. 355). Huttenlocher argued that "the 'meanings' which became linked to word-sounds formed unitary cohesive elements of experience before that linkage occurred" (p. 356). In other words, children had already worked out the nonlinguistic relationships encoded in the words that they were able to comprehend; therefore, they had no trouble recalling the relationships. Instead their problem was one of retrieving the word (Huttenlocher's interpretation of why the children were unable to produce words was discussed earlier, on p. 103).

Somewhat later in development there is evidence of production preceding comprehension for word order (Chapman and Miller's (1975) subjects ranged in age from 1:8 to 2:8 with MLUs of 1.53 to 3.11) and for certain words—color terms, as reported in this study, the names of objects (Nelson and Bonvillian, 1978) for children ages 12 to 28 months, and the observation that words such as "why" and "how" are often produced before comprehended (Blank, 1974). This apparent difficulty mastering comprehension may be related to the nature of the relationships to be recalled. Blank (1974, pp. 241–242) argues that the reason the child produces certain terms before he comprehends them is that his nonlinguistic conceptual knowledge that is available on a sensorimotor level is not adequate for deriving the meanings. Instead the child has to find another way of deriving meanings, that of using the word itself to get environmental feedback. Such an account is consistent with the notion that the child does not comprehend a word because he is unable to access the relationship for which it stands.

However, Nelson and Bonvillian's (1978) data pose some complications. Their children demonstrated a pattern of production first in the acquisition of object words. Knowledge of objects, especially those that can be manipulated (as used by Nelson and Bonvillian), is generally regarded as within the sensorimotor techniques available to the young child. Blank (1974, p. 241) presumes that object words are comprehended first, then produced, and that this order of acquisition reflects the child's sensorimotor knowledge. It is the words that are not readily portrayable visually, such as "why" and "how" that can be expected to follow a production, then comprehension, sequence. Evidently the first assumption, that of comprehension first for object words, is not accurate. The remaining questions are whether or not some general sensorimotor knowledge, presumably acquired as the children handled the objects, was indeed mastered and, if so, was directly linked to the word meanings. Nelson and Bonvillian report indirect evidence regarding a possible link between measures of general cognitive knowledge and word acquisition: weak positive correlations were found between several measures of word learning and a "bracketed mental score" consisting of three sensorimotor measures and three verbal items adapted from the Stanford-Binet Intelligence Test. More importantly, Nelson and Bonvillian did not measure specific object knowledge that could be directly linked to particular word meanings. Such information could have helped account for why some children were more likely to produce first, then comprehend, than other children, and why some word meanings were learned by a particular child in one sequence whereas other words were learned in the other sequence.

What about the correct production of word order strings coexisting with incorrect comprehension? The interpretations that have been proposed focus on possible comprehension strategies that are dependent upon situational contexts (e.g., Chapman, 1978). However, this explanation did not apply to the production/comprehension differences evident in the subjects who learned color terms. Perhaps children can produce but not comprehend word order strings because of the different recall/recognition demands of the different tasks. For example, when the child is asked to "Tell me what's happening" (production task) as a toy man pushes the car, he has to recall the words and recognize the relationship. But when the task requires him to "Show me...man push car" (comprehension task) he has to recognize the words and recall the relationship. It may be easier for him to recall the words than it is to recall the relationship, particularly if he does not firmly "know" the relationship to begin with. There is reason to suspect that the more abstract relationships that exist between words may pose some learning difficulties for young children.

The idea that production may precede comprehension when the underlying nonlinguistic relationship is such that it is more difficult to recall than the word is at the level of interesting speculation. Additional evidence of production/comprehension relationships in other content domains, and at differing levels of linguistic acquisition, are needed before serious consideration of this theory is warranted. However, the hypothesis is intriguing in its potential for interrelating several aspects of the obviously complex relationship existing between the production and comprehension modes of performance.

A conservative interpretation of the findings of the study reported here suggest that one way of achieving greater accuracy in describing the relationship between cognition and language is to look at cognition in terms of nonlinguistic categorization strategies, and to differentiate between the performance and comprehension modes of language performance. Inherent in this finding is another one: the explicit training of word meanings allows for the unraveling of interrelationships that may not be observable under other circumstances. The value of studying early semantic acquisition in naturalistic settings has been established; this study attests to the value of investigating semantic acquisition within a training context. Information about how children's cognitive and linguistic knowledge influence their training performance is important for two reasons: it can increase our understanding of what is involved when children spontaneously acquire word meanings, and it can increase our effectiveness in training children who are unable to acquire language in the normal, spontaneous fashion. It is the latter situation that is addressed in the next chapter. The findings of this study, along with other recent psycholinguistic evidence pertaining to how normal children acquire the meanings of words, is applied to such clinical questions as: what vocabulary items to teach, how to teach word meaning, and how to assess word meaning. Theoretical issues are presented according to these topic areas, with related clinical questions and pertinent evidence.

Chapter 6
THE TRAINING
OF WORD MEANINGS

The training of word meanings reported in this study belies any assumptions that the training of color terms is a rather uninteresting, simple matter. In fact, several of the outcomes run contrary to some commonplace assumptions. For example, the subjects' patterns of learning in the explicit training circumstances closely paralleled what has recently been reported about how children spontaneously acquire color terms (Bartlett, 1977, 1978). There was evidence that the children first learned semantic relationships among color terms and later worked out correct reference to colored objects. Some children spontaneously generalized from production training to correct comprehension while other children did not; furthermore, those who did not correctly generalize lacked specific cognitive knowledge that the others demonstrated.

Since this attempt to explicitly teach young children the referential meanings of words within a structured training situation turned up some unexpected findings, it suggests the need to stop and reconsider other training circumstances. Of particular interest is the status of the training of word meanings within language-training programs designed to develop communication skills in children having difficulty acquiring language. What is the role of word meanings within currently available language-training programs? How are word meanings taught?

THE ROLE OF WORD MEANINGS
WITHIN CURRENT LANGUAGE-TRAINING PROGRAMS

The role of word meanings within language-training programs must be considered within the broader framework of the general purpose of the program. The goal of most programs is to train the child so that he can spontaneously generate novel, grammatically correct, complete utterances. The emphasis has been upon the development of a structural competence, i.e., control of the relationships among words in a sentence. The training status of word meanings has reflected that emphasis.

Many of the programs developed in the late 1960s accentuated the mastery of surface grammatical forms. The words that were explicitly

117

trained were those that functioned as grammatical units (e.g., pronouns, auxiliary verbs, prepositions, or negation markers). The content words (e.g., nouns, verbs, adjectives, and adverbs) were relegated a secondary status. The only explicit training provided was that necessary to build a minimal set of content words (usually an arbitrary amount, such as 50 words) that could be used as some sort of plug-in units for the syntactic training. Such a programming strategy is exemplified in the Monterey Language Training Program (Gray and Ryan, 1973). The lack of interest in content words is apparent in Harris's (1975) review. She notes: "Generally the subject is first taught noun labels and then other forms of grammar" (p. 571). She then never mentions the "noun labels" again; the subsequent review and discussion addresses studies in which a variety of grammatical forms were trained (e.g., prepositions, verb tenses, plurals, and complex and compound sentences).

With the psycholinguistic shift of attention to semantic relations as a way of characterizing early word combinations, instead of grammatical units, the role of content words in training programs also changed. Words were taught as expressions of semantic functions and relations, e.g., recurrence, nonexistence, disappearance, agent, action, object, possession, and so on (Bricker and Bricker, 1974; Miller and Yoder, 1974; Stremel and Waryas, 1974; Bloom and Lahey, 1978). As in the programs based on a grammatical unit strategy, the reference-making function of words is not emphasized. Nevertheless, the child must know two components of word meaning in order to successfully use words to express semantic relations, i.e., the lexical meaning of the word itself plus the more abstract relational meaning of the word in combination with another word. The training programs generally emphasize the combinatorial meanings. The former, the lexical meaning, is treated as if it were evident at the beginning of training for the words in question, or could be readily taught in simple training activities such as pairing a word with a referent. Indeed, Miller and Yoder (1974) imply that the referential meaning of a word can be acquired incidentally as the clinician is training the word's semantic function.

In addition to the emphasis upon word order and grammatical meanings, there is another factor that may contribute to the relative neglect of content words in training programs: it is not feasible to standardize a particular set of words to be taught to all children. The words that serve a grammatical function (e.g., pronouns, prepositions, and auxiliary verbs) constitute a small set of words that each child must master, making it possible to standardize the linguistic forms and their sequencing within a particular training program. However, content words are not amenable to such standardization. Each child has the choice of many possible vocabulary items that are appropriate to the communicative context. Each child builds his own set of content words based on his own unique environment and communicative needs. Instead of specifying a standardized vocabulary for a training program to be taught in the same sequence to all children, the designers of language-training programs must deal with more general principles for the selection of lexical items for a particular child.

The problem of deciding what words to teach has been addressed in regard to the beginning stages of language training. However, the training of word meanings is still cast within the context of combinatorial meanings. Holland (1975) offered some guidelines for which words to teach and in what contexts. Holland's considerations for lexical training were tuned to the needs of the language programs designed to teach a semantically based grammer (MacDonald and Blott, 1974; Miller and Yoder, 1974). She emphasized that children's use of words revealed many functions other than naming (reference) and that the words to be trained should be chosen with an eye toward facilitating communication within context, with maximal potential for combinations with other words according to a given set of a priori semantic relations. Her consideration of reference per se was only to make the point that the clinician's job is more than just teaching the referential function (p. 516). Presumably, it is understood that the clinician already knows how to go about teaching the referential meanings of words.

Lahey and Bloom (1977) have expanded Holland's suggestions with some additional reflections about which words to teach at the beginning stages, and how to organize a first lexicon. Like Holland, they accentuated the communicative usefulness of particular words for a child, and the desirability of selecting and organizing lexical items to express various categories of semantic content, e.g., recurrence of objects and actions, attributes, actions, objects, and so on. In addition, they introduced two new considerations that bear on the referential aspects of word meaning. The first was the suggestion that words to be trained be chosen on the basis of how easy they are to demonstrate in the nonlinguistic context. Lahey and Bloom (1977) observed that much needs to be learned about how to present referents for a child to label. They recommend that concepts (word meanings) that are easy to demonstrate nonlinguistically should be presented before those more difficult to depict. The assumption appears to be that the learning of referential meanings would be easier if the referents could be easily depicted nonlinguistically.

The second new consideration was that of linguistic context, in this case the number of contexts in which a word could be used. Lahey and

Bloom advised that words be selected for training that have a "broad application to many objects and events" (p. 342). In other words, words that have a wide range of referents, and/or may carry several different word meanings, have greater utility than words with more limited meanings.

However, Lahey and Bloom, like Miller and Yoder (1974), do not specifically address the training of the referential meanings of the linguistic forms. Instead the focus is upon the more abstract content categories with linguistic forms regarded as expressions of those categories:

> Forms are presented in contexts that illustrate the content categories, for example, acting on object, locating objects, and rejecting objects. As the child observes or participates in these contexts, the clinician provides relevant linguistic forms to code content. Goals for two-word utterances can be derived from combinations of the known forms in the same contexts, while new lexical forms are also gradually added (p. 348).

The secondary status of word meanings is further apparent in Bloom and Lahey's (1978) comprehensive plan and goals for language training, where information about the training of lexical items is limited to a few very general observations (e.g., the choice and rate of training lexical items depends on the particular child; add new lexical items gradually and continually throughout the program, p. 385) and considerations for selecting the first words to train (pp. 582–585). The training they describe is structured according to content categories; the primary emphasis is upon relational categories.

Since the training of linguistic forms is embedded in the context of higher-order content categories, the apparent supposition is that an explicit training step to teach the referential meaning of a lexical item is not necessary—that the child can simultaneously learn the lexical meaning of the word and its more abstract relational meaning. Or perhaps the assumption is that clinicians know how to teach the lexical meaning and only need to be reoriented to consider the relational meanings that are described as semantic functions or semantic relations.

How valid are these assumptions? Obviously, the writers of language programs operate from the premise that clinicians know how to teach lexical referential meanings, since there is seldom a specific set of training procedures devised for this purpose, especially beyond the earliest stages of language acquisition. The training of lexical items is almost always viewed as the establishment of a core of items that can serve as units in the presumably more important task of learning to put words together (cf. Holland, 1975; Lahey and Bloom, 1977; Bloom and Lahey, 1978). But perhaps these assumptions are not accurate. Conceivably the training of the referential meaning of particular lexical items (nouns, verbs, adjectives, prepositions, etc.) is more complicated than assumed, complex enough to warrant explicit training procedures directed to this level of word meaning alone. Maybe clinicians do not know how to teach lexical meanings—possibly they could benefit from an orientation to some of the complexities involved in working out the relationship between a word's meaning and the category of real world information that it represents.

Much of what clinicians know about the training of word meanings would seem to be based upon informal clinical lore of an intuitive nature, since there have not been any writings directed to the issue. Somehow we just "clinically pick up" how to train words, and which words to train. While Holland (1975), Lahey and Bloom (1977), and Bloom and Lahey (1978) have offered some guidelines for which words to train first, based upon the normative psycholinguistic literature, their total lexicon is quite small (approximately 35 words). Beyond these specific words, the clinician is left with the more general guidelines, again based on the normative literature, that can be paraphrased in an oversimplified fashion by the admonition to "choose vocabulary to match the cognitive and environmental needs of the child."

This researcher suspects that in actual application many language interventionists choose to train vocabulary items that are depicted in pictured stimuli available in language development kits and materials catalogs, in lieu of more structured principles for teaching vocabulary to children more linguistically advanced than the very beginnings of language. These procedures probably do no harm (for example, the strategy of teaching to the materials is consistent with Lahey and Bloom's suggestion to teach first the forms that can be nonlinguistically depicted), but they seem rather imprecise and limited compared to the picture emerging from child language studies. A number of child language investigators have looked at different aspects of the referent relationship between words and real world objects, events, relationships, and experiences. There is evidence of subtle and complex categorical equivalences underlying a wide range of semantic categories at the earliest stages of word acquisition and beyond. Many of the findings have implications for how to go about training word meanings, although few of the psycholinguistic writings have addressed this line of application.

It is an appropriate time to think carefully about vocabulary acquisition within the clinical setting. It is a time of considerable potential for enhancing our effectiveness in teaching a relatively neglected yet particularly important linguistic skill, the mastery of referential word meanings. Exciting theoretical developments in the study of word acquisition are available, combined with a willingness among speech clinicians to broaden their clinical procedures to include cognitive and social context.

This chapter relates various theoretical issues that have been addressed in the psycholinguistic literature to the general clinical questions of what lexical items to teach, how to teach word meaning, and how to assess word meaning. Within each of these three inclusive questions particular theoretical issues are discussed, with their own, more specific clinical questions and whatever pertinent evidence is available. The topics are presented in an unrelated order; there is no attempt to tie them together into a logical or hierarchical sequence. Rather, they constitute a topical mosaic of interrelated issues pertaining to the acquisition of word meaning.

A comprehensive review of the literature that describes how normal children acquire various word meanings is not provided; several excellent reviews are now available and heartily recommended for the reader who is interested in a more general overview (e.g., Clark and Clark, 1977, Chapter 13, pp. 485–514; Bowerman, 1978b, pp. 120–134; de Villiers and de Villiers, 1978, Chapter 5, pp. 121–150). Only those portions of the available literature that were perceived as having a bearing on clinical matters are discussed here. The intent is to increase awareness of what may be involved in the business of teaching a child how to use a particular word to refer to particular bundles of real world information. At this stage of knowledge it is only possible to conjecture about possible answers to many of the clinical questions; however, such speculation may help us begin to define the parameters of the task, a necessary step before one can go about devising appropriate means of training.

CLINICAL QUESTIONS, THEORETICAL ISSUES, AND IMPLICATIONS FOR INTERVENTION

What Lexical Items to Teach?

The content of this section is not designed to be a direct extension of the guidelines offered by Holland (1975) or Lahey and Bloom (1977). As pointed out earlier, their consideration of lexical items was in the context of a first lexicon, and how those words could expedite the development of multi-word combinations. In contrast, the present discussion of which lexical items to teach extends beyond the first words and also concentrates on the referential meanings of individual lexical items.

An additional caveat must precede the discussion of *what* words to teach. Although the section following this one takes up the question of *how* to teach word meanings, it is impossible to crisply distinguish between these two aspects of training. Instead, in actual practice, the two questions involve interactive considerations of each—it is not a matter of first considering what words to teach, arriving at some particular lexical items, and then considering how to teach them. The consideration of what words to teach is influenced by how they could be taught and the how to teach question is influenced by the content. In the discussions to follow the questions are separated only for the convenience of emphasis; considerable overlap is inevitable.

Theoretical Issue: Is the Relationship Between Cognition and Language the Same in Language-Disordered Children as is Apparent When Studying Normal Children?   A number of clinical questions are directly tied to this issue. How literally can we apply normal acquisition findings to determining a first lexicon for language-disordered children? What if children having problems acquiring language also indicate patterns of underlying categorical equivalences different from those evident in normal children? Could words be taught first, as representatives of nonverbal categories? If so, could the first lexical items be arbitrarily selected on the basis of the clinician's observation of possible communicative need?

The available normative literature and evidence has centered almost exclusively on the earliest stages of word acquisition, in part because that is where considerable differences of opinion have developed. The various theoretical positions were reviewed earlier. To summarize briefly, the predominant interpretation has been that children's earliest word meanings serve to represent meanings that they have already worked out nonlinguistically (Clark, 1973, 1977; Nelson, 1973, 1977, 1978). However, there is also evidence that linguistic input can trigger a search for a conceptual grouping that might not have otherwise occurred to a child (Blank, 1974; Schlesinger, 1974, 1977; Wells, 1974; Bowerman, 1976, 1977b; Braunwald, 1978; Gruendel, 1977).

What do we know about language-disordered children that is relevant to this issue? The verbal communication of language-impaired children is highly similar to that of younger normal children (see Rice, 1978, and Leonard, 1979, for reviews of the literature). This comparison suggests that other factors may be implicated when children have difficulty acquiring language. Since nonlinguistic representational behavior appears to parallel language development (cf. Bates et al., 1977a, 1977b), it has been suggested that this may be the factor that accounts for the comparability of the language performances of language-impaired children with that of younger normals. Morehead and Ingram (1976, pp. 227–228) reviewed evidence for the possibility that language-disordered children may have a specific cognitive deficit in more general aspects of representational behavior. Leonard (in press) has pursued this possibility with the proposal that "language impairment should no longer be viewed as a strictly linguistic deficit, but rather as a deficit associated with a delay in the development of a number of representational abilities."

Let's return to a consideration of the clinical questions. If language-disordered children, or, perhaps, just *some* language-disordered children, do indeed have problems acquiring representational abilities, can we assume that the relationship between cognition and language that they may demonstrate is the same as that accounting for normal development? Two aspects of the cognition/language relationship are involved in this issue. First, does underlying cognition account for the word meanings of language-disordered children? It has generally been assumed that the first word meanings used by normal children reflect underlying nonlinguistic categorical equivalences (Clark, 1973, 1977; Nelson, 1974, 1977, 1978). This conclusion is based upon such evidence as the systematic use of words by children to refer to real world information in a manner unlike adults' usage (that is, the underlying concept guides the use of the word) and systematic nonlinguistic strategies for interpreting word meanings (i.e., nonlinguistic knowledge of "the way things are" determines the comprehension of the word). However, there is no evidence to confirm such a systematic influence of underlying nonlinguistic information to direct the use of words by language-disordered children, nor to disconfirm it. The second question is whether the underlying cognitive organization of children having trouble acquiring language is the same as that apparent in normally developing children. Among the research findings cited as evidence for cognitive differences in language disordered children there are reports of difficulties solving matching tasks (Inhelder, 1966, 1976). Such matching abilities are central to the child's ability to construct equivalences among nonlinguistic objects and events, a process that is basic to language. There is at least some reason to suspect that there may be different strategies for forming nonlinguistic categorical equivalences for some language-disordered children as compared to normal children.

Insofar as underlying nonlinguistic equivalences influence word meanings and the language-disordered child is prone to form groupings different from a normal child, one cannot assume that introducing the words that normal children first acquire to the child having difficulty acquiring language will automatically result in the close match between linguistic forms and underlying cognition that is apparent in the normal child's use of words. Two implications for training follow from this observation.

Instead of adhering to the cognition-first hypothesis, the clinician could follow the interactionist model of the relationship between language and cognition. In place of matching words to underlying concepts the clinician might deliberately choose to teach certain lexical meanings as a way of introducing to the child possible nonlinguistic categorical groupings that he might not otherwise spontaneously develop. However, the findings of the study reported here suggest some justification for caution. The training of color words did not exert much influence on the children's strategies for equating multi-attribute objects (see pp. 66–67). Also, while nonlinguistic knowledge was not a prerequisite for the children learning to *produce* color terms, it did play an important role in their spontaneous acquisition of correct comprehension. It may well be that linguistic input can just suggest concepts that the child is already capable of forming, but cannot play the stronger role of teaching a nonlinguistic concept, a conclusion consistent with Bowerman's (1977b) position. It seems that the idea of choosing those words to train that could introduce certain concepts may have serious limitations.

The second clinical implication involves training according to the cognition-first hypothesis, but without a priori assumptions as to the nature of underlying nonlinguistic knowledge. Instead of assuming such knowledge to be like that most typical of normal children, the interventionist could try to deduce the apparent categorizational strategies of the individual child and choose lexical items to match them. This strategy has been suggested by Bowerman (1978b, pp. 169–170), based on a different rationale. She observed that there is no uniform system of nonlinguistic information common to all normal children; instead there are discernible patterns of individual differences in how normal children organize experiences. Presumably children having problems with the acquisition of language could differ not only from a normal child but also from another individual child with language disorders. Indeed, it is reasonable to predict greater variability within the language-disordered group of children than in a comparable group of normal children.

What value does the normative literature have for determining what words to teach? There is reason to suspect that the relationship between cognition and language may not be the same for language-disordered children as that apparent in young normal children's first uses of words. Given that there may be differences, is the literature describing patterns of language acquisition in normal children to be dismissed as having no proven value (as evident in Harris's (1975) paper)? On the contrary, what is known about how normal children link up nonlinguistic information and the meanings of words can serve as a valuable heuristic for how to choose words to train and how to train them. The descriptions of the interrelationships evident in the linguistic and conceptual competencies of young normal children provide valuable clues for what to consider when trying to assist a child build a language system who cannot manage to do so on his own.

An awareness of normal cognitive and language development can serve as a guide for a reasonable match between a child's conceptual knowledge and particular linguistic forms. The greater the discrepancy between what a child knows conceptually and the meaning of particular words, the less likely it is that the child will be able to master the word's meanings. For example, Bloom and Lahey (1978, p. 546) point out that the use of activities designed to teach opposites, superordinate categories, and verbal analogies with a child who cannot yet express ideas in simple sentences runs counter to what is known of how normal children code nonlinguistic information. Opposites, superordinate categories, and verbal analogies draw upon more sophisticated cognitive knowledge than do the relational meanings encoded in simple sentences, such as actor-action-object strings. It seems more reasonable to follow the normal order of linguistic coding of concepts unless there are other factors involved (such as some constraint on the child's ability to produce multi-word utterances coexisting with other signs of cognitive readiness for more abstract concepts).

To return to the more specific question of what words to teach, it is probably more useful to rely on the normative literature as a guide for which words *to* teach, rather than which words *not to* teach. Many of the meanings of the first words acquired by normal children are based upon some very basic cognitive notions, such as identity (proper nouns), recurrence and negation (relational terms), and similarities and categories of similarities (substantive words like "dog"), which also happen to have considerable communicative import for a young child. Such words certainly seem like a reasonable place to start teaching words to a child lacking them. The ubiquitous appearance of words like "more" and "no" in the first lexicons of normal children is testimony to their ease of acquisition and immediate communicative usefulness. It is difficult to imagine a language-disordered child with a minimum of cognitive competence who would not be able to learn the word "more" and be able to use it to communicate meaningfully.

On the other hand, some words are noticeably absent in the first lexicons of young normal children. It could be argued that these absences can serve as guides for which words not to teach first to children having trouble acquiring words. For example, Lahey and Bloom (1977) suggest only a very limited set of attribute words in the first lexicon on the grounds that "attribution, in general, makes up a small part of the language used by young children and should not be overemphasized" (p. 347). While this certainly is an accurate observation of the patterns of language use evident in young normal children, it is still conceivable that such words might be appropriate for individual children with language differences. It is usually the case that language-disordered children at the earliest stages of training are older than the age at which normal children neglect attribute words. The language-disordered child may be particularly tuned to specific attribute dimensions in his strategies for forming nonlinguistic equivalences. Or it just may be that the training of the referential meanings of attribute words may help introduce the more general notion of linguistic mapping of nonlinguistic equivalences specific to objects. Furthermore, attribute words may have more communicative significance for the older language-disordered child than the younger normal child. For example, it is possible to think of social situations where the child would benefit from knowing both "big" and "little," or both "dirty" and "clean," instead of having only "not big" or "not dirty" available for his use.

At any rate, the interventionist must determine which words to teach which individual child. The normative literature's usefulness as a guide is most evident when determining what words to teach first—the relationship between nonlinguistic concepts and word meanings beyond the earliest stages of acquisition is relatively unmapped. The available literature can only serve as a first approximation of what words to teach to a particular language-disordered child. Considerations of what the child knows nonlinguistically, his particular interests and communicative needs, can suggest the training of words that are quite different from the patterns of normal acquisition.

Theoretical Issue: How Are Semantic Categories Organized Internally? Are categories of word meanings organized according to singly defined attributes or according to complex associations with one centrally defining example? (When the word is held constant for differing referents, are those referents equated on the basis of similarity to prototype or equivalence of single attributes?) For hierarchical semantic structures, are the various levels equally informative of the categorical structure, or is one level more informative than others? (When the referent is constant and the word can vary, do some words have greater communicative utility than others?)

The clinical questions that follow from this theoretical issue are: Should the first lexical items be chosen to generalize along lines of prototypicality (central to peripheral exemplars) or single attributes (for single attribute matching)? When teaching lexical items that are hierarchically nested (such as rose / flower / plant or collie / dog / animal), should the lexical items be chosen to represent a specific-to-general direction of training, or general-to-specific, or middle-to-specific-to-general, or other possible options?

The possibility that semantic categories are organized according to principles different from the matching of single defining attributes has been raised by the findings of Rosch and her colleagues (reviewed earlier, pp. 35–36). In regard to the first aspect of the development of word meanings (word constant, referents vary),[1] there is evidence that some of children's first word meanings are organized according to a prototype, or one best exemplar of the cluster of attributes that comprise the groupings (Bowerman, 1977b; Anglin, 1977). Furthermore, the prototypic referents for a word appear to be learned first; that is, children first attach the word meaning to a centrally defining exemplar, with other, less typical referents acquired later. These less typical referents share one or more of the attributes of the prototype; the more the number of attributes held in common, the more likely the referent is to be named with the same word used to refer to the prototypic exemplar. Bowerman (1978b, p. 170) suggests that prototypicality be considered when deciding which referents to use when teaching a particular word meaning.

The second aspect of the development of word meanings involves situations in which the referent is constant and the word can vary. Another of Rosch's findings has a bearing on deciding which lexical items to teach when there are different available ways of naming a particular referent. When dealing with a hierarchy of categories, Rosch maintains that there is a basic level of semantic category (defined by possessing significant numbers of attributes in common, used by same motor programs, similar in shape, and can be recognized from average shapes of members of the category). This basic level is described as that of the "basic object" (see p. 35). She predicts that children will first learn words at this level. For example, in the case of the referent dog, a child could refer to it as "collie," "Spot," "dog," or "animal." In this case, "dog" would represent the basic object level and would be the most likely first lexical item for that referent. Anglin (1977, p. 237) found that children first named objects at an intermediate level of generality, consistent with Rosch's predictions.

---

[1]See Brown (1978) for an integration of his earlier work on reference (1958), including the distinction between two lines of development (words versus referents, fixed versus variable), with the recent work defining basic objects and prototypes.

Rosch has emphasized the importance of multi-attribute processing in the formation of children's meanings of words. There is some additional evidence to support that notion. Recall that in the study reported here, all the subjects could match colored blocks (single-attribute matching). The grouping strategies for equating multi-attribute real world objects were what differentiated the two groups. Furthermore, the knowledge that color could be a criterial attribute for equating objects when competing criteria were available was a central factor in the children's ability to spontaneously generalize from production training to comprehension.

Carey's work (1978) also supports the role of multi-attribute processing. She has considered the process whereby children acquire the full and complete meaning of a word. She differentiates between the initial, partial, fast mapping of conceptual information into a lexical unit, and the slower-developing full coordination of lexical organization and conceptual information involved in a full mapping of meaning. In order to account for this process of lexical acquisition, she has distinguished between two kinds of semantic information: one that is part of an integrated representation of a particular object and another that is coded as discrete features. She proposes that the acquisition of meaning is characterized by the gradual addition of defining features, plus the information available in "haphazard example," that is, unanalyzed units of interrelated linguistic and nonlinguistic information. While the notion of "haphazard example" is not intended to account for the same linguistic information that prototypes do, both notions involve multi-attribute processing of bundles of correlated nonlinguistic information.

How can these observations about how semantic categories are organized help a clinician decide which words to train? When deciding which word among several hierarchically related words to train, the notion of a truest name, a basic level, can serve as a guiding principle. In this case, the interventionist's intuitive judgment is closely related to theoretical proof. The notion that the basic object level is somehow most useful corresponds well to actual clinical practice. For example, Coleman and Anderson (1978, pp. 250–253) have reported a list of lexical items used in a training study. Most of the items in their "noun corpus" represent an intermediate level of generality. Indeed, the close congruence between the intuitive basis for the selection of which words within a hierarchy to train first and the theoretical description of the basic object level is additional confirmation of the theory itself.

However there is an obvious limitation to the available literature. The studies of the internal organization of semantic categories conducted by Rosch and her colleagues and Anglin have been limited to object words,[2] and only a small number of categories of these (i.e., animal, vehicle, furniture, fruit, weapon, vegetable, clothing, food, plant). Of course, the language-disordered child needs far more than just the names of objects in order to successfully communicate. The interventionist is once again in the position of having to understand the basic principles and move beyond the available data base into intuitive judgment of which words, out of several candidates for referring to the same actions, states, experiences, and so on, represent the psychological equivalent of "basic object." Since Rosch's theoretical model seems to substantiate intuitive notions of basic objects, the use of intuition to determine which words to teach in other linguistic domains may not be as weak an approach as it may first appear.

Once words at the basic object level were taught, the interventionist could systematically introduce other words at different levels of abstraction to refer to the same nonlinguistic information. There is no clear evidence suggesting whether the second step should be toward greater abstraction or greater specificity. It seems to depend at least in part upon the naming practices of adults and the particular semantic domain being considered. For example, Anglin (1977) found that the names that mothers chose to label a picture representing a hierarchy of words, such as food, fruit, apples, for their young child almost always coincided with the name used by young children (p. 87). Although most names were at an intermediate level, for some categories the word was at the most specific level, e.g., "pineapple," or "grasshopper" (p. 79) while for others the word was at the most general level, e.g., "money" as opposed to "coin" or "dime" (p. 98).

After the word to be trained has been selected, the choice of which referents to present for a particular word meaning could be directed by a consideration of prototypicality. Within such a rationale, the order of presentation would be prototypic referents trained first, then generalization structured to follow the progression from central to peripheral category members. For example, when teaching the word "dog" (at the basic object level), the first exemplars could be German shepherds or collies, followed by beagles, then poodles, and finally more peripheral members, such as Pekinese, Great Dane, or other exotic breeds. As with basic objects, the clinician would have to draw upon intuitive judgment to supplement the available literature for lexical domains other than object words.

---

[2]Bowerman (1976, 1977b) reported a prototypic organization of referents for her daughter's acquisition of the action words "kick" and "open."

Once again clinicians' intuitive judgment seems to parallel what has been established on theoretical grounds. The idea that prototypes are the most salient referents coincides nicely with what clinicians actually do. Most of the time, language trainers seem to intuitively select the prototypic member of a particular category as the referent for word training, for example, a red apple to train "apple," or a wooden kitchen chair to train "chair," on the assumption that these referents are somehow "easiest." The commercial training materials certainly attest to the propensity to use clearly illustrated prototypes as stimulus materials. Insofar as clinicians are more likely to choose prototypic referents, everyday pedagogical practice supports the theoretical position, as in the case of the basic object.

One important point about both basic objects and prototypic exemplars is that they require multi-attribute processing. Therefore, generalization items would not have to be designed to move along a gradation of a singly-defining attribute. In fact, a sequencing that requires a shifting in the criterion for equivalence may be the preferred means of enhancing generalization within a category or across levels of a particular category.

Careful specification of the stimulus dimensions of generalization items has been a central tenet of behavior modification technology. However, this appears to be changing. Stokes and Baer (1977, pp. 357–358) offer a suggestion very similar to the one presented here, for different reasons. They advocate a loosening of control over the stimuli presented in a "train loosely" strategy as a means of facilitating generalization. However, the idea suggested above, that of shifting attributes for equivalence groupings to correspond to the organization of attributes packaged in a prototype, suggests more structure than "train loosely" implies. Generalization items would be selected according to a systematic consideration of attributes. For example, when training "dog" generalization items could first be chosen to represent an attribute most representative of the category, such as size, that is; all exemplars would be medium-sized but might vary in color, length of tail, and other attributes. Later generalization items could share the same color, length of tail, or other attributes, and vary along the size dimension.

Theoretical Issue: Do Children First Learn the Relationship between Words and Real World Information (Reference) and Later the Connections between Lexical Meanings, or Vice Versa? When this question is extended to the clinical situation, it has implications for the selection of words to teach and their order of presentation. Should the words represent a family of items, e.g., color terms, that would later be tied to correct reference, or should words be selected to teach specific referent relationships, with a later introduction of additional words of the lexical family?

Children evidently learn color terms first as a family of related words and only later do they work out how the word meanings correspond to visual properties. The major source of evidence for this conclusion is Bartlett's work (described earlier, pp. 42–47). The findings of the training study reported here are consistent with this interpretation of the sequence of normal acquisition. The training subjects first learned which words were appropriate responses to the question "What color is this?" Far more training trials were required to establish to which color the given color term referred.

The idea that semantic organization precedes referential meaning runs counter to other interpretations of certain linguistic phenomena evident in how children use words. Bowerman's (1974, 1977a, 1978c) analysis of errors of overregularization of various word meanings, and Kuczaj's (1978) interpretation of the acquisition of the progressive inflection -ing (see earlier discussion, pp. 46–47) are both predicated on the idea that children first learn words as relatively isolated lexical units representing referential information; the knowledge of similarities across words is developed later.

The characterization of children's word acquisition as a process of moving from initial referential mapping to a later, more sophisticated understanding of how words are linguistically related has high intuitive appeal. However, the evidence from the domain of color terms is quite convincing. Several additional factors may be at work. It could be that what kind of knowledge is acquired first depends on the lexical domain and the kinds of nonlinguistic conceptual knowledge available to the child. For those words that represent nonlinguistic information that the child has already completely or partially worked out, it is reasonable to predict that the referential meaning will be evident in the first uses of the word. However, for words representing nonlinguistic equivalences that for some unknown reason are more difficult for the child to master (such as groupings of like-colored objects), the first uses of the word may be based on equivalences within the lexical organization, or the communicative situation. Examples are the knowledge that a small set of words are appropriate responses to questions such as "What color is this?" or the use of a small set of words to serve particular communicative functions such as "Why?" or "What?" as a means of obtaining adult attention (even before the meanings of "Why" or "What" are fully understood).

Not only is the nature of the available nonlinguistic information a possible factor; so too is the nature of the linguistic equivalences. There are certainly different degrees of difficulty or abstractness involved in working out the relationships among linguistic forms. Some, such as the superordinate/hyponymic relationship evident among color terms (see p. 43), may be relatively easy to acquire, and may certainly be expected to precede nonlinguistic information that is difficult to master. On the other hand, other linguistic equivalences, such as different semantic and syntactic means for expressing causative meanings, may require far more sophisticated linguistic processing and could conceivably lag far behind the referential mapping of nonlinguistic knowledge that was worked out comparatively early.

What value do these considerations have for the decision of what words to train a child with difficulties acquiring language? There are several relevant points. First, the teaching of referential meanings may not always be the most useful first step; there may be some categories of lexical meaning in which words can first be taught as a family of related items. If this is the case, then the selection of words to teach would be on the basis of their family membership. The second and more basic point is that the relationship between nonlinguistic knowledge and how to express meanings linguistically is an important factor in language learning at levels of acquisition more complex than that of the first words. The choice of what words to teach can be influenced by a consideration of the relative abstractness of the nonlinguistic meanings as compared to the abstractness of relationships between and among words.

Theoretical Issue: How Does the Child Extend His Initial Word Meanings into More Sophisticated Ways of Expressing the Same Basic Meanings such as learning semantically equivalent but linguistically different means of expressing a given content, or learning how to juxtapose reference and context for the invention of uniquely appropriate semantic expressions (metaphors, humor)? The clinical implications for this issue take us beyond the first fifty words, beyond the initial lexicon, into considerations of what words to choose for training more advanced knowledge of word meanings. The training literature has virtually ignored the needs of communicatively handicapped children beyond the level of constructing syntactically correct utterances. Yet there is much important linguistic learning beyond that level, and the bulk of this later learning seems to involve knowledge about word meanings. For the language-disordered child to acquire anything near normal functioning in verbal communication and language based academic subjects (reading, social studies, history, and so on), he must master more complex ways of expressing semantic information. The interventionist's first task is to decide what words to teach: Which words have the greatest semantic productive potential, that is, which words can be related to equivalent meanings framed in different syntactic structures? Which words can be trained to serve as metaphors? What words merit explicit training as expressions of humor (riddles, puns)?

The theoretical issue raised here is at present for all practical purposes an unmapped area of child development. It has yet to be the object of widespread investigative efforts. Nonetheless, there is some current work that opens a passageway into the tangled interrelationships of more advanced semantic knowledge.

Bowerman has compiled detailed records of the language acquisition of her two daughters, Christy and Eva. She has been especially sensitive to how her daughters learned to express semantic information. Her careful documentation of how particular words were used to express certain meanings at differing levels of her daughters' linguistic development allowed for the observation of systematic regularities in Christy's and Eva's packaging of semantic information. One particular kind of meaning has turned out to be especially informative about how children learn to express equivalent meanings in linguistically different structures. The meaning is that of causation, of some event causing the occurrence of another event. There are several possible ways to linguistically express the notion of causation, with the differences dependent upon the explicitness of the semantic material and the amount of compression of semantic elements into single words. Two simple means of representing underlying causative relationships would be "John made the door open" or "John opens the door," in which case the causing event is left unspecified. More complex linguistic mapping is necessary in order to specify the causing event, such as "John pulled on the door and that made it come open," or, with greater semantic compression, "John pulled the door open."[3] (See Bowerman, 1974, 1977a for a more complete discussion of the linguistic representation of causation.) There are a number of constraints on the formation of such causative constructions in English. As Christy and Eva Bowerman talked about causative events and relationships, their utterances revealed systematic errors in the means they chose to linguistically map causative meanings (see Bowerman, 1974, 1977a for detailed examples of the errors).

Bowerman has interpreted her daughters' errors, supplemented with observations of other children's causative errors, as evidence of the ability

---

[3]This representation of linguistic relationships is based on the premise that lexical items are not the basic units of meaning. Instead, the lexical items are composed of smaller semantic units referred to as components, features, and so forth. These components may be shared by different words (e.g., McCawley, 1971).

of young children to extract underlying rules and regularities governing how semantic material can be put together in lexical items. Furthermore, children's analyses of the meanings of individual words are intimately connected to their syntactic development. In Bowerman's data, errors involving compressed or conflated semantic material were preceded by or co-occurred with the correct production of syntactic constructions that explicitly spelled out the relationship between a causing event and a resulting event. For example, Christy first used novel conflated sentences like "I'm pulling it unstapled" 2 months after sentences with the correct use of "because," and at the same time as sentences like "The boy pushed the witch in the oven and that made her dead." (Bowerman, 1977a). In other words, children seem to start with particular meanings they wish to express, such as causal relationships. They not only learn how to express that meaning in a particular lexical item; they also are capable of figuring out more general patterns governing how semantic material gets packaged into lexical items, such that they predict that words with certain meanings are possible. Children also learn how to manipulate syntactic structures to express equivalent meanings, all within the same time frame.

The implications for language training of Bowerman's interpretations of how children acquire causative verbs is nothing less than profound. The available language-training programs are designed to teach sentence construction as an isolated area of linguistic learning. "John made the door open" and "John opened the door" would be taught in separate and probably unrelated training steps, since different grammatical structures are used, even though the meanings are equivalent; the related pairs "John pulled on the door and that made it come open" and "John pulled the door open" would also most certainly be widely separated in training sequences. Yet the artificiality of such separateness is striking when compared with the preceding account of how children learn to express notions of causation.

How can such meaning equivalences be incorporated into training? Perhaps it would be feasible to start with the underlying meaning and then systematically train alternative ways of expressing it. Certain words appear to have considerable semantic productive potential; that is, they can be reframed in different linguistic constructions to represent the same underlying meanings. The example for which there is the most information is that of causative verbs. One could start with a small set of verbs capable of expressing causative relationships, such as "open," "break," and "warm." The meaning of the words could be taught by the demonstration of appropriate actions combined with the modeling of semantically equivalent but syntactically different structures. When teaching the child to produce the particular word meanings, the interventionist could encourage the production of different syntactic structures for equivalent meanings. Of course, the complexity of syntactic structuring would depend upon the skills of the particular child.

Another factor is when to consider a particular word meaning as being "taught." If we assume that the child will continue to work out regularities underlying equivalent but different means of expressing the same notions, we would need to be prepared to return to particular content that was trained at an earlier time to a certain level, reintroduce the content in the context of more sophisticated ways of saying the same thing, and go on to train the child to a higher level of competence. Such considerations will certainly increase the complexity of language-training programs. On the other hand, the awareness that the child's analysis of certain word meanings (most probably those involving relational components, such as verbs) is connected to syntactic development may be a very important consideration in improving the effectiveness of language training.

Later lexical growth involves more than working out how words relate to syntactic structures. It also involves working out additional complexities in what words can mean. For example, children have to learn that the same words can have different meanings (polysemy). (We can *run*; we *run* errands; we can *run* a campaign; water *runs*; noses *run*; nylon stockings *run*; colors *run* from red to violet, and we could *run* on and on with this example.) Children also have to learn that words sometimes do not mean what they seem to mean. Sometimes phrases acquire meanings that are independent of the meanings of their component words (idioms). "Kick the bucket," "Put one's foot in one's mouth," and "Mind your p's and q's" have meanings unlike their literal interpretation. Idioms are sometimes traceable to metaphors that have lost their original connections, such as having "a frog in your throat." Metaphors involve the placement of a word in an improbable context, where the word suggests one reference, the context another (Brown, 1958, p. 142), in order to suggest a common element. A well known example is "a mighty fortress is our God." "Don't be a pig" might be an example more familiar to children. Such mismatches of context and reference serve as the basis for much of the humor evident in riddles and puns, such as "What is the best way to make pants last? Make the coat first."

Little is known about how normal children acquire all the nuances and complexities involved in situations requiring knowledge of more than one meaning for a word, although a number of investigators have recently turned their attention to the topic (see Gardner et al., 1978, for a review of the literature). It is apparent that some knowledge of multiple word meanings is acquired relatively early. Around the ages of 7 and 8 children demonstrate emerging comprehension of multiple word meanings. In lab studies they are able to sort out the different senses of such adjectives as "sweet," e.g., "the sweet one" to refer to a piece of candy or a person, and are able to match appropriate pictures to verbal metaphors.

These findings correspond well with the observation by many elementary school teachers that it is around second or third grade when children first begin to be fascinated by riddles and simple jokes. My 7-year-old daughter certainly has confirmed this impression, with her recently acquired enthusiasm for telling jokes. The papers she brings home from school demonstrate that knowledge of multiple word meanings is required for correct responses on second-grade reading assignments.

The mastery of nonliteral meanings is generally regarded as a progression of competence from these beginnings in the early elementary years to a later-appearing and more sophisticated adult level of knowledge. Preschoolers' knowledge has been regarded as negligible. However, recent studies suggest that preschoolers may comprehend something of multiple meanings if the assessment task is appropriate (Gardner et al., 1978, p. 10). Furthermore, some investigators suggest that the creative applications of word meanings evident in young children's utterances can be regarded as metaphoric in nature (e.g., Gardner et al., 1978). As with other areas of linguistic skill, it appears that normal children's acquisition of nonliteral meanings is more complex than traditionally assumed.

Virtually nothing is reported in the literature about how children with difficulties acquiring language manage these more advanced applications of word knowledge. Those of us who have worked with such children can recall numerous examples of incomplete communication because the child did not understand a nonliteral use of a word meaning. Language-disordered children routinely miss the humor in riddles and puns, and have little facility for creative slang terms (but their aptitude for expletives is well known). Such difficulties with word meanings could lead to social embarrassment or ostracism for the language-disordered child (even if he had mastered the necessary grammatical skills) among children as young as 6 or 7 years of age.

While the language-training literature has overlooked the development of more advanced word meanings, there is evidence suggesting that metaphorical understandings can be trained in normal children. For example, Kogan (1979) reports that the provision of verbal labels facilitated elementary children's ability to match pictures according to metaphorical relationships. Such a technique is readily adaptable to a clinical setting.

Another consideration related to the training of metaphors is the choice of lexical items. The suggestion of Lahey and Bloom (1977, p. 342) to select words that have broad application to many objects and events is an appropriate first step in selecting a lexicon. Beyond the earliest stages, the interventionist could choose words to train that have multiple meanings or have frequent metaphorical extensions. Body parts are examples of words that are often used to suggest metaphorical equivalences, for example, "the foot of the mountain," an employee serving as "the boss's right arm," the "eyes and ears of the world," "he's a real heel," a piece of pipe referred to as "an elbow," the "heart of the matter" and so on.

Obviously, the training needs to be matched to the child's ability to figure out the nonlinguistic and linguistic equivalences involved. Granted that not all children with language disorders may be capable of such linguistic learning (such as the severely mentally retarded), it seems to this writer that many of the children enrolled in training could benefit greatly from explicit training of multiple word meanings, metaphors, idioms, slang, riddles, and puns. For at least some of the children, the ability to handle the manipulation of word meanings may make the difference between communicating like a normal child or appearing to be vaguely lacking in communicative competence.

How to Teach Word Meanings?

Theoretical Issue: What Is the Role of Reference in How Children Use Words?   Questions that follow from this one include: what is meant by reference? Do young normal children use words to refer to objects, events, or experiences, or do they intend other functions for what may appear to be labels for referents?

The significance of this issue for the training of word meanings bears on the question of how to teach word meanings—should reference be taught first and other communicative functions later, or should the word be taught first in the context of particular communicative functions? What referents should be selected to teach particular word meanings?

Let's begin with a consideration of what is meant by "reference." It is a term that has been used frequently throughout this book, pops up repeatedly in the literature about how children acquire word meanings, and yet demonstrates different shades of meaning in different situations. There appear to be two different interpretations of reference: a more general one, encompassing a variety of real world information, and a more limited interpretation, restricted to the naming of objects or visual events. The more general interpretation is evident in definitions offered by Clark and Clark (1977), "The reference of a word, its extension, is the set of things the word applies to in any real or imaginary world—the objects, states, events, or processes in that world" (p. 410), and Brown (1958),

". . . not all referents are objects with size, shape, and weight. Actions like dropping and kissing are referents and so are such qualities as large and small or red and green" (p. 8); "Reference may be said to exist wherever occurrences of a name are coordinate with occurrences of some other kind" (p. 9). The accounts of children's acquisition of word meanings put forth by Bowerman (e.g., 1976, 1978a) and Schlesinger (e.g., 1977a, 1977b, in preparation) are consistent with such a broad definition of "reference."

The more limited sense of reference is evident in Gentner's (1978, pp. 989–990) distinction between nouns and verbs. She describes simple nouns as being "referential," that is, with the function of pointing to an object, whereas verbs are "relational," that is, expressing abstract concepts in which no particular action is connected with a particular verb. For example, the meaning of "give" is not tied to any one particular action. Instead, verbs can represent relationships among noun arguments. In the case of "give" these relationships involve notions like possession, do, and cause.

The sense in which the term "reference" has been used throughout this book is that of the more general meaning, encompassing objects, states, attributes, events, and processes evident in the real world. That sense is the intended meaning in the ensuing discussion. However, Gentner's (1978) point is well taken. Not all verbs refer to actions in the world in the same sense that "jump" does. Indeed, upon close inspection the correct use of many word meanings may require more abstract processing than would be supposed at first glance. It is important to keep this in mind when thinking about the meanings of words that children must learn.

Are children's first word meanings based upon reference? Many of the words that children first understand and use demonstrate a referential relationship to real world information. For example, in her study of what words children first comprehend, Huttenlocher (1974) reports:

> The earliest words to which the children responded systematically designated individual objects, classes of objects, and perceptible acts. All of these words involved referents that could easily be pointed out by an adult speaker (p. 355).

The words that children first produce are also predominately referential in nature. Nelson (1973, p. 20) found that 71% of the first 50 words of her 18 subjects fell into the category of "nominals" (a category defined as "words used to refer to the 'thing world' " (p. 16)). Such findings tend to substantiate the commonly held assumption that a child's first word learning consists of naming or labeling objects or actions in his world. However, the reference-making function does not account for all of children's earliest mastery of word meanings. Bowerman (1976, p. 114) points out that children early on learn words such as "hi," "good-night," and "goody" that do not "represent" or "stand for" some object, event, or property. Nelson (1973) also reported the use of words that were non-referential in nature (albeit in small percentages of the first 50 words), such as "personal-social" words (e.g., "thank you," "please") and "function" words (e.g., "what," "for").

Not only do children have words that are not literally referential, there have been a number of investigators who have noted that children may not always intend for such ostensibly referential words as object names to serve a referential function.[4] This observation has come out of attempts to account for how children first use their words, at the stage of single words or early two-word combinations. Labeling or naming is only one of many speech functions that single words may serve for the child. Children may use object words to request, reject, command, comment upon nonexistence, hypothesis-test for appropriateness, or serve as an information-gathering strategy (e.g., Bates, 1976; Greenfield and Smith, 1976; Braunwald, 1978; Nelson, 1978).

What implications do these observations about reference have for the training of word meanings to children unable to master them on their own? In recently developed language-training programs (Bricker and Bricker, 1974; Miller and Yoder, 1974; Stremel and Waryas, 1974; Bloom and Lahey, 1978) the reference-making function of words has been overlooked. Instead the word's relational meaning in combination with other words, the semantic relational meaning, has been emphasized. As discussed earlier (pp. 118–121), the referential meaning of a word is given only secondary consideration, if at all. Holland's (1975, p. 516) point that the clinician's job is more than just teaching the referential function of words carries the connotation that reference is somehow restricted to limited usefulness for the child. Leonard (1978, pp. 74, 85) has recently suggested that words "first be taught to emphasize their performative function (e.g., *Mommy* taught as a form to request the assistance of the mother) rather than their referential function (e.g., *Mommy* taught while pointing to the mother)" (p. 85).

But let's take a more careful look at these recent perspectives on the training of referential word meanings. Two factors may be implicated in

---

[4]Nelson (1973, p. 15) took this possibility into account in her system of classifying children's first 50 words. How the child used a word determined its classification, e.g., "door" could be used to designate a door (nominal word) or to ask to have the door opened to go outside (action word).

the relative lack of importance attributed to the training of referential word meanings: first, what is regarded as training activities for referential word meanings may involve a very limited notion of reference; second, the significance of the referential meanings for pragmatic functions or semantic relations may be underestimated.

The traditional procedure for teaching children words that refer to real world information is to present the child with a visual stimulus (real objects or pictured objects), say the word while pointing or otherwise designating the correct referent, and then asking the child to do so. The prototypic language form in such teaching is a noun; occasionally verbs are taught within such a format (with the clinician modeling the action or showing a picture allegedly depicting the action in question), along with attribute words and some relational words (most likely the spatial prepositions "in," "on," and "under"). At least one language-training program (Guess, Sailor and Baer, 1974, pp. 547–550) has formalized this procedure into a structured training step. The referential relationships that are taught are limited to things and actions at the first step; colors, size attributes ("big"/"little"), and spatial prepositions ("on"/"under") are added later (pp. 552–555).

Such concrete training procedures seem to reflect a limited notion of reference, i.e., constrained to referents that can be depicted visually. This traditional clinical interpretation of reference seems to be the target of Holland's (1975) comment:

> Thus it is not enough to teach the child to say or to recognize "go" in relationship merely to naming the behavior of running or of so labeling a picture of a fast moving vehicle that will accomplish his learning only the referential function. "Go" must be taught also as an action of his own body, as the act of "making go" a small car across a table, as well as the act of leaving a room, and the more abstract notion of people leaving in contrast with people arriving, and so on (p. 516).

If reference is defined only as a matter of "establishing object-word correspondence" (Holland, 1975, p. 516), I would agree with Holland's admonition. However, a different notion of reference leads to a different interpretation of the clinical value of teaching reference. When reference is defined in broader terms, Holland's other examples for the meaning of "go" can be interpreted as being part of the referential function. Certainly the referential meaning of "go" excludes neither actions of one's own body, nor leaving the room. People leaving in contrast with people arriving still involves reference to movement, along with additional factors of directionality, and, possibly, intent. In short, reference is more than the traditional clinical training procedures would indicate. Instead, reference involves the use of a word to represent or stand for a set of things in the real world, where such things can be objects, states, events, processes, attributes, feelings, relationships between objects, and so on. Reference certainly is not limited to that information that can be depicted visually or auditorially.

Such words as "me," "happy," "off," and "want" represent non-linguistic information that is not susceptible to visual representation, yet these are referential words that appear in children's first lexicons. Not only does the traditional clinical interpretation of reference represent a limited notion of reference, it also does not correspond to the apparent subtleties of reference of which young normal children are capable early on in their acquisition of word meanings.

Another aspect of reference with implications for the clinical situation is its role in relation to other communicative meanings, i.e., pragmatic functions. Is it possible to train words as indicators of pragmatic intentions, such as request, independent of and prior to their referential meaning? Would it be advantageous to first train "Mommy" as a form to request mother's assistance and later as a word to refer to the mother (Leonard, 1978a, p. 85)? Several questions arise. If the child does not know who "Mommy" is, how can he use "Mommy" as a form to request mother's assistance (unless she's the only available source of assistance in the environment)? Why use the word "Mommy" as a form to request assistance? Presumably any appropriately stressed vocalization would suffice if the referential meaning were not important, even nonsense syllables. What difference would it make if the child understood the referential meaning for "Mommy" in comprehension tasks but did not use the word in production as either a label or request?

It seems that it would be possible to incorporate both aspects of meaning into the training situation (especially if the child demonstrates comprehension of the word). Such a combined approach certainly would have advantages over trying to train the pragmatic function without the referential meaning. Obviously, the child needs to know who his mother is in order to elicit her attention or enlist her help. It seems reasonable to teach him the appropriate word to refer to her while at the same time demonstrating that the word can be used to achieve some control over her actions. Presumably, the child would already demonstrate the pragmatic functions of requesting in his gestural communication. It would be a matter of attaching a linguistic form to his request, designating who he wants to attend to him. If it is a matter of learning a linguistic form as a means of eliciting attention or assistance (irrespective of who provides it), it would be more referentially accurate to teach the child to say "help."

The question of what referents should be selected to teach particular word meanings has already been touched upon in the earlier discussion of prototypes (see pp. 127–131). Some additional observations are offered here in regard to two different aspects of how to choose referents: 1) when the particular word meaning has a referent that can be depicted, and 2) when the information that a given word represents does not lend itself to nonlinguistic illustrations. This differentiation is inherent in Lahey and Bloom's (1977, p. 342) suggestion to choose as first words to be learned those that involve concepts that are easily demonstrated, with concepts that are more difficult to illustrate deferred until later in training. It is interesting to note that while this suggestion generally coincides with the kinds of word meanings that normal children first acquire, it also has been observed that some of the first words used by normal children involve referential meanings that are more difficult to depict, such as "me" and "want."

Some guidelines are possible for how to structure the clinical situation in order to teach the referential meanings of words. Particular stimuli can be selected as referents on the basis of their prototypicality for the category in question. Bowerman (1976, p. 167; 1978b, p. 169–170) has proposed additional considerations for the selection of referents and how to go about contriving referent situations. The first is in regard to object words. The suggestion is to choose referent objects that can act spontaneously or be acted upon by the child, and that also look quite similar. Another suggestion with implications for how to structure referent contexts deals with words for directional motion ("up," "down,"), bodily activities ("night night," "sit," "walk"), and words like "more" and "all gone." These words all share a common characteristic—their first appearance in the comments of normal children are in relatively limited circumstances. Words for directional motion and bodily activities are first used to refer to activities of the child's own body, then with the bodies of other people and later with actions involving inanimate objects. "More" and "all gone" often appear first to request additional food or drink, and only later get extended to other exemplars. Bowerman (1976, p. 167) suggests that a similar sequence be followed when the clinician presents referents for these particular words.

But what about those early-appearing words without easily depicted referent objects or situations, such as "want," or many of the more advanced word meanings that present similar illustrative problems? The child must have at least some notion of the bundle of real world information that is being represented before he can learn the word that labels it. The child also needs to learn those word meanings that are not easily depicted. There does come a time, we hope, when words can be used to teach the meanings of other words. But before this time, and probably for some word meanings after that level of symbolic competence has been attained, it will be necessary to come up with some means of representing the nonlinguistic information involved. To suggest that the answer to this dilemma lies in the clinical creativity and intuitive knowledge of word meanings possessed by the language interventionist borders on a cop-out. Yet that is the best source available.

No formal language-training program will ever be able to come up with explicit and standardized procedures for how to train all of the various possible word meanings. And the word meanings that will surely be saved for last are those that are difficult to depict. But that does not mean that words such as "me" and "want" and "hope" are impossible to teach. Instead it means that each interventionist will have to devise unique teaching procedures based upon what she or he knows about the particular child plus the interventionist's ideas of what aspects of the meanings of "want," for example, that she or he wishes to teach. It may involve devising contexts built around the child's desire for a favorite object, entity, or activity. It could involve only the child and the trainer, or the use of other children and the trainer in a modeled situation, or the use of puppets to depict a context. It may involve an intensive period of training in a short time interval, or occasional instances of teaching interspersed with other content over a long time interval. It most surely will require a wide variety of contexts, activities, and training procedures, especially for the more difficult words.

An example comes to mind. I once had the opportunity to observe a very creative clinician teach the meaning of sexual reproduction (in reference to chickens) to a 10-year-old boy with a severe hearing loss from birth, limited linguistic abilities, but considerable intellectual competence. The youngster had brought up the topic during a therapy session, asking the clinician for information. The clinician proceeded to train the meaning of the term "sexual reproduction." The training encompassed several different 30-minute sessions. Various means of illustrating the nonlinguistic information were used, involving pictures, gestures, actions, other words, and toy objects. It certainly presented the opportunity for creative use of therapy contexts and materials, and the clinician made full use of novel and yet appropriate procedures. Most important of all, the clinician was not inhibited by any concern for the "right way" to teach the content. The youngster, who happened to live on a farm, learned what the term "sexual reproduction" meant—an understanding that later served him well both in his home environment and in his academic coursework (biology).

To summarize, the teaching of the referential meanings of words certainly has great intrinsic value. However, the specifics of how to go about teaching reference are largely undefined when one gets beyond simple pairings of object words with real world objects or pictures of objects.

Theoretical Issue: What Is the Relationship Between Lexical Meaning and Semantic Relations? The clinical question that arises from this issue is: How should the referential meaning of words be trained—embedded in their relational meanings (multi-word utterances) or as a separate training step prior to introducing word combinations?

The distinction between lexical meaning and the semantic roles that words can play can be quite subtle, especially when used to describe the earliest stages of linguistic competence. The literature discussing these notions is complicated further by differing senses for the same terms. It is appropriate to preface the discussion of the relationship between these two kinds of semantic knowledge with a consideration of some theoretical distinctions and corresponding terms.

The basic distinction is that between the meanings of particular words (linguistic forms) and the different meanings evident in combinations of words. For example "Mary admires Sue" does not mean the same as "Sue admires Mary." The meanings of the words stay the same, but the meaning relating the words, when combined, is different for the two statements. The meaning between the words is often referred to as "relational" or "combinatorial" meaning. These combinatorial meanings[5] have been described in terms of the semantic roles played by the linguistic components, variously referred to as semantic roles, semantic relations, semantic functions, or content categories. Describing linguistic components in terms of semantic roles makes it possible to relate grammatical structure closely to meaning (Fillmore, 1968). It has been widely accepted as an appropriate means of describing the rules of word combination evident in children's first multi-word utterances (e.g., Bloom, 1970; Schlesinger, 1971; Bowerman, 1973; Brown, 1973). Various semantic roles have been proposed, such as "agent," "instrument," "possessive," and others, with some variation in the classification systems proposed by different investigators. These grammatical concepts[6] involve two kinds of abstract categorization—cognitive and linguistic. The cognitive categorization entails the knowledge of "agentness" or "possessiveness," of real world persons or objects, that is, what actions, events, or relationships constitute the concept of "agent" or "possession." Schlesinger (1977b, p. 156) provides a detailed example of what

---

[5]More precisely, the relations of noun phrases to verbs (Fillmore, 1968).

[6]The use of the term "grammatical concept" is not intended to suggest a merging of grammatical relations (subject, verb, object, and so on) and semantic relations. As Brown (1973, pp. 121–123) points out, the two notions are not the same. "Grammatical concept" is used here to refer to relationships of word order in a general sense.

might be involved in the child's learning of the boundaries of the agent concept: What is an agent—Mommy handing the bottle to the child, Mommy holding the bottle, and/or the bottle containing the milk? The linguistic categorization is evident in the set of possible linguistic components that can serve to represent a particular semantic function. At the level of words (as opposed to phrases or clauses), one group could serve as agents, another group as actions, and so on. Some words are more restricted in their possible semantic roles than are others; for example, "Mommy" could serve as agent, dative (the animate being affected by the state or action of the verb), possessor, or experiencer, whereas words like "key" and "more" are more likely to be limited, the former to the instrumental category, the latter to express recurrence. In addition, the word meanings themselves are also categorical in nature; that is, words represent distinguishably different bits of information that are regarded as equivalent for the purposes of word meanings. Therefore, when considering word meanings and semantic relations, two levels of categorization are involved with one nested inside the other; the word meanings are nested within grammatical concepts, the nesting fluid enough to allow movement of some words across grammatical categories. And, of course, there is an additional level of abstraction that comes into play, that of rules for combining words which build upon the categories of semantic relations. These rules of word combination are beyond the scope of the discussion here.

Sometimes words are dichotomized as "substantive" (referring to particular objects or to categories of objects) versus "relational" (referring to a relationship between objects, including such parts of speech as verbs, adjectives, and prepositions) (Bloom, 1973; Lahey and Bloom, 1977; Bloom and Lahey, 1978). A similar distinction has been extended to the more abstract groupings of the semantic roles that words can play. For example, Miller and Yoder (1974, pp. 514–516) differentiate between "relational functions" and "substantive functions." "Relational functions" are regarded as not referent-specific and consist of categories such as "recurrence," "nonexistence," and "existence;" "substantive functions" involve closer ties to referents and are expressed in categories such as "agent," "object," "actions," and "possession."

Miller and Yoder's differentiation is also closely related to Brown's (1973, pp. 170–172) distinction between "operations of reference" and semantic functions or relations. "Nomination," "recurrence," and "nonexistence" were the three operations of reference that were frequent in children's Stage I utterances. Brown regarded these operations of reference as qualitatively different, in the sense of less abstract, than categories of semantic relations such as "agent," "action," "possession" and so on. One of the differences is that each operation tends to be linked with just a few words: for nomination, "this," "that," "see," "there," "here"; for recurrence, "more," "another"; for nonexistence, "all gone," "no more," "no." Another difference is that the operations of reference demonstrate a wide range of applicability: "Any thing, person, quality, or process can be named, can recur, and can disappear. In this respect words like that, more, and all gone are quite different from such narrow-range words as green, sit, swim, slow, and the like" (Brown, 1973, p. 170).

Another distinction that is drawn is that between the child's grammatical competence at the single-word level and later stages of word combinations. The notion of semantic relations usually describes how word combinations express meanings. Whether or not single-word utterances express such combinatorial meanings is a matter of current controversy. Some authors use different terms to describe the semantic intent of single-word utterances as compared to word combinations. For example, Miller and Yoder (1974, pp. 514–515) use the term "functions" for single words and "relations" for multi-word combinations.

The variability in terminology evident in different writings is no trivial matter. For example, the words "relations" and "relational" bear careful watching. The ideas expressed in "semantic relations," "relational meanings," "substantive" versus "relational," and "relational functions" versus "substantive functions" all involve subtle but important distinctions. Throughout the following discussion, "relational meaning" is used to refer to the meanings evident in word combinations, "semantic relations" to refer to categories of linguistic components defined by semantic role or intent, and "semantic functions" to refer to the categories of semantic intent evident in single-word utterances.

With the warning about terminology out of the way, let's return to the question of the nature of the relationship between lexical meaning and semantic relations. Two aspects of meaning are involved in the semantic relations evident in the combinations of words: the meanings of the lexical items themselves, plus the additional meanings represented in their combination. To use a famous example, "Mommy sock" (Bloom, 1970, pp. 5–14) can represent two different relational meanings: possessor-object (Mommy's sock) or agent-object (Mommy puts on the sock). However, both of these relational interpretations depend upon the correct referential meaning for each of the lexical items. The child must know who Mommy is and also what a sock is in order to know that Mommy can own a sock or that Mommy can put on a sock. Notice that some knowledge of the real world is necessary for correct linguistic interpretation, e.g., that Mommy can own a sock, whereas the sock cannot own Mommy. Miller (1978) has argued that such nonlinguistic practical knowledge is packaged into lexical meaning.[7] In this sense, the lexical meaning constrains the combinatorial possibilities. For example, "girl sing" is a workable combination, but "chair sing" is not, because in the real world girls can sing but chairs cannot. In order to come up with word combinations that make sense, the child must understand the lexical referential meaning and some additional nonlinguistic knowledge about events in the real world.

In the language acquisition literature, word meanings and relational meanings have been regarded as separate areas of study; that is, studies have investigated either acquisition of word meaning or acquisition of relational meanings (usually in the contexts of semantic roles and rules for word combination), but seldom are they considered as a unified area of learning. However, Bowerman (1976, pp. 106–107) has pointed out that the distinction between lexical meaning and relational meanings can become blurred, especially for some categories of semantic relations. She notes that the relational meanings are sometimes involved in both kinds of knowledge. For example, the words "my," "mine," and "in" all encode the relational notion as part of the lexical meaning. Other examples could include "more" and "no." Bowerman (1976) accentuated the relatedness of the semantic developments affecting the acquisition of word meanings and of the rules for word combinations.

The nature of the relationship between the two kinds of semantic knowledge, lexical and relational, has immediate implications for how to go about training such linguistic knowledge. Two training strategies are possible:

1. Train lexical meanings in an explicit training step preceding the training of word combinations
2. Embed the training of individual lexical items in the training of word combinations

The first strategy would be consistent with the notion that the meanings of individual lexical items and semantic relations are different enough to warrant separate training, whereas the second would be in line with an emphasis upon the close relationship between lexical and relational semantic knowledge. The suggestions of Holland (1975) and Lahey and Bloom (1977) exemplify the second strategy, i.e., choose lexical items that will readily plug into various word combinations and train them within the context of those word combinations.

---

[7]There are some difficulties with this interpretation of lexical meaning. See discussion on p. 149.

The former strategy could be regarded as the more conservative one, where the meanings of individual lexical items are regarded as prerequisite, simpler components of the more complex linguistic task of combinatorial meanings. The latter strategy could be characterized as more concerned with expediency, assuming that a separate training step (and the time involved) is not necessary, that by teaching the more complex kind of semantic meaning (relational meanings), the simpler kind of meaning (lexical meaning) is also learned in the process.

Is a separate training step for lexical meaning necessary, or is this a situation where a language trainer can "get something for nothing"? Is one general training principle feasible, or are different training strategies more or less appropriate for different contexts? How can we go about sorting out the relationship between lexical and combinatorial meanings in training circumstances? One means of doing so is to carefully consider the training tasks and what the child must learn in order to master them. Since the more expedient approach, that of training both kinds of semantic knowledge, is currently being advocated, let's take a detailed look at what this training strategy requires of the child.

For the purpose of illustration, consider the training of the meanings involved in the semantic relations of action-object, where the agent is understood to be the child, that is, (child)-action-object. Since semantic relations are categories of linguistic forms, the first step is to select the linguistic forms, in this case, words, to be trained. Within the strategy of training both meanings simultaneously, it would not be necessary to choose lexical forms that the child already knows. We will assume that he does not know the forms we choose. Let's start with "push car." The language interventionist's job becomes one of providing appropriate contexts and corresponding linguistic labels. Presumably this would involve a toy car and the action of pushing. The adult could push the car, probably with her or his hands, while the child observes and the adult says, "push car." Then the adult could hand the car to the child and say, "push car." The goal behavior would be for the child to choose a car from among several toys and push it when the adult says, "push car," or for the child to say, "push car" when the adult demonstrates the appropriate activity and asks, "What am I doing?" What does the child know at this point? Does he have the meaning for "car" or "push" or "push car"? It is impossible to conclude if he does, since less complete kinds of knowledge could also account for correct performance under these conditions. For example, he could regard "push car" as a single lexical unit designating the nature of the game, along the lines of "do this with this object"; or he could regard "push car" as the object name, in the sense of "trolley car"; or he could regard "push car" as the name of the action, in the sense of "pushcar-ing." Further contrasts are necessary before we could conclude that he had mastered either the individual lexical items or the semantic relations.

The next step would be introducing a contrasting lexical form for either the action or object, or both. For illustrative simplicity, let's contrast only one, that of the object. The procedures would involve pushing with a variety of toy objects, presumably all capable of being pushed (teaching "push house," for example, seems to run contrary to information packed into the lexical items). Criterion for this step would be correct performance with "push car," "push bus," "push chair," "push box," and whatever other objects were used. Now what does the child need to know in order to perform correctly? He would have had to separate the two words; if "push" is to apply to various objects, he cannot manage with an unanalyzed "pushcar" strategy. Does he know the meaning of "push"? Presumably he could have tied the word "push" to the action that was demonstrated with each of the objects, but he also could still be operating with a "this is what you do with the objects in this game" strategy, in which case he would only have to have worked out the correspondence between the object name and the toy objects used. Does he know "car," "chair," etc.? Presumably he would know the referential relationship between "car" and the toy object(s) used. If only one toy car were used, the meaning of "car" may be limited to that one particular toy. If more than one car were used, with variations in size, color, and other noncriterial dimensions, the child could have learned that "car" refers to a category of toy objects. Since it is unlikely that a real car would be used in the context of "push car" (with a human as an agent, at least), one could not be sure that the child knew that "car" referred to real automobiles without checking if that generalization had occurred. Similar constraints would apply for the meanings of "chair" and other possible object names.

The next logical step would be to introduce the second contrast, in this case that of the action words. This would involve different actions with different objects, across all combinations, e.g., "push car," "push chair," "hit car," "hit chair," and so on. Now the child would have to fully differentiate the action words from the object words. What does he know about the lexical items now? His knowledge of the meanings for the action words would be limited by the same constraints as applied to the object words, i.e., the number of referents provided and the attributes of those referents. If "push" were only demonstrated with the hands doing the pushing, this may be part of the meaning ascribed to "push," or if "push" were only used with toy objects, the nature of the objects that can be pushed may be part of the child's perception of the meaning of that lexical item. Additional probes would be necessary to determine how far the child could extend the meaning of "push," i.e., to what kinds of actions, for what kinds of objects.

Assuming, for the moment, that this kind of training procedure accomplishes the training of semantic relations, can we conclude that the training of lexical items occurs simultaneously? The answer depends upon several factors: the criterion for acquisition of word meaning, the nature of the word meanings and semantic relations being trained, and the linguistic and cognitive abilities of the child. If word meanings are regarded only as a matter of matching a word to a particular object-referent, then it seems quite feasible for such "meanings" to be learned within the training conditions described. However, if word meanings are regarded as categorical in nature, mastery of a particular word meaning would entail the correct use of the word in a set of referential circumstances that represented the full meaning of the word. For example, "car" would not be considered as fully learned until the child knew that it referred to real cars as well as toy cars, that cars are distinguished from buses and trucks, that cars are used to transport people, and so on. "Push" would not be regarded as mastered until the child knew that it involved a pressing against an object so as to move it, that different entities can push (e.g., people, trucks, bulldozers), that "push" is distinguished from "hit," and so on. If the full meanings of lexical items are to be taught in the context of semantic relations (word combinations), it would require careful selection of stimulus objects and events to represent the full range of the word's meaning and/or systematic probing for generalization to untrained referent objects or situations or events.

An alternative would be to approach the training of lexical meanings somewhat differently. It could be argued that it would be possible to teach restricted word meanings within the initial teaching of semantic relations, where the goal of training focused on rules for combining words. After the child learned "push car," "hit truck," etc., in the appropriate order of action-object, then the clinician could go back and expand the meanings of the lexical items to more closely correspond to the full meaning of the word. Either strategy seems to have merit, depending upon the immediate goals of training. The important point to keep in mind is that what the child actually knows about the words as a function of the training needs to be considered when training word meanings embedded in word combinations, a point that is not stressed in the available language-training suggestions (e.g., Miller and Yoder, 1974; Holland, 1975; Lahey and Bloom, 1977; Bloom and Lahey, 1978).

Another factor to be considered is the nature of the word meanings and semantic functions or relations being taught. As pointed out earlier, sometimes the two kinds of semantic knowledge are closely related, whereas in other circumstances the two are more distinct. In the case of a close relationship, e.g., "more" to express recurrence, or "my" or "mine" to express possession, or "in" to express location, it seems to be most appropriate to teach the lexical meaning in the context of word combinations. Indeed, the meanings of the words "more," "my," and "in" are virtually impossible to depict to a child without being related to appropriate objects or entities. On the other hand, many words have meanings that are relatively independent of their possible combinatorial meanings, such as object categories or the names of persons. Whether or not these word meanings can be acquired simultaneously with combinatorial meanings seems to depend upon such additional factors as the nature of the referents, the abstractness of the word meanings, and the frequency of the words in the child's environment. It is feasible to predict that words that have referents that are easy to depict or denote, that are more literal than abstract in meaning, and that are frequently used by speakers in the child's environment are words that will be relatively easy for a child to learn. Such words may well be mastered simultaneously with combinatorial meanings. However, insofar as particular words refer to information that is difficult to depict (e.g., words such as "like," "happy," "see," "hurt," "hungry"), are more abstract in meanings (e.g., "give," "take," "bring," "clothing," "food"), and/or are less frequently heard by the child, these words may require training at the level of lexical meaning before introducing combinatorial meanings. This distinction of words easy to teach and words difficult to teach roughly corresponds to words young normal children learn first versus those words acquired somewhat later in development. As a general rule, then, perhaps at the very earliest stages of language training, the simple word meanings being taught at that level could be embedded in combinatorial meanings (assuming that training is based upon the developmental model). The important point to confirm is that a particular word meaning is, in fact, simple in nature for the individual child being trained. (See the earlier discussion pp. 123–127 of the value and limits of the normative literature for selecting what words to train.)

A third factor is that of the child being trained, more specifically, the conceptual and linguistic knowledge and skills that he brings to the training tasks. Word meanings that correspond to his preexisting cognitive organization and communicative intents may well be taught within the context of combinatorial meanings, since they presumably would be relatively easy to master. However, it is not always possible to ascertain underlying cognitive or pragmatic readiness, or there may be occasions when word meanings are taught even though prior cognitive or pragmatic knowledge is known to be lacking. At these times, specific training for lexical meanings may well be appropriate. Furthermore, children vary in their abilities to generalize cognitive and linguistic information. Some groups of language-disordered children, in particular, those who are mentally retarded, may have considerable difficulty with the generalization required for mastering word meanings, for example, learning the category of real world objects that are referred to as "car." It may be necessary to provide separate training steps for lexical meanings prior to, or in conjunction with, training of combinatorial meanings for children with such limited cognitive and linguistic skills.

To return to the initial question, is it feasible to train the referential meanings of words embedded in relational meanings? One can conclude that it is probable, under some circumstances, that word meanings can be taught simultaneously with relational meanings. If one wishes to "get something for nothing" that is certainly the more viable approach—it is less likely that the training of word meanings alone (in most cases) will result in spontaneous acquisition of combinatorial meanings. However, there are legitimate cautions for the clinician to keep in mind when pursuing the strategy of expediency: just how much of a word's meaning is being learned under the training circumstances, how amenable the particular word meanings and semantic functions or relations are to simultaneous training, and the cognitive and linguistic abilities of the child to differentiate and generalize cognitive and linguistic information. There will be some training circumstances that call for a separate training step for teaching individual lexical meanings, prior to, or in conjunction with, the training of combinatorial meanings.

Before leaving the issue of the training of word meanings and semantic relations, let's briefly consider the training of semantic relations from the perspective of the relationship between the two kinds of semantic knowledge. Recall that semantic relations are distinguished from word meanings in that the semantic classifications of agent, object, and so on, consist of a category of different linguistic forms that can serve to represent that particular semantic intent. However, this theoretical distinction seems to be blurred in the language-training literature. For example, Miller and Yoder (1974) report the training of the semantic concept of recurrence using the word "more" (p. 521), and the semantic function of action using the word "eat" (p. 523). If a semantic relation or function category is represented by only one word, how does one know that the child has any semantic knowledge more abstract than the meaning packaged in the lexical item? Instead of a notion of "recurrence" that can be expressed by different words, such as "more" or "another" or "again," the child may only know the more limited semantic knowledge represented in the meaning of "more."

While this theoretical distinction does not affect the content or procedures for training, i.e., the training of "more" certainly has intrinsic merit, it does affect the interpretation of what the child knows. Just as careful distinctions are drawn between word meanings, semantic relations, rules for word combinations, and grammatical relations in the theoretical literature, these distinctions can help us clarify precisely the goals of training, the content to be trained, criteria for completion of training, and the interpretation of what the child knows. The current state of the art of training semantic concepts is such that there is considerable blurring of the distinctions between various kinds of semantic knowledge and how this knowledge is utilized in the child's acquisition of rules for word combinations. The earlier example of "push car" was discussed in terms of the meanings of individual lexical items and relational meanings. Also wrapped up in that example is information about rules for combining words (usually the primary focus of therapy) and information about grammatical concepts such as "action" and "object" or "verb" and "noun." The training task is certainly facilitated by the simultaneous presentation of so much information. Much of the time children seem to be able to master several kinds of linguistic information simultaneously, on a subconscious level. However, it is when training breaks down, when the content is either not mastered at all or only mastered incompletely, that it becomes necessary to follow the lines of a careful delineation of the different kinds of linguistic knowledge involved in the training task, where such distinctions as lexical meanings, semantic relations, and rules for word combinations assume a very practical significance.

Theoretical Issue: How Do Nonlinguistic Categorical Equivalences Influence the Acquisition of Word Meanings?   The importance of categorical groups of real world information in the formulation of word meanings has served as a major premise throughout this book. The idea that the cognitive process of categorization is basic to learning a language has been accepted by students of child language for some time, beginning with Brown (1956), reemphasized by Lenneberg (1967), and more recently evident in the interpretations of the nature of the meaning expressed in children's first words. Words serve to represent sets of distinguishable but linguistically equivalent objects, events, relationships, and so on. Just how the nonlinguistic information gets connected with the meanings of words is unclear.

What relevance do categorical groups have for determining how to go about teaching word meanings? Several points of application are possible. How can nonlinguistic categories be tied to word meaning within the training setting? Should nonlinguistic categories be trained? How many referent exemplars of a linguistic category should be trained—how does the language interventionist determine when to stop?

The question of how to tie nonlinguistic categories to word meanings involves the various issues of measurement discussed in Chapter 2. Two characteristics of the categorization/word meaning relationship present difficulties for the training situation: Many of the bundles of equivalent information that become encoded in words are not readily observable, and only some of the nonlinguistic categorical equivalences eventually get tied to particular word meanings. The semantic domain of color words was selected for the study reported here because it appeared to be especially suitable for the measurement considerations; that is, it allowed for a relatively straightforward measurement of nonlinguistic categories within the format of a sorting task, and reasonable assurance that the information needed to perform on the sorting task was equivalent to the information represented in the word meanings.

However, the nature of most word meanings is probably such that a precise link with measurable nonlinguistic categorizational strategies is not likely. Yet there are at least two different means of getting at the relationship between underlying categories and word meanings that are available to interventionists. The first involves an alertness for those word meanings that have characteristics that may make it possible to devise a specific, measurable connection to nonlinguistic equivalences. It seems unlikely that color terms are the *only* word meanings where such a link can be demonstrated. For example, spatial adjectives appear to be a likely candidate.

A number of linguists and psychologists (e.g., Miller and Johnson-Laird, 1976) have observed that the features underlying spatial adjectives (and also other lexical domains, including spatial prepositions and verbs of motion) correspond to bundles of perceptual information. Carey (1978) provides a detailed discussion of the nature of the conceptual underpinnings of spatial adjectives and how that information is represented in the process of acquiring the meanings of the words. The spatial adjectives include: big, little; long, short; tall, short; wide, narrow; thick, thin; deep, shallow; and high, low. There is a well established order of difficulty for the set of pairs, with big/little acquired first and deep/shallow the last to be learned (see de Villiers and de Villiers, 1978, pp. 136–143 for a review of the literature describing order of acquisition). Two aspects of lexical meaning are encoded in spatial adjectives. The first is a core comparative structure requiring a dimension of comparison (height for "tall"), a standard of comparisons (what is usual for "tall"), and a direction from the standard (greater than or less than). This core comparative structure is also evident in other relative adjectives, such as fast/slow. The second aspect of lexical meaning for spatial adjectives is that of dimensional features that differentiate the pairs, such as height (tall/short) or width (wide/narrow) or length (long/short).

It is possible to construct an array of objects to visually represent the perceptual information encoded in the word meanings. Carey (1978) describes several such arrays that were used in a series of studies investigating what children knew about the word meanings. Such tasks are readily adaptable to the clinical purpose of determining what nonlinguistic equivalences children have worked out that could be used as a basis for training word meanings. If the child was unable to respond correctly when asked to "Show me the big one" or "Show me the tall one," the clinician could follow this with a check of nonlinguistic equivalences by asking the child to "Show me another one like this one" or demonstrating matching behaviors and encouraging the child to match various stimuli.

Carey's (1978) account of how spatial adjectives are acquired has further implications for the role of nonlinguistic equivalence information in the training of word meanings. She argues that children first map words onto the core comparative structure. Later they map dimensional information. That is, children first learn big/little and initially interpret the other spatial adjectives in those terms, respecting the polarity of the correct response (e.g., interpreting "wide" as "big," and "low" as "little"). In other words, the relationship between nonlinguistic concepts and the meanings of spatial adjectives involves a hierarchical ordering, such that the more general conceptual information (the comparative core) is mapped first into words that have a broad range of reference. As the conceptual information becomes more differentiated, with greater awareness of perceptual (dimensional) differences, new word meanings appear to map the new distinctions.

Another family of words demonstrates a similar pattern of acquisition. The verbs of possession (give, take, pay, trade, spend, buy, and sell) are comparable to spatial adjectives in that they form a set of words that are linked by common components of meaning and are acquired in order of complexity. When learning the words, children seem to interpret the more complex verbs as if they were the simpler verbs (Gentner, 1978), similar to the pattern of acquisition evident with spatial adjectives. However, the nonlinguistic information encoded in these verbs is quite abstract, involving such notions as transfer of possession, obligations, and mutual contracts (Gentner, 1978). Such abstract nonlinguistic knowledge does not readily lend itself to measurement independent of the word meanings. Obviously, this does not rule out teaching these word meanings to language-disordered children; it just means that the interventionist may not be able to specifically assess or explicitly demonstrate the nonlinguistic equivalences but will probably have to rely somewhat on verbal description to determine what the child knows and to help get the meaning across.

In the case of such a hierarchical relationship existing within a family of words, the order for training the words can parallel the mapping of more general conceptual information followed by the more specific, e.g., train "big" and "little" before "wide" and "thin," or "give" and "take" before "buy" and "sell." When dealing with words that are part of a related hierarchy, the assessment of nonlinguistic information (where possible) can provide the clinician with cues for when and how to train an entire set of words, not just one particular word meaning.

While some words, such as color terms and spatial adjectives, can be tied to perceptual information, most word meanings depend upon more abstract equivalences. What options are available to the clinician who is trying to teach word meanings that correspond to nonlinguistic information that does not lend itself to categorization tasks? It certainly is not necessary for those who train children to be bound to the same rigorous requirements for measurement that are necessary for formal investigations. Instead they can rely upon less complete evidence of a child's probable nonlinguistic knowledge. For example, the observation of Stremel and Waryas (1974) that a head shake can serve to indicate denial or rejection certainly seems to be appropriate kind of evidence from which to infer the child's ability to equate certain nonlinguistic events and relationships that correspond to the meaning of "no."

The precise measurement of underlying categories is not as important as is the consideration of the possible nature of the underlying nonlinguistic categories for the word meanings to be trained, and how that nonlinguistic information corresponds to what is known about the child's level of functioning. Considerations of how cognition links up with linguistic knowledge can serve a valuable heuristic function in deciding how to train word meanings. For example, if a word is being trained that has more than one meaning, it is important to take into account the differences in categorizational information addressed. Words such as "more" can be used by a child to designate recurrence, or to compare relative amounts. Such a distinction appears to be obvious on the linguistic level but perhaps not so obvious in the implications for how to structure training experiences. It would seem to be important for the interventionist to be quite clear about which of the two meanings were being trained and to devise training experiences to correspond to that meaning. When training recurrence, situations involving the appearance of additional substances or repetition of actions would be appropriate. However, in the case of the comparative meaning of "more" it would be necessary to present differing amounts (numbers) of the same substances (things). The nonlinguistic information represented in a word's meaning provides rather direct cues for how to structure training experiences to depict that meaning. If the child does not demonstrate nonlinguistic knowledge commensurate with that required to teach the word meaning, the chances for successful training may be reduced.[8]

Another example of how careful consideration of the link between underlying concepts and word knowledge can influence clinical decisions is to be found in a reconsideration of one of the recommendations put forth by Lahey and Bloom (1977). They proposed that clinicians train only one member of a pair of contrastive adjectives; for example, train "big" but not "little." This recommendation was based on earlier evidence that normal children learn one adjective of a polar pair before another (Clark, 1970). Therefore, they reasoned, it might confuse children to teach opposites at the same time. However, Carey (1978) reports evidence that children learn both members of a contrastive pair at the same time. Carey argues that the simultaneous mastery of both elements of a pair is a function of how underlying conceptual knowledge gets matched up with word meanings—the words are mapped onto a core comparative structure. The contrast between the two words is important information in establishing the comparative structure. If Carey's interpretation is correct, Lahey and Bloom's (1977) conclusion that opposite pairs should not be trained at the same time is misleading. Instead, both members of the pair would need to be trained at the same time in order to complete the comparative contrast.

The next question related to nonlinguistic categories is whether or not to train them as a prerequisite step before training the corresponding word meanings. The preceding section explored various measurement considerations and looked at how the interventionist could use available information as a guide for how to train word meanings. If nonlinguistic categories are so important, shouldn't they be trained as a preliminary step, or should one wait for evidence of spontaneous mastery of appropriate knowledge?

---

[8]A possible example may be found in Coleman and Anderson's (1978) study. They reported (p. 244) that some children did not learn spatial prepositions such as "above," "in," and "on" even after intensive training. They also reported that "the children's concept of spatial relationships appeared to exist on an all-or-none basis." One cannot help but wonder if these two pieces of information are causally linked.

Unfortunately, the reported psycholinguistic studies of how word meanings are acquired by young children have not looked at this particular question. The training study reported here did not involve the training of nonlinguistic categories, although the measurement tasks and the domain of color terms seem well suited to such an inquiry.

Several factors appear to be involved. The first is whether or not it is possible to train categories to language-disordered children. The answer to that will most certainly hinge on the general cognitive competencies of the child in question. In the case of severely retarded children, training even simple categorization skills may involve tremendous expenditures of time and effort, if the task can even be accomplished at all. On the other hand, for those language-disordered children whose difficulties appear to be limited to particular linguistic processing abilities, the training of categorizational strategies may be managed quite readily.

Related to the issue of whether it is possible to train categories is the length of time required. How much time should be spent in this phase of training? And what should be done if there is no apparent success? It is possible that there are inherent features of the categorization tasks that make them difficult for a child to master, yet he may have some notion of the underlying concepts that the tasks purport to measure. If this be the case, the child could conceivably learn a word to express the notion, while still unable to perform correctly on categorization tasks. If the interventionist persisted in training categorization tasks even though the child knew the word, it would be comparable to the teacher who insists that a child who is having trouble with phonics continue with his phonics workbook, even though he can read well, on the grounds that phonics is important to reading. In other words, while evidence of categorizational skills can indicate readiness for word training, a lack of such skills does not rule out the possibility that the word can be learned. The results of the training study reported here offer evidence that is consistent with this conclusion. Two of the children who did not demonstrate the targeted categories were able to learn to produce the words quite readily; other subjects without such categorical knowledge eventually learned to produce color terms correctly. The question of whether or not to train nonlinguistic categories, and for what proportion of clinical time, as a procedure for training word meanings, suggests a number of possible studies. In the meantime, those professionals who train language-disordered children will have to rely upon their own good judgment and an understanding of the issues involved.

The final question pertaining to underlying categorization bears on how many referent exemplars should be trained. If word meanings are based on categories of different environmental objects, events, and so on, that are regarded as equivalent for the purpose of word meanings, then the teaching of word meanings would involve more than one exemplar or referent—a set of equivalent referents would be involved. While this observation may appear to be obvious, it does run counter to some common clinical procedures. Often the meaning of a word is trained almost exclusively with one referent, such as a red rubber ball for "ball." But as the description of all the different kinds of balls (see p. 31) demonstrated, the word "ball" refers to a set of perceptually different objects. A clinical procedure that would be in line with the notion that categorical structure underlies word meanings would start with a referent stimulus that was prototypic or centrally defining for the category, and then continue to train the word/referent relationship through different exemplars until reaching referents with borderline membership. For example, if training the meaning of "fruit," such centrally defining exemplars as "apple" and "orange" could be trained first, with the subsequent presentation of exemplars gradually less central, until such borderline members as "tomato" and "pumpkin" were trained. This notion can also be described in behavioral terms: it is appropriate to build a stimulus class, i.e., a group of dissimilar stimuli that elicit the same response; a simple stimulus-response association will serve to represent only a few unique cases of word meaning (such as proper names, if identity sets are not considered as stimulus classes or categories).

Underlying categorical equivalences have a further and very important influence upon language training. There is some evidence that the different performance modes, production versus comprehension, tap underlying nonlinguistic knowledge at different levels (see p. 113). This issue is discussed in the following section.

Theoretical Issue: What Is the Relationship among Production, Comprehension, and Categorical Equivalences?   The role of cognition in accounting for the discrepancies between production and comprehension competencies of young normal children at different stages of language acquisition is a matter of growing interest among those who study how children learn the meanings of words. Since the normative literature has already been discussed in some detail, it will not be reviewed here. Suffice it to say that the nature of the relationship between underlying cognition and the two different linguistic performance modes appears to be a matter of considerable complexity of which little is known at present.

A number of clinical questions relate to this issue. How can the role of cognition influence the order of training for comprehension and production? Can production training be accomplished without correct comprehension or appropriate nonlinguistic knowledge? Is cognition necessary for correct comprehension but not for correct production of words? Does cognition account for spontaneous generalization from production training to comprehension?

The question of the order of training comprehension and production addresses a well known controversy in the language-training literature. A number of different orderings have been proposed with different sources of supportive evidence. The traditional operant approach has involved the training of imitation first, then comprehension, and then production (e.g., Bricker and Bricker, 1974; MacDonald, 1976). An alternative order of training has been developed by Winitz and Reeds (1976), who argue that there is no need for the initial imitation training; comprehension training alone is sufficient to establish both comprehension and production competence.

While the order of imitation and comprehension is an issue, there is agreement that comprehension training for a given linguistic form is to precede production training. The presumption is that it is easier for children to learn to comprehend particular linguistic information than it is to express that information in production. However, that certainly was not the case for the two subjects in the study reported here who successfully completed production training for color terms and who subsequently failed comprehension training.

How can the role of cognition in production/comprehension discrepancies be considered when one is determining the appropriate order for training the different performance modes? The interpretation of the production/comprehension gap proposed in the study reported here offers some clues for what to take into account. If ease of acquisition of production versus comprehension tasks varies according to the nature of the nonlinguistic relationship to be encoded (see pp. 113–116) the order of training could be structured accordingly. For example, if the nonlinguistic relationships are comparatively easy to master, and it is likely that the child already knows them, a comprehension, then production sequence of training would be well suited to the relationship existing between nonlinguistic knowledge, comprehension, and production. However, if the nonlinguistic relationship is difficult for a child to attain, and there is reason to believe that the child has not completely worked out the nonlinguistic information before training, it actually may be easier for him to learn to produce than comprehend. In order to ensure comprehension, additional steps may be necessary, i.e., the training of the nonlinguistic information. In such a case, two different orders are possible—production, then nonlinguistic concepts (see earlier discussion, p. 158, of considerations for the training of nonlinguistic categories), and then comprehension, or the second alternative, nonlinguistic training, then comprehension, and then production. Of course it is possible to modify these orders by training production and concepts concurrently, or comprehension and concepts concurrently. To train comprehension without some prior or concurrent training of conceptual knowledge could be a time-consuming task.

Closely related to the question of the order in which to train comprehension and production are questions pertaining to the nature of the training for each of the performance modes individually. In regard to production, it is possible to train a child to be able to produce a word correctly in referential context while at the same time the child is unable to comprehend the same word (see Ruder and Rice, 1977, for documentation of this phenomenon). While this set of circumstances provides valuable information about the nature of the linguistic learning process, it does not represent an appropriate training goal in and of itself. No one would argue that correct production alone constitutes full mastery of the meaning of a word; it is debatable whether production alone or comprehension alone would have the greater communicative value. However, there may well be circumstances when production alone could serve as a means of training other knowledge, such as following production training with concurrent categorization training. The learned production response could then be used to label the categorizational information being trained, an association that could presumably have facilitating effects for some children. The value and specific effects of such concurrent training remain to be seen.

The relationship between underlying nonlinguistic categories and comprehension that was evident in the study reported here has two implications for training. The first is that such categorical knowledge appears to be more of a prerequisite for correct comprehension than correct production. Subjects lacking a color-sorting strategy did not perform correctly on comprehension tasks but could do so on production tasks; subjects with a color-sorting strategy demonstrated competence for both comprehension and production. The close tie between comprehension and conceptual knowledge has also been alleged to exist in young normal children's first word meanings (Nelson, 1978).

When applied to the clinical setting, this information leads to the conclusion that comprehension training without appropriate nonlinguistic knowledge may be a difficult task. Before undertaking comprehension training, it would be wise to probe relevant cognitive competencies. If such knowledge is not evident, the clinician could then decide on the feasibility of teaching it, either as an independent step prior to comprehension training, or to train cognitive strategies concurrent with comprehension, or to train correct production and use the child's productive responses to help train the conceptual information.

Another aspect of comprehension training is revealed in the following question: When does it appear spontaneously? Those subjects in the training study reported in Chapters 4 and 5 who spontaneously generalized to correct comprehension from production training were those who indicated mastery of relevant nonlinguistic information. The implications for training are rather obvious. When one wishes to get something (i.e., comprehension) for free, one makes sure the child has the appropriate conceptual knowledge and then trains production, and it is quite likely that the child will spontaneously master the comprehension performance mode also.

A careful look at the role of conceptual knowledge in the acquisition of linguistic competence in both performance modes has resulted in some interesting implications for training. It is apparent that the easiest training circumstances exist when the child has already mastered the nonlinguistic meaning. Matters become much more complex when the child does not know the nonlinguistic information to be encoded in the words. Perhaps the facilitating role of underlying cognition, and its apparently stronger influence on comprehension than production, has been the unknown factor that has confounded the controversy over which training procedures work best.

Theoretical Issue: What Is Involved in Learning the Full Meaning of a Word?   When children learn word meanings, with how much of the meaning do they begin? Both Clark (1973) and Nelson (1974) have observed that children do not begin with fully complete word meanings. What is involved in the child's later and more complete mastery of a word meaning? Is a long time interval involved or a relatively short one?

Carey (1978) has analyzed the entire course of learning the meaning of words and the various perceptual, conceptual, and linguistic processes that are involved. She distinguishes between an initial "fast mapping" of a word's meaning and a full awareness of the word's meaning that is acquired later. The fast mapping includes information such as the fact that the new word is a word, along with some of its syntactic and semantic properties. The subsequent full mapping of the word involves the restructuring of the lexicon in order to insert the new word in its proper place, and the restructuring of the conceptual domain to correspond to the perceptual and cognitive distinctions encoded in the new word. In the case of color terms, one of the domains studied by Carey, the full mapping sometimes required as much time as several months. Carey argues that the complete acquisition of the word's meaning involves more than adding features until the full entry is achieved (as proposed by Clark's (1973) semantic feature hypothesis). Carey describes evidence of how children learn spatial adjectives that is not readily accounted for within the semantic feature hypothesis. Carey offers an alternative interpretation of how children go about learning words, an explanation that accounts for the initial fast mapping and the later, more time-consuming attainment of the full meaning. Carey calls the model the missing-feature-plus-haphazard-example theory.

Children's initial but partial meanings of words include not only some of the components of adult meaning for the word but also more specific information about some particular objects to which each adjective applies. The child may know that "tall" is an adjective, is used for comparison, involves physical extent, represents a positive pole, applies to buildings and refers to the distance from the ground up, and applies to people in reference to the distance from head to toe. But he may not know that "tall" also can apply to towers or ships. The dimensional information encoded in the initial entries is in an unanalyzed form. With further experience with the word in different contexts the child extracts the semantic features, the aspects of the conceptual system that are relevant to the lexical domain, and how to map those semantic features onto words. Carey proposes that these processes go on in unison. Both the nonlinguistic and linguistic contexts serve as important sources of information for the child as he works out the full meaning of the word.

What does such an account have to offer the training of word meanings in a clinical setting? Two of Carey's points have immediate relevance: 1) word meanings are acquired in two phases, and 2) context (both nonlinguistic and linguistic) is important in helping a child acquire the full meaning.

Procedures for the training of word meanings have not included a consideration of two phases of acquisition, an initial partial fast mapping and a more gradually acquired full mapping. My hunch is that most of our training efforts have resulted in acquisition at the level of initial, partial, fast mapping. As a general rule, the kind of extensive probing that would be necessary in order to document full acquisition of a word's meaning has not been done. However, the notion of training to a full meaning has been implicit at other times in this discussion, e.g., the desirability of training a category of referents and consideration of alternative ways of expressing the same meaning. One of the new clinical implications to be found in Carey's work follows from her observation that the full mapping may entail a long time interval during which the child can be restructuring his conceptual and lexical structures. Therefore, it might be desirable to plan for an extended period of training for a particular word meaning. The first stage would consist of intensive, structured clinical experiences within a relatively short time interval. The second stage would entail systematic probes of the child's understandings of the word, with intermittent presentation of appropriate nonlinguistic and linguistic contextual information. The second stage could conceivably be stretched over a long time interval, particularly for more complex words. It appears to be misleading to consider the training "done" when the child demonstrates acquisition of some of the defining components—that initial training may only represent a partial mapping of the full meaning that will only be apparent when the child is confronted with novel linguistic or nonlinguistic contexts.

Carey's second point of clinical value is that contexts, both nonlinguistic and linguistic, are important sources of information about word meanings. This is reassuring, because context is something the interventionist has control of in a training situation. It is also consistent with the considerable emphasis upon nonlinguistic context evident throughout this discussion, e.g., which referents to choose, the desirability of moving from centrally defining to peripheral members of a category, and so on. However, the linguistic context has received less attention as the source of important information for a child learning words.

The aspects of word learning that would seem to be most dependent upon linguistic contexts is the restructuring of the lexical structure, that is, deciding the word's relationship to other words. If the child knows "big" and "little," this information can help him learn "tall." "Tall" would have similar privileges of occurrence in grammatical structure (the child could notice its structural similarities to "big" and "little"); "tall" also applies to spatial dimensions and therefore combines with only certain words that are quite similar to words modified by "big" and "little." These and other cues from linguistic contexts would help the child work out the linguistic relatedness of certain words, indicating the proper placement of a word in the lexical structure.

The consideration of how a child learns the linguistic aspects of word meaning is closely related to how children learn to express the same meanings in different linguistic forms, i.e., the equivalence of certain word meanings and syntactic constructions (see pp. 134–135). Much of the learning in both of these instances involves abstracting common linguistic components from different linguistic contexts.

The same training strategy would appear to be appropriate for both aspects of lexical restructuring. The procedures would involve providing the child with appropriate linguistic contexts for a targeted word or meaning. The word or meaning could be incorporated into different sentence structures and compared and contrasted with other words used in the same linguistic slot. Instead of presenting only one or a few linguistic examples, demonstrating the "right way to say it," it would probably be more suited to the nature of the learning involved if a number of examples were presented, demonstrating various similarities and differences. Such verbal stimulation could accompany the relevant nonlinguistic context, allowing the child maximal opportunity to extract the relevant information to be encoded in the word.

The distinction between "partial" and "full" acquisition of the meaning of words presumes that there is a means of determining just what the child knows about the word in question. However, this presumption obscures a matter of considerable complexity—the assessment of a child's understanding of word meanings. In the next section the question of how to assess word meanings is examined more carefully.

How to Assess Word Meanings?

The assessment of a child's knowledge of word meanings is an integral part of the training of that area of linguistic competence. Assessment plays two roles in programming for language-disordered children. The first is that of identification, i.e., determining if a child does have problems acquiring language as compared to normally developing children. In the case of word meanings, this would involve a judgment about whether a particular child's knowledge of word meanings was consistent with expectations for his chronological or mental age peer group. Theoretically, it would be possible to conclude that a child had a language disorder solely on the basis of his knowledge of word meanings, even if other aspects of his language development were normal, although that would be quite unlikely in actual practice.

The second role played by assessment is that of providing information for therapy decisions. What the child knows about word meanings would determine where to begin therapy (what words need to be taught) and how to know when particular content is mastered (what the child needs to know before moving to the next program step, or determining that therapy is concluded).

The discussion to follow considers the second role of assessment, that of information for therapy. The neglect of the first role, that of identification, is not because the topic is unimportant. On the contrary, the determination of which children have problems acquiring language and with what particular aspects of language, is a matter of central significance that has generally been neglected in the language-training literature (see Rice, 1978, for a consideration of some of the issues). However, the information presently available about the acquisition of word meanings is such that it is more appropriate to conjecture about possible means of application to the less formal, ongoing assessment during therapy than to the development of more formal criteria for judging normal versus disordered. The discussion of the second role of assessment, of course, raises issues to be considered in the identification and behavioral description of children with language disorders.

An additional disclaimer is necessary. The discussion of assessment of word meanings is not intended to represent a comprehensive consideration of the various issues involved in assessment of linguistic competence. Several recent publications provide overviews of the literature and issues (e.g., Lloyd, 1976; Minifie and Lloyd, 1978; Miller, 1978). The purpose of the following discussion is to raise some questions about clinical assessment of lexical understandings from the perspective of recent information reported in the child language literature. The emphasis will be on introducing new considerations; such familiar issues as production versus comprehension competence and elicited versus spontaneous samples are only alluded to.

Theoretical Issue: How Is Meaning Packaged into Words?   After this rather extended discussion of word meanings, what word meanings to teach and how to teach them, it is the issue of assessment that brings us to the heart of the matter: How is meaning packaged into individual lexical items? The answer to this question has a direct bearing on how to go about assessing what a child knows about word meanings. Ideally, assessment procedures would be designed to measure a child's knowledge of the defining aspects of the meaning of a particular word. It would also be very convenient if the same organizational principles for packaging meaning into words were common to all words. If such were the case, one means of assessing word meanings would be equally applicable to different words.

A comprehensive theoretical model of the structure of meaning within lexical units could serve as a framework for the development of assessment tasks. Is such an account of word meaning available? Unfortunately, no. Instead there are several different models of word meanings available, each with different strengths and weaknesses and with several important inadequacies common to all. It is appropriate at this point to take a brief look at the different theoretical versions of the structure of word meaning before considering their implications for the development of assessment tasks.

The theoretical literature addressing word meanings spreads across the disciplines of linguistics, psychology, and philosophy and can be quite abstract and complex in nature. An excellent integration and summary of the literature, along with evaluative comments, has recently been completed by Clark and Clark (1977, pp. 408–448). They describe three major views of how meaning is mapped into lexical units:

1. The encyclopedic view—The mental encyclopedia corresponds to what has been referred to throughout this paper as "nonlinguistic concepts," i.e., all of one's knowledge about the world, presumably stored as categories. In this view of word meaning, the meaning slot in the lexical entry would be comprised of one's encyclopedic entry for that word; in other words, all of one's nonlinguistic knowledge gets packed into the linguistic meaning. Nelson's (1974) account of the nature of children's first word meanings seems to be consistent with this view of word meaning, along with Miller's (1978) view of lexical meaning (mentioned earlier on p. 148).

2. The componential view—Within this account, word meanings consist of a list of the defining properties or features. For example, "man" would be defined as human, male, and adult. Only a small part of one's nonlinguistic knowledge (the encyclopedic entry) is represented in the word's meaning, just the necessary attributes for the word in question. This view has been widely applied to studies of children's acquisition of word meanings, e.g., Clark's semantic feature hypothesis (1973), Bowerman's analysis of causative verbs (1974, 1977a), and Gentner's studies of verb acquisition (1978).

3. The nominal view—This version of word meanings is like the first in that lexical meaning is closely tied to encyclopedic information. However, it is argued here that the lexical entry for a word contains no information per se; it merely "names" the category labeled by that word, with the category information residing in the mental encyclopedia. Word meanings do not entail necessary attributes or properties; they label already existing categories. Rosch Heider's (1971, 1972; Heider and Olivier, 1972; Rosch, 1973, 1975) characterization of the meaning of color terms, where color words serve to label independently formed perceptual categories (discussed earlier on p. 40), appears to be consistent with this theoretical perspective.

Each of these views has its own strengths and weaknesses in accounting for various aspects of word meaning. In addition, all are unable to account for more complex characteristics of word meaning, such as multiple meanings (senses) for the same word, the bundling of words into idiomatic expressions, where a phrase assumes a single unit of meaning, and the phenomenon of lexical creativity, that is, the creation of novel words or new uses for old words in order to convey meanings never before associated with them.

What implications would such different ideas about the nature of word meaning have for the assessment of what children know about word meanings? One immediate consideration is the role of the mental encyclopedia, the nonlinguistic conceptual knowledge of the child. If one subscribes to the encyclopedic or nominal views of word meaning, assessment would involve describing a child's nonlinguistic knowledge, since word meanings and encyclopedic information correspond closely. In order to find out what a child knew about "house," for example, it would be necessary to obtain such nonlinguistic information as what it looks like, the category of real world things that are equated as being houses (presumably involving some form of a nonlinguistic categorization task), the function of houses, and real world characteristics (e.g., inanimate, immobile, susceptible to fire).

Given this set of circumstances, assessment could run into several problems. How would we know if a child knew the meaning of a word? If the word's meaning is the same as the nonlinguistic conceptual meaning, is everyone's meaning for the word different, since no two people would have the same nonlinguistic information? Does the meaning of "house" change if the child learns something new about houses? (This question and the preceding one were raised by Clark and Clark, 1977, p. 413.) If a child knew only what a house looked like, does this constitute enough information? Just how much of the potentially large amount of nonlinguistic information needs to be assessed? Presumably, the assessment could become downright ponderous if all possible aspects of relevant nonlinguistic knowledge were to be assessed.

Even if the nonlinguistic information is limited to categories (the nominal view), there are still potential problems for assessment. For example, if the child uses the word "dog" only to refer to stuffed toy animals, do we conclude that he does not know the natural category of dogs, or that he knows the natural category and is misapplying the label, or does he just have a linguistic category of "dog" (stuffed toy animals) without knowledge of the natural category? Thorough assessment of the child's nonlinguistic categories would be necessary in order to sort out these relationships. Another question is how do we know which words label preexisting categories of real world information? It's difficult to imagine that natural categories exist for words like "hot," "happy," and "no." What do we do with such words that do not seem to label categorical information in the same sense as words that name natural categories, such as animals, plants, and minerals?

Can we avoid some of the problems posed by the measurement of encyclopedic knowledge by following the componential view? Not all of the nonlinguistic knowledge is involved in word meanings according to this view, just those properties or features that are defining. For example, when assessing what a child knows about the meaning of "man" it would only be necessary to determine what he knows about its defining components, male, adult, human. This has the effect of limiting what needs to be assessed to more manageable portions. However, the problem of nonlinguistic knowledge has not been entirely solved. Each feature or component, such as "male," consists of nonlinguistic information with a corresponding list of necessary properties. Can we have a component called "male," or do we need to subdivide "male" into its defining features? How do we know how finely to draw the list of attributes? (This question is discussed in detail by Bolinger, 1965.) In order to measure what a child knows about "male," what defining nonlinguistic features do we need to assess?

A second problem arises with those words or concepts that do not seem to be definable in terms of necessary attributes, such as "house." It is difficult to come up with any one particular defining feature that would unequivocally designate a structure or building as a "house." Well known examples of such categories that seem to defy definition by necessary properties are "game," "thinking," and "playing."

All three approaches to word meaning—encyclopedic, componential, and nominal—pose problems of what to assess (how much nonlinguistic knowledge) and how to assess those word meanings that are not accounted for by the theoretical model. Furthermore, there are limitations common to all three. None of them provides direction or a systematic set of principles for the assessment of multiple meanings for the same word, idiomatic expressions, or lexical creativity.

So how are we to proceed when we are faced with a child lacking language skills and we need to ascertain what he knows about work meanings? Obviously, the available theoretical models have significant limitations. While it would be desirable to design assessment tasks and procedures according to systematic guidelines derived from a theoretical model, that framework is not likely for some time. However, there are some more general considerations to be derived from the theoretical literature. Since no one theory accounts for all aspects of word meaning for all words, an eclectic approach is justified. Different approaches may be used for different words. For example, assessment tasks could be structured to get at what a child knows about defining components for words that lend themselves to that model (e.g., spatial adjectives, verbs of possession) and what he knows about natural categories for other words (e.g., color terms). It is apparent that nonlinguistic information plays a central role in word meanings; therefore, assessment should include a means of tapping the knowledge available in a child's mental encyclopedia (subject to the considerations discussed in Chapter 2.) A final general observation is that the assessment of more complex semantic information, such as that expressed in idioms, multiple word meanings, and creative uses of words, will have to be based upon our adult, common-sense knowledge of the meanings involved.

Such sweeping generalizations only suggest general directions for assessment. What about specific procedures and methods of obtaining information about a child's knowledge of word meanings? These are explored in the following section.

Theoretical Issue: How Can We Determine What Children Know about Word Meanings?   Investigators of child language acquisition have had to deal with this problem in their studies of how young children acquire word meanings. Since young children are neither linguistically nor cognitively able to report or analyze their own linguistic knowledge, investigators must rely on indirect evidence from which to infer children's linguistic competence. A similar situation exists when one is dealing with children who have language deficiencies and who may or may not also exhibit cognitive deficits—they are generally unable to report their own linguistic knowledge. The techniques developed by child language investigators to determine what young children know about word meanings can be related to such clinical questions as: Are the standardized point-to-the-picture tests adequate for measuring children's word meanings? What other means can be devised to explore what a child knows about particular words? How are errors of word usage to be interpreted?

By far the most commonly used clinical procedure for assessing a child's understanding of lexical items is some form of a point-to-the-picture or name-the-picture task. Standardized tests, such as the Peabody Picture Vocabulary Test (Dunn, 1965), a point-to-the-picture task, frequently constitute the only assessment of word knowledge in an entire battery of tasks to determine a child's linguistic competence. Yet when we consider this format for assessment in terms of what we now know about the nature of word meanings and what young children can know about such meanings, the information obtained from such tasks seems very limited. For example, what about word meanings that are not susceptible to visual representation, such as "more" or "want," or, at more advanced levels, "fix," "free," "salary," "save," or "schedule"? What about the categorical aspect of word meaning: If a child can correctly point to or name one exemplar of a category, such as "toy," does that mean he understands the meaning of "toy" or is he operating with a lexical meaning that entails just one particular instance?[9] What about words with multiple senses, such as "rest" ("I want to rest" versus "I want the rest") or "train ("See the train" versus "See him training")? Although it would be possible to increase the informative value of point-to-the-picture or name-the-picture tasks by careful selection of stimuli and increased items for particular words, there are real limitations inherent in the nature of the task.

However, the techniques of child language investigators suggest other means of getting information about a child's lexical competence. One particularly rich source of information is a child's understanding and production of words in informal, everyday communication settings. While context is not controlled, in the sense of careful specification and presentation of stimuli as during a formal testing situation, it is carefully observed and serves as a source of information from which to infer intended meanings. Studies looking at young children's comprehension of word meaning (e.g., Huttenlocher, 1974) and their word productions (e.g., Bowerman, 1974, 1977a, 1977b; Gruendel, 1977; Braunwald, 1978) have been based on data collected in informal, naturalistic settings, with contextual information serving as cues to what the child meant to say.

The underlying reasoning is that repeated observations of a child's extension of a word (the set of objects or actions or relationships in the real world to which the word refers) will reveal his intension for the word (the properties or features or information that define the word). For example, Bowerman (1978a) observed that her daughter Eva used the word "off" only in connection with separation of things from the body. Given such a pattern of extension, it is reasonable to conclude that Eva's intension for "off" involved objects being removed from the body.

The big advantage to this technique is that the determination of a child's linguistic competence is not confounded by the constraints imposed by an elicitation format, constraints involving task requirements and/or stimulus limitations. For example, a child might spontaneously say "train" when he saw one but yet not be able to designate the appropriate picture when asked to "Show me train," either because he didn't understand the task or because his notion of "train" involved dynamic

---

[9]The assessment of categorical knowledge is not discussed here because it has been addressed in considerable detail elsewhere. However, it should certainly be kept in mind that the measurement of a child's understanding of nonlinguistic and lexical categories is an important component of the assessment of word meanings.

movement or other features not represented in the picture, or both. The disadvantages are the amount of time involved in collecting the information—diary studies are generally not feasible for children enrolled in language therapy—and the inherent subjectivity involved in interpreting the child's intended meanings.

While it is unlikely that naturalistic observations could serve as the sole source of information for the determination of a language-disordered child's lexical competence, such techniques could serve as a source of supplementary information in certain situations like the following: when detailed information about a particular word meaning is needed (a potential item for training or for determining when training has been completed); to obtain information about word meanings that do not lend themselves to visual representation; to learn more about the competencies of a child unable or unwilling to perform in formal assessment situations; or to investigate a child's knowledge of multiple word meanings, idioms, or evidence of lexical creativity.

Even though such data collection is time consuming, it may well serve as a source of information otherwise unavailable to the interventionist. The area of word meaning is a linguistic competence that may prove to be more elusive than other linguistic skills in a structured assessment situation, especially for young or severely disabled children. Some system of obtaining naturalistic information, to be collected by the interventionist, parents, older siblings, or aides, would seem to be a necessary component of a training program to teach word meaning.

Another important source of information that has been utilized by investigators of child language and largely overlooked by those who provide language training is the nature of the child's errors. Fromkin (1973, pp. 215–269) has argued that speech errors provide information about linguistic knowledge that is not evident in correct performance. That certainly has proved to be the case with young children's errors of word meaning. Such error phenomena as over- and undergeneralization of word meanings (discussed earlier on p. 32) have provided valuable insights into children's lexical and cognitive knowledge.

Errors can not only indicate what a child does not know, but they can also provide evidence of linguistic progress. Bowerman (1978c, pp. 381–391) provides evidence of "progressive regression," i.e., errors that reveal growth in linguistic competence via the child's creation of novel forms according to patterns of perceived regularities and similarities among words (discussed earlier on p. 46). Recall that she describes three types of progressive errors that children have been observed to make: those involving causative verbs (discussed in detail on pp. 134–135), those using nouns as verbs (e.g., "Barrette my hair back," "I can't zipper it," "I am crackering my soup" (Bowerman, 1978c, p. 386)), and those interchanging semantically similar words (e.g., substitutions of "put," "take," "bring," and "give" for one another (p. 389)).

The implications for assessment are obvious—if we only record a child's response as correct or incorrect, we will miss out on a great deal of important evidence. How would we know what kind of errors were made: those that represent a lack of knowledge, or novel creations reflecting an awareness of systematic regularities among linguistic forms? Even if we determine that the errors were based on a lack of knowledge, it would be important to know the nature of the error. For example, was a word's extension too narrow, or too broad, or based on nondefining features?

Another consideration is the nature of the circumstances in which informative, creative errors of word meaning are likely to occur. While some such errors may be observed in a formal therapy setting (due to chance or careful structuring of the circumstances), most of the reported data have come from spontaneous comments in informal settings, frequently in children's dialogues with each other. The implication is that it is necessary to not only collect information about the nature of errors evident in children's performance on tasks assessing word meaning, but to also collect information about errors in naturalistic settings. It may well be feasible to train parents to observe and record such errors, thereby increasing the available data base for determining what a child knows about word meanings.

There is one more procedure employed by those who have studied young children's lexical knowledge that may be applicable to the clinical setting in the case of children with some linguistic performance skills. If one wants to know what a child knows about the meaning of a word, the most direct route is to ask the child. Anglin (1977) did just that with children ranging in age from 2:8 to 6:7. The children were asked questions such as "What is a _____?", "Tell me everything you can about a _____," "What kinds of _____s are there?" and "Tell me a story about a _____," concerning 12 words (dog, food, flower, vehicle, animal, apple, rose, car, collie, fruit, plant, and Volkswagon). He reported (p. 190) that children 3 years of age or older were able to manage the task, and relayed a considerable amount of information about the meanings of particular words (a finding also reported by Nelson (1978, p. 52) for a similar task with children 3:6 to 4:6). Furthermore, the children's responses yielded an interesting finding: their definitions (intensions) did not control their classification behaviors (extensions); that is, the two kinds of performance did not coincide with each other. For example, a child who may have correctly defined food as "something you eat" nevertheless did not classify a picture of catsup or a sucker as "food" even thought he may have known that catsup or suckers could be eaten. Anglin (p. 235) attributes this discrepancy to a child's lack of conscious, reflective, analytic processing of information when asked to classify objects.

Anglin's findings suggest several points of importance for the purpose of clinical application: a child's understanding of word meaning may not be fully revealed by his extension of the word (the set of objects to which he applies the word); the discrepancy is not apparent without directly tapping a child's knowledge of the word; and even very young children (3 years of age and over) are capable of providing relevant information.

Obviously, such a procedure would not be appropriate for children with very limited language competencies. However, it may well be workable for many children enrolled in language therapy at moderately advanced levels of skill. Furthermore, such direct questioning may be the most feasible way of determining what a child knows about idioms, metaphors, multiple word meanings, novel uses of words, or other more complex lexical knowledge. Presumably, the children for whom this information would be sought are children at more advanced levels of linguistic competence, such that they could handle the task format.

In sum, our traditional clinical means of assessing a child's knowledge of word meanings, i.e., point-to-the-picture or name-the-picture tasks, have inherent limitations that require supplemental sources of evidence. Observations of the child's use of words in a natural setting (from which to determine his extension of the word and infer his intension), careful analysis of the nature of errors, and direct inquiries about the child's understanding of particular words are all potential sources of valuable information.

SUMMARY AND CONCLUDING REMARKS

The purpose of this chapter was to explore the clinical implications of current information about how young normal children learn word meanings. The content represented a topical consideration of various issues that have been raised in the psycholinguistic literature that may have a bearing on how word meanings could be taught to children having difficulties acquiring language. Three clinical questions were addressed: what lexical items to teach, how to teach word meanings, how to assess word meanings.

In regard *to what lexical items to teach,* the following issues and corresponding clinical implications were discussed:

1. While the relationship between cognition and language in normal children is not clear, the nature of this relationship in children with language deficiencies is unknown. It is probably more useful to rely on the normative literature as a guide for what words *to* teach, rather than which words *not to* teach.
2. Semantic categories may be organized according to bundles of correlated attributes instead of singly defining attributes, with some levels of semantic organization more salient than others. Words to be trained could be selected according to their psychological salience, with "basic object" level words trained first. The decisions of which words to train within a category, and which referents to choose for a particular word could be made according to prototypicality (representative grouping of attributes).
3. Some words may be learned first as a family of words, with the referential mapping taking place later. For such words (e.g., color terms), the selection of words to teach could be on the basis of family membership, introducing all the words in the family as a group, then emphasizing the referent relationship.
4. Children relatively early on learn more complex semantic skills, such as semantically equivalent but linguistically different means of expressing a given content, and how to juxtapose reference and context for the invention of uniquely appropriate semantic expressions (e.g., metaphor, humor). Words to be trained might include those selected on the basis of semantic production potential, that is, words that can be related to equivalent meanings framed in different syntactic structures and on the basis of possible use as metaphors or expressions of humor (double word meanings).

The discussion of *how to teach word meanings* can be summarized as follows:

1. The reference of a word entails the set of things to which the word applies, with "things" including objects, states, events, or processes. While most of young children's word meanings are referential in nature, they also learn some nonreferential meanings and use some referential words in a nonreferential manner. The training of referential word meanings need not be limited to referents that can be depicted visually. The training of nonreferential communicative intentions for referential word meanings seems to depend upon the child's knowl-

edge of the referential meaning. The nature of the referents evident in young, normal children's use of words can serve as a guide for how to choose referent objects, events, and relationships when teaching word meanings.

2. Lexical meanings interrelate with the meanings expressed in word combinations in a complex fashion. While it may sometimes be possible to train lexical meanings embedded in word combinations, there also may well be circumstances when a separate training step for individual word meanings is necessary, prior to training the word in combination with other words.

3. Categorical groupings of real world information underlie word meanings. It may be possible to tie nonlinguistic categories directly to some word meanings within a clinical setting, such as color terms and spatial adjectives, but it appears that for most word meanings indirect assessment, such as behavioral indicators, may have to suffice. The question of whether nonlinguistic categories should be trained, and at what point in a training sequence, remains a matter of conjecture, as does the question of how many referent exemplars of a linguistic category should be trained.

4. There is growing awareness of a complex interrelationship between the two performance modes, comprehension and production, and cognition (categorical equivalence). A child's cognitive knowledge may influence the order of training: if the child knows the nonlinguistic relationships, then a sequence of comprehension, then production, may be most effective; if he has not worked out the nonlinguistic information, then production first followed by comprehension may be more appropriate. It is possible to train correct production without correct comprehension or appropriate nonlinguistic knowledge. Therefore, cognitive information may only be necessary for correct comprehension but not correct production of words. Furthermore, underlying cognitive knowledge may account for spontaneous generalization from production training to comprehension.

5. The acquisition of the full mastery of a word's meaning can involve a long time interval (e.g., several months for color terms) and includes knowledge of a word's relationship to other words. The training of word meanings could be designed to take into account the initial, fast, and partial mapping of word meanings, along with the later, more time-consuming, full mapping. Training procedures could also incorporate appropriate linguistic contexts as a means of facilitating the child's learning where to place a particular word in his families of words.

The last question considered was that of *how to assess word meanings*. Two issues were raised:

1. The question of how meaning is packaged into words remains unresolved. While several theoretical models have been proposed, none is sufficiently robust to serve as a framework for the development of comprehensive assessment procedures. An eclectic approach to clinical measurement is justified, with different theoretical models applicable to different word meanings. For more complex semantic knowledge, e.g., idioms, metaphors, and novel uses of words, the clinician's own common-sense knowledge of the meanings involved may serve as the best guide for what is being assessed.
2. Young children and children with limited linguistic competence have a trait in common: it is usually difficult to determine precisely what they know about word meanings. Psycholinguistic investigations of young normal children's lexical competence suggest considerations for clinical assessment: point-to-the-picture or name-the-picture tasks give a very limited idea of what a child may know about word meanings; much information can be gleaned from records of children's spontaneous use of words in their natural environment, an analysis of the nature of their errors, and direct inquiries of those children able to tell someone what they know about a word's meaning.

It is evident that the content of this chapter does not constitute a well integrated, internally consistent model for the training of word meanings.[10] Nor has that been its purpose. Instead, the intention has been to raise some issues for thought, to make the point that there is presently a wealth of information about the acquisition of word meanings in normal youngsters that has not been applied to language training, and that we are no longer justified in overlooking the systematic development of an area of linguistic competence that is of central importance for a child trying to learn to communicate effectively. It is time to incorporate explicit training steps for word meanings into language-training programs, as an integral part of the training of linguistic competence, from the earliest stages through the acquisition of a vocabulary commensurate with a child's linguistic and cognitive competencies and social needs. The complexities of the linguistic and cognitive knowledge involved are such that this may turn out to be the area of linguistic competence that poses the greatest challenge to language trainers. However, it also offers the promise of full communicative competence for those children learning language in training circumstances.

---

[10]Indeed, if one looks very closely, some considerations seem to contradict others.

APPENDIX A
Score Sheet

Name _____   Reliability observer _____

Date _____

Testing site _____

Opening instructions:

Stimuli: Entire stimulus set

E: "I have some toys here for us to do some things with. See, here's one, and here's one (etc.)." (E points to or picks up each object in such a way as to elicit a glance from child at each object).
"I'm going to put these away for now (E removes all but stimuli for Task 1) and now we're going to play with these."
(Move directly to instructions for Task 1.)

TASK 1

Trial 1

Stimuli: Red sheep   ____ ____   Yellow sheep   ____ ____
          Red sheep   ____ ____   Black cow   ____ ____
          Red man   ____ ____   Green sheep   ____ ____
          Red chicken   ____ ____   Green sheep   ____ ____
          Red goat   ____ ____   Blue man   ____ ____

Directions: "Put all the other ones like this one in here (pointing to box)."

Model stimulus: *Red* sheep

Criterion for classification by color/animal/random: All red (or same animal) in first four choices, or not all the same

Criterion for identical match: First 2 choices if subsequent 2 not color

Response classification: Color
                          Animal
                          Identical
                          Other

Trial 2

Stimuli: Green goat   ___ ___   Yellow goat   ___ ___
           Green goat   ___ ___   Black horse   ___ ___
           Green pig   ___ ___   Red goat   ___ ___
           Green chicken   ___ ___   Red goat   ___ ___
           Green sheep   ___ ___   Blue man   ___ ___

Directions: "Put all the other ones like this one in here (pointing to box)."

Model stimulis: *Green* goat

Criteria: Same as trial 1

Response classification: Color
                           Animal
                           Identical
                           Other

Trial 3

Stimuli: Yellow pig   ___ ___   Green pig   ___ ___
           Yellow pig   ___ ___   Red pig   ___ ___
           Yellow goat   ___ ___   Red pig   ___ ___
           Yellow dog   ___ ___   Black cow   ___ ___
           Yellow sheep   ___ ___   White man   ___ ___

Model stimulus: *Yellow* pig

Criteria: Same as trial 1

Response classification: Color
                           Animal
                           Identical
                           Other

TASK 2

Trial 1

Stimuli: 1 green dog   ___ ___   1 yellow goat   ___ ___
           1 red dog   ___ ___   1 red pig   ___ ___

Directions: "Put all the other ones like this one in here (pointing to box)."

Model stimulus: *Red* sheep

Criterion for classification: Color—first 2 choices, same color; non-color: first 2 choices not same color

Trial 2

Stimuli: 1 green sheep   ___ ___   1 red dog   ___ ___
           1 green goat   ___ ___   1 yellow sheep   ___ ___

Model stimulis: *Green* pig

Trial 3

Stimuli: 1 yellow sheep   ___ ___   1 red sheep   ___ ___
           1 yellow pig   ___ ___   1 green dog   ___ ___

Model stimulus: *Yellow* goat

TASK 3

Trial 1

Stimuli: 3 red pigs   ___ ___   3 green goats   ___ ___
           3 yellow dogs   ___ ___   1 black cow   ___ ___

Directions: "Give me a red one."
  random   "Give me a green one."
  order, 3   "Give me a yellow one."
  per color

Criterion: Correct on 2/3 per color item

		Correct	Incorrect
Response:	Red	_____	_____
	Green	_____	_____
	Yellow	_____	_____

TASK 4

"What color is this?" Random order, 3 trials
Criterion: 2/3 correct for 3 trials

Response:

	Yes	No
Red	_____	_____
Yellow	_____	_____
Green	_____	_____
Blue	_____	_____
White	_____	_____
Black	_____	_____

TASK 5

Block matching (for subjects with no evidence of color matching, i.e., no color classification on any of previous trials)

Stimuli: 3 red blocks, 3 green blocks, 3 yellow blocks, 2 blue blocks

Model stimulus: Red blocks, etc.

Directions: "Which goes with this?"

Criterion: Correct match on 2/3 blocks for 3 different colors, random order

Total number of trials: 9

		Yes	No
Response:	Red	_____	_____
	Yellow	_____	_____
	Green	_____	_____

Summary Score Sheet

Subject: _____

TASK 1

	Color	Animal	Identical	Other
Trial 1	_____	_____	_____	_____
Trial 2	_____	_____	_____	_____
Trial 3	_____	_____	_____	_____

TASK 2

	Color	Other
Trial 1	_____	_____
Trial 2	_____	_____
Trial 3	_____	_____

Color-concept user: Two or more color sorts summed across Tasks 1 and 2, on two out of three occasions

TASK 3

	Correct	Incorrect
Red	_____	_____
Green	_____	_____
Yellow	_____	_____

TASK 4

	Number correct
Names of color	_____

TASK 5

		Yes	No
Block matching	Red	___	___
	Yellow	___	___
	Green	___	___

APPENDIX B
Pilot Study: Sorting Tasks

SUBJECTS

The subjects were 12 preschool children, ages 2:1 to 4:1. Eleven were en-rolled in day care / preschool and one was in the care of a private babysit-ter. All subjects were presumed normal in terms of physical, social, and intellectual development on the basis of reports of teachers / caregivers. Almost all of the children verbalized freely. The younger ones used intel-ligible 2–3-word phrases. The older ones talked in complete sentences. Potential subjects were eliminated if they were able to correctly name or comprehend "red," "green," or "yellow."

RESULTS*

Feasibility of Tasks

The children were able to complete the sorting tasks within one session of approximately 15–20 minutes. Their response patterns revealed different sorting strategies consistent with the design of the task, i.e., some sort by color, some by animal, and some by identical match. Such findings indi-cated that the series of sorting tasks were operationally feasible for the target age group.

Criterion for "Color-Concept-User"

The critical question was how to differentiate color-concept-users from non–color-concept-users. Six of the children sorted by color on Tasks 1 or 2, i.e., two or more color sorts summed across both tasks, and the other six sorted by color on the blocks only. With such a cut, not only did the data divide evenly, but the ages of the children were also equivalent, rul-ing out a possible confounding by chronological age. This differentiation also had a reasonable theoretical rationale, in that it could be argued that the selection of color among several attributes as a meaningful attribute for matching real world objects is qualitatively different from using color as a means of visually matching otherwise undifferentiated objects.

---

*The data describing how the children grouped objects on the sorting tasks are pre-sented in Chapter 4, pooled with the data for the training subjects.

The probability of being a color-sorter by chance, i.e., of randomly selecting objects corresponding to a color-sorting strategy, on the basis of two or more color sorts summed across Tasks 1 and 2, is 0.0236 for one color sort on Task 1 and one color sort on Task 2, 0.000925 for two color sorts on Task 1, and 0.0645 for two color sorts on Task 2. Such low probabilities rule out a chance explanation. Of course, more than two color sorts decreases the probability even further, e.g., three color sorts on Task 1, 0.0000077, three color sorts on Task 2, 0.00427 (Hogg and Craig, 1970).

A further consideration for establishing the criterion of color-concept-user versus non–color-concept-user that emerged as a recommendation from the pilot study was some evidence of stability over time. With such young children, there would be a strong possibility of occasion-to-occasion variability in such a preference procedure. Therefore, the criterion for the training study was amended to stipulate performance on two out of three occasions, spread over at least 2 days' duration. The highest chance probability of being a color-sorter on two out of three occasions is 0.0235, which is sufficiently low to rule out chance as a viable factor (Hogg and Craig, 1970).

Naming of Stimuli

An additional bit of information sought in the pilot study was whether or not the subjects could name the stimuli. It was found that few could name very many and most could name only one or two of the animals. Ability to name did not seem to be predictive of sorting preference. Anglin (1977, p. 166) reported similar findings: his child subjects could not name a wombat or an aardvark but could correctly classify them as animals. Given this finding and because the naming task took considerable time, it was dropped from further use.

APPENDIX C
Probe Sheet

PROBES

Name _____

Training *Red*

Objects	1	2	3	4
Balloon				
Barrette				
Cup				
Bowl				
Pencil				

Colors	1	2	3	4
Black watch				
Blue ribbon				
White comb				
Green spoon				
Yellow plate				

Training *Green*

Objects	1	2	3	4	5	6	7
Balloon							
Barrette							
Cup							
Bowl							
Pencil							

Colors	1	2	3	4	5	6
Black ribbon						
Blue comb						
White watch						
Yellow spoon						

Training *Yellow*

Objects	1	2	3	4	5	6	7	8
Balloon								
Barrette								
Cup								
Bowl								
Pencil								

Colors	1	2	3	4	5	6
Black comb						
Blue spoon						
White plate						

Red versus *Green*

Objects		1	2	3	4	5	6	7	8
Balloon	R								
	G								
Barrette	R								
	G								
Cup	R								
	G								
Bowl	R								
	G								
Pencil	R								
	G								

Colors

Same as for Training Yellow step

Red/Green/Yellow

Objects		1	2	3	4	5	6	7
Balloon	R							
	G							
	Y							
Barrette	R							
	G							
	Y							
Cup	R							
	G							
	Y							
Bowl	R							
	G							
	Y							
Pencil	R							
	G							
	Y							

Colors

Same as for Training Yellow step

APPENDIX D
Individual Subjects' Trials to Criterion

Training Steps

CC/NCC	Subject	Red	Green	Red/Green	Yellow	R/G/Y	Total
NCC	Rhonda	38	19	430	19	50	556
CC	Kathy	73	19	306	30	168	596
CC	Steven	57	46	420	19	61	603
CC	Valerie	68	40	410	29	102	649
NCC	David	235	43	283	36	60	657
CC	Melinda	30	39	732	38	86	925
NCC	Sherry	18	50	1000	29	244	1341
NCC	Ronnie	121	41	1000	29	382	1573
NCC	Arlene	94	56	1000	71	663	1884
NCC	Helen	115	168	1004	214	520	2021

REFERENCES

Anglin, J. 1977. Word, Object and Conceptual Development. W. W. Norton & Co., New York.

Barrett, M. D. 1978. Lexical development and overextension in child language. J. Child Lang. 5:205–220.

Bartlett, E. J. 1977. Semantic organization and reference: Acquisition of two aspects of the meaning of color terms. Paper presented at biennial meeting, Society for Research in Child Development, March 17–20, New Orleans.

Bartlett, E. J. 1978. The acquisition of the meaning of color terms: A study of lexical development. In: R. Campbell and P. Smith (eds.), Recent Advances in the Psychology of Language IVa pp. 89–108. Plenum Press, New York.

Bates, E. 1976. Language and Context: The Acquisition of Pragmatics. Academic Press, New York.

Bates, E., Benigni, L., Bretherton, I., Camaioni, L. and Volterra, V. 1977a. From gesture to the first word: On cognitive and social prerequisites. In: M. Lewis and L. Rosenblum (eds.), Interaction, Conversation, and the Development of Language, pp. 247–307. John Wiley & Sons, New York.

Bates, E., Benigni, L., Bretherton, I., Camaioni, L., and Volterra, V. 1977b. Cognition and communication from 9–13 months: A correlational study. Program on Cognitive and Perceptual Factors in Human Development Report No. 12, Institute for the Study of Intellectual Behavior, April, University of Colorado, Boulder, Col.

Berlin, B., and Kay, P. 1969. Basic Color Terms: Their Universality and Evolution. University of California Press, Berkeley.

Blank, M. 1974. Cognitive functions of language in the preschool years. Dev. Psychol. 10:229–245.

Bloom, L. 1970. Language Development: Form and Function in Emerging Grammars. The MIT Press, Cambridge, Mass.

Bloom, L. 1973. One Word at a Time: The Use of Single-Word Utterances Before Syntax. Mouton Publishers, The Hague.

Bloom, L., and Lahey, M. 1978. Language Development and Language Disorders. Wiley & Sons, New York.

Bolinger, D. 1965. The atomization of meaning. Language. 41(4):555–573.

Bolinger, D. 1967. Adjectives in English: attribution and predication. Lingua. 78:1–34.

Bornstein, M. H. 1973. Color vision and color naming: a psychophysiological hypothesis of cultural difference. Psychol. Bull. 80:257–285.

Bornstein, M. H. 1975. Qualities of color vision in infancy. J. Exp. Child Psychol. 19:401–419.

Bower, T. G. R. 1974. Development in Infancy. W. H. Freeman & Co., San Francisco.

Bowerman, M. 1973. Early Syntactic Development: A Cross-Linguistic Study with Special Reference to Finnish. Cambridge University Press, London.

Bowerman, M. 1974. Learning the structure of causative verbs: A study in the relationship of cognitive, semantic and syntactic development. Papers and Reports on Child Language Development, Stanford University Committee on Linguistics, 8:142–178.

Bowerman, M. 1975. Commentary on "Structure and Variation in Child Language" by L. Bloom, P. Lightbown, and L. Hood. Monogr. Soc. Res. Child Dev. 40(2), Serial No. 160:80–90.

Bowerman, M. 1976. Semantic factors in the acquisition of rules for word use and sentence construction. In: D. Morehead and A. Morehead (eds.), Normal and Deficient Child Language, pp. 99–179. University Park Press, Baltimore.

Bowerman, M. 1977a. The acquisition of rules governing "possible lexical items": Evidence from spontaneous speech errors. Papers and Reports on Child Language Development, Stanford University Committee on Linguistics 13:

Bowerman, M. 1977b. The structure and origin of semantic categories in the language learning child. Paper presented at the Burg Wartenstein Symposium #74, Fundamentals of Symbolism, Wenner-Gren Foundation for Anthropological Research, July 16–24, New York.

Bowerman, M. 1978a. The acquisition of word meaning: an investigation of some current conflicts. In: N. Waterson and C. Snow (eds.), Proceedings of the Third International Child Language Symposium. John Wiley & Sons, New York.

Bowerman, M. 1978b. Semantic and syntactic development: A review of what, when and how in language acquisition. In: R. L. Schiefelbusch (ed.), Bases for Language Intervention, pp. 97–189. University Park Press, Baltimore.

Bowerman, M. 1978c. Words and sentences: Uniformity, individual variation, and shifts over time in patterns of acquisition. In: F. D. Minifie and L. L. Lloyd (eds.), Communicative and Cognitive Abilities—Early Behavioral Assessment, pp. 349–396. University Park Press, Baltimore.

Braine, M. D. S. 1976. Children's first word combinations. Monogr. Soc. Res. Child Dev., Vol. 41 (1), Serial No. 164.

Brainerd, C. J. 1976. Does prior knowledge of the compensation rule increase susceptibility to conservation training? Dev. Psychol. 12:1–5.

Brainerd, C. J. 1977a. Cognitive development and concept learning: An interpretive review. Psychol. Bull. 84(5):919–939.

Brainerd, C. J. 1977b. Learning research and Piagetian theory. In: L. S. Siegel and C. J. Brainerd (eds.), Alternatives to Piaget. Academic Press, New York.

Braunwald, S. R. 1978. Context, word and meaning: Toward a communicational analysis of lexical acquisition. In: Andrew Lock (ed.), Action, Gesture, and Symbol: The Emergence of Language. Academic Press, London.

Bricker, W. A., and Bricker, D. D. 1974. An early language training strategy. In: R. L. Schiefelbusch and L. Lloyd (eds.), Language Perspectives: Acquisition, Retardation, and Intervention, pp. 431–468. University Park Press, Baltimore.

Brinker, R. P. and Bricker, D. D. Teaching a first language: Building complex structures from simpler components. In: J. H. Hagg and P. M. Mittler (eds.), Advances in Mental Handicap Research. John Wiley & Sons, New York. In press.

Brown, R. 1956. Language and categories. In: J. S. Bruner, J. J. Goodnow, and G. A. Austin (eds.), A Study of Thinking, pp. 247–312. John Wiley & Sons, New York.

Brown, R. 1958a. How shall a thing be called? Psychol. Rev. 65:14–21.

Brown, R. 1958b. Words and Things. The Free Press, New York.

Brown, R. 1973. A First Language: The Early Stages. Harvard University Press, Cambridge, Mass.

Brown, R. 1976. Reference in memorial tribute to Eric Lenneberg. Cognition 4:125–153.

Brown, R. 1978. A new paradigm of reference. In: G. A. Miller and E. Lenneberg (eds.), Psychology and Biology of Language and Thought: Essays in Honor of Eric Lenneberg, pp. 151–166. Academic Press, New York.

Bruner, J. S., Goodnow, J., and Austin, G. 1956. A Study of Thinking. John Wiley & Sons, New York.

Bruner, J. S., Olver, R., and Greenfield, P. 1966. Studies in Cognitive Growth. John Wiley & Sons, New York.

Burling, R. 1959. Language development of a Garo and English speaking child. Word 15:45–68.

Carey, S. 1978. The child as word learner. In: M. Halle, G. Miller, and J. Bresnan (eds.), Linguistic Theory and Psychological Reality. The MIT Press, Cambridge, Mass.

Carroll, J. B. 1976. Promoting language skills: the role of instruction. In: David Klahr (ed.), Cognition and Instruction. Lawrence Erlbaum Associates, Hillsdale, N.J.

Cazden, C. B. 1977. The question of intent. In: M. Lewis, and L. Rosenblum (eds.), Interaction, Conversation and the Development of Language. John Wiley & Sons, New York.

Chapman, Robin S. 1978. Comprehension strategies in children. In: J. F. Kavanagh and W. Strange (eds.), Speech and Language in the Laboratory, School and Clinic. The MIT Press, Cambridge, Mass.

Chapman, R. S., and Miller, J. F. 1975. Word order in early two and three word utterances: Does production precede comprehension? J. Speech Hear. Res. 18:355–371.

Chomsky, N. 1957. Syntactic Structures. Mouton, The Hague.

Chomsky, N. 1959. A review of *Verbal Behavior,* by B. F. Skinner. Language 35:26–58.

Chomsky, N. 1965. Aspects of the Theory of Syntax. The MIT Press, Cambridge, Mass.

Clark, E. 1973. What's in a word? On the child's acquisition of semantics in his first language. In: T. Moore (ed.), Cognitive Development and the Acquisition of Language, pp. 65–110. Academic Press, New York.

Clark, E. 1975. Knowledge, context, and strategy in the acquisition of meaning. In: D. Dato (ed.), Developmental Psycholinguistics: Theory and Applications. 26th Annual Georgetown University Roundtable. Georgetown University Press, Washington, D.C.

Clark, E. 1977. Strategies and the mapping problem in first language acquisition. In: J. Macnamara (ed.), Language Learning and Thought, pp. 147–168. Academic Press, New York.

Clark, E. 1978. Strategies for communicating. Child Dev. 49(4):953–959.

Clark, E. V., and Garnica, O. K. 1974. Is he coming or going? On the acquisition of deictic verbs. J. Verb. Learn. Verb. Behav. 13:556–572.

Clark, H. 1970. The primitive nature of children's relational concepts. In: J. Hayes (ed.), Cognition and the Development of Language. John Wiley & Sons, New York.

Clark, H., and Clark, E. 1977. Psychology and Language. Harcourt Brace Jovanovich, New York.

Coleman, R. O., and Anderson, D. E. 1978. Enhancement of language comprehension in developmentally delayed children. Language, Speech and Hearing Services in Schools 9(4):241–253.

Conklin, H. C. 1955. Hanunóo color categories. Southwestern J. Anthropol. 11:339–344.

Cooper, J., Moodley, M., and Reynell, J. 1978. Helping Language Development. Edward Arnold, London.

Corrigan, R. 1978. Language development as related to stage 6 object permanence development. J. Child Lang. 5:173–189.

Cromer, R. F. 1974. The development of language and cognition: The cognition hypothesis. In: B. Foos (ed.), New Perspectives in Child Development, pp. 184–252. Penguin Books, Baltimore.

Cromer, R. F. 1976a. The cognitive hypothesis of language acquisition and its implications for child language deficiency. In: D. Morehead and A. Morehead (eds.), Normal and Deficient Child Language, pp. 283–333. University Park Press, Baltimore.

Cromer, R. F. 1976b. Developmental strategies for language. In: V. Hamilton and M. Vernon (eds.), The Development of Cognitive Processes, pp. 305–358. Academic Press, London.

Cromer, R. F. 1979. Reconceptualizing language acquisition and cognitive development. Paper presented at the Early Language Intervention conference, May 23–25, Sturbridge, Mass.

Cruse, D. A. 1977. A note on the learning of colour names. J. Child Lang. 4: 305–311.

Curcio, F., Kattef, E., Levine, D., and Robbins, O. 1972. Compensation and susceptibility to conservation training. Dev. Psychol. 7:259–265.

Dale, P. 1976. Language Development: Structure and Function. 2nd ed. Holt, Rinehart & Winston, New York.

Denney, N. W. 1972a. A developmental study of free classification in children. Child Dev. 43:221–232.

Denney, N. W. 1972b. Classification in preschool children. Child Dev. 43: 1161–1170.

Denney, N. W., and Acito, M. A. 1974. Classification training in two- and three-year-old children. J. Exp. Child Psychol. 17:37–48.

de Villiers, J. G., and de Villiers, P. A. 1973. Development of the use of word order in comprehension. J. Psycholing. Res. 2:331–341.

de Villiers, J. G., and de Villiers, P. A. 1978. Language Acquisition. Harvard University Press, Cambridge, Mass.

Dore, J. 1975. Holophrases, speech acts and language universals. J. Child Lang. 2:21–40.

Dunn, L. M. 1965. Peabody Picture Vocabulary Test. American Guidance Service, Circle Pines, Minn.

Ervin-Tripp, S. 1971. An overview of grammatical development. In: D. Slobin (ed.), The Ontogenesis of Grammar. Academic Press, New York.

Faulkender, P., Wright, J., and Waldron, A. 1974. Generalized habituation of concept stimuli in toddlers. Child Dev. 45:1002–1010.

Fillmore, C. J. 1968. The case for case. In: E. Bach and R. T. Harms (eds.), Universals in Linguistic Theory. Holt, Rinehart & Winston, New York.

Fraser, C., Bellugi, U., and Braun, R. 1963. Control of grammar in imitation, comprehension, and production. J. Verb. Learn. Verb. Behav. 2:121–135.

Fromkin, V. A. 1973. Speech Errors as Linguistic Evidence. Mouton, The Hague.

Gardner, H., Winner, E., Bechhofer, R., and Wolf, D. 1978. The development of figurative language. In: K. Nelson (ed.), Children's Language, Vol. I, pp. 1–38. Gardner Press, New York.

Gentner, D. 1978. On relational meaning: The acquisition of verb meaning. Child Dev. 49(4):988–998.

Ginsburg, H., and Opper, S. 1969. Piaget's Theory of Intellectual Development: An Introduction. Prentice-Hall, Englewood Cliffs, N. J.

Goldin-Meadow, S., Seligman, M. E. P., and Gelman, R. 1976. Language in the two-year-old. Cognition 4:189–202.

Gray, B., and Ryan, B. 1973. A Language Program for the Non-Language Child. Research Press, Champaign, Ill.

Greenfield, P. M., and Smith, J. H. 1976. The Structure of Communication in Early Language Development. Academic Press, New York.

Gruendel, J. 1977. Referential extension in early language development. Child Dev. 48(4):1567–1576.

Guess, D. 1969. A functional analysis of receptive language and productive speech: Acquisition of the plural morpheme. J. Appl. Behav. Anal. 2:55–64.

Guess, D., and Baer, D. M. 1973. An analysis of individual differences in generalization between receptive and productive language in retarded children. J. Appl. Behav. Anal. 6:311–329.

Guess, D., Sailor, W., and Baer, D. 1974. To teach language to retarded children. In: R. L. Schiefelbusch and L. L. Lloyd (eds.), Language Perspectives: Acquisition, Retardation, and Intervention, pp. 529–563. University Park Press, Baltimore.

Harris, S. L. 1975. Teaching language to nonverbal children—with emphasis on problems of generalization. Psychol. Bull. 82(4):565–580.

Heider, E. R. 1971. "Focal" color areas and the development of color names. Dev. Psychol. 4:447–455.

Heider, E. R. 1972. Universals in color naming and memory. J. Exp. Psychol. 93:10–20.

Heider, E. R., and Olivier, D. C. 1972. The structure of the color space in naming and memory for two languages. Cog. Psychol. 3:337–354.

Hogg, R., and Craig, A. 1970. Introduction to Mathematical Statistics. MacMillan, London.

Holland, A. 1975. Language therapy for children: Some thoughts on context and content. J. Speech Hear. Disord. 40(4):514–523.

Huttenlocher, J. 1974. The origins of language comprehension. In: R. L. Solso (ed.), Theories in Cognitive Psychology: The Loyola Symposium, pp. 331–368. Lawrence Erlbaum Associates, Potomac, Md.

Ingram, D. 1978. Sensorimotor intelligence and language development. In: A. Lock (ed.), Action, Gesture and Symbol: The Emergence of Language. Academic Press, New York.

Inhelder, B. 1966. Cognitive development and its contribution to the diagnosis of some phenomena of mental deficiency. Merrill-Palmer Q. 12:299–319.

Inhelder, B. 1976. Observations on the operational and figurative aspects of thought in dysphasic children. In: D. Morehead and A. Morehead (eds.), Normal and Deficient Child Language, pp. 335–343. University Park Press, Baltimore.

Inhelder, B., and Piaget, J. 1964. The Early Growth of Logic in the Child. Harper & Row, New York.

Kogan, N. 1976. Cognitive Styles in Infancy and Early Childhood. John Wiley & Sons, New York.

Kogan, N. 1979. A cognitive style approach to metaphoric thinking. In: R. Snow, P. A. Federico, and W. Montague (eds.), Aptitude, Learning and Instruction: Cognitive Process Analyses. Lawrence Erlbaum Associates, Hillsdale, N.J.

Kuczaj, S. A. 1978. Why do children fail to overgeneralize the progressive inflection? J. Child Lang. 5:167–171.

Lahey, M., and Bloom, L. 1977. Planning a first lexicon: Which words to teach first. J. Speech Hear. Disord. 42:340–349.

Lenneberg, E. H. 1967. Biological Foundations of Language. John Wiley & Sons, New York.

Leonard, L. B. 1978. Cognitive factors in early linguistic development. In: R. L. Schiefelbusch (ed.), Bases of Language Intervention, pp. 67–96. University Park Press, Baltimore.

Leonard, L. B. 1979. Language impairment in children. Merrill-Palmer Q. 25: 205–232.

Lloyd, L. L. 1976. Communicative Assessment and Intervention Strategies. University Park Press, Baltimore.

McCawley, J. D. 1971. Prelexical syntax. In: R. J. O'Brien (ed.), Monograph Series on Languages and Linguistics, 22nd Annual Round Table. Georgetown University Press, Washington, D.C.

McCawley, J. D. 1974. (Dialogue with) James McCawley. In: H. Parret (ed.), Discussing Language. Mouton, The Hague.

MacDonald, J. D. 1976. Environmental language intervention programs for establishing initial communication in handicapped children. In: F. B. Withrow and C. J. Nygren (eds.), Language Curriculum and Materials for the Handicapped Learner. Charles E. Merrill Publishing Co., Columbus, Oh.

MacDonald, J. D., and Blott, J. P. 1974. Environmental language intervention: A rationale for a diagnostic and training strategy through rules, context and generalization. J. Speech Hear. Disord. 39:244–256.

McLean, J. E., Yoder, D. E., and Schiefelbush, R. L. (eds.). 1972. Language Intervention with the Retarded: Developing Strategies. University Park Press, Baltimore.

Macnamara, J. 1972. Cognitive basis of language learning in infants. Psychol. Rev. 79(1):1–13.

Macnamara, J. 1977. Problems about concepts. In: J. Macnamara (ed.), Language Learning and Thought, pp. 141–145. Academic Press, New York.

Mandler, J. M. Categorical and schematic organization in memory. In: C. R. Puff (ed.), Memory, Organization and Structure. Academic Press, New York. In press.

Marquesen, V. 1975. Establishing multiple stimulus classes in preschool children. Unpublished doctoral dissertation, University of Kansas, Lawrence.

Marmor, G. S. 1978. Age at onset of blindness and the development of the semantics of color names. Child Psychol. 25:267–278.

Mecham, M. 1958. Verbal Language Development Scale. American Guidance Service, Circle Pines, Minn.

Mervis, C. B., Catlin, J., and Rosch, E. 1975. Development of the structure of color categories. Dev. Psychol. 11:54–60.

Miller, G. A. 1978. Practical and lexical knowledge. In: E. Rosch and B. B. Lloyd (eds.), Cognition and Categorization. Lawrence Erlbaum Associaties, Hillsdale, N.J.

Miller, G. A., and Johnson-Laird, P. N. 1976. Language and Perception. Harvard University Press, Cambridge, Mass.

Miller, J. 1978. Assessing children's language behavior. In: R. L. Schiefelbusch (ed.), Bases of Language Intervention, pp. 269–318. University Park Press, Baltimore.

Miller, J., and Yoder, D. 1974. An ontogenetic language teaching strategy for retarded children. In: R. L. Schiefelbusch and L. L. Lloyd (eds.), Language Perspectives: Acquisition, Retardation, and Intervention, pp. 505–528. University Park Press, Baltimore.

Minifie, F. D., and Lloyd, L. L. (eds.). 1978. Communicative and Cognitive Abilities—Early Behavioral Assessment. University Park Press, Baltimore.

Moore, T. E., and Harris, A. E. 1979. Language and thought in Piagetian theory. In: L. S. Siegel and C. J. Brainerd (eds.), Alternatives to Piaget, pp. 131–152. Academic Press, New York.

Morehead, D. M., and Ingram, D. 1976. The development of base syntax in normal and linguistically deviant children. In: D. M. Morehead and A. E. Morehead (eds.), Normal and Deficient Child Language, pp. 209–238. University Park Press, Baltimore.

Morehead, D. M., and Morehead, A. 1974. From signal to sign: a Piagetian view of thought and language during the first two years. In: R. L. Schiefelbusch and L. L. Lloyd (eds.), Language Perspectives—Acquisition, Retardation, and Intervention, pp. 153–190. University Park Press, Baltimore.

Nelson, K. 1973a. Some evidence for the cognitive primacy of categorization and its functional basis. Merrill-Palmer Q. 19:21–39.

Nelson, K. 1973b. Structure and strategy in learning to talk. Monogr. Soc. Res. Child Dev. 38, Serial No. 149.

Nelson, K. 1974. Concept, word and sentence: Interrelations in acquisition and development. Psychol. Rev. 81:267–285.

Nelson, K. 1976. Some attributes of adjectives used by young children. Cognition 4:13–30.

Nelson, K. 1977. The conceptual basis for naming. In: J. Macnamara (ed.), Language Learning and Thought, pp. 117–136. Academic Press, New York.

Nelson, K. 1978. Semantic development and the development of semantic memory. In: K. E. Nelson (ed.), Children's Language, Vol. I, pp. 39–80. Gardner Press, New York.

Nelson, K. E. and Bonvillian, J. D. 1978. Early language development: Conceptual growth and related processes between two and 4 1/2 years of age. In: K. Nelson (ed.), Children's Language, Vol. I, pp. 467–556. Gardner Press, New York.

Nelson, K., Rescorla, L., and Gruendel, J. 1978. Early lexicons: What do they mean? Child Dev. 49(4):960–968.

Olver, R., and Hornsby, J. 1966. On equivalence. In: J. S. Bruner, R. Olver, and P. Greenfield (eds.), Studies in Cognitive Growth. John Wiley & Sons, New York.

Papert, S. 1977. Concepts and artificial intelligence. In: J. Macnamara (ed.), Language Learning and Thought, pp. 137–140. Academic Press, New York.

Piaget, J. 1970. A conversation with Jean Piaget. Psychol. Today 25–32.

Piaget, J. 1964. Development and learning. In: R. Ripple and V. Rockcastle (eds.), Piaget Rediscovered. Cornell University, Ithaca, N.Y.

Piaget, J., and Inhelder, B. 1969. The Psychology of the Child. Basic Books, New York.

Report on the Legislative Council. 1977. Asha 19:138.

Report on the Legislative Council. 1979. Asha 21:190.

Ricciuti, H. 1965. Object grouping and selective ordering behavior in infants 12–24 months old. Merrill-Palmer Q. 11:129–43.

Rice, M. 1978. Identification of children with language disorders. In: R. L. Schiefelbusch (ed.), Language Intervention Strategies, pp. 19–55. University Park Press, Baltimore.

Richards, M. M. 1976. Come and go revisited: Children's use of deictic verbs in contrived situations. J. Verb. Learn. Verb. Behav. 15:655–665.

Rosch, E. 1973. On the internal structure of perceptual and semantic categories. In: T. E. Moore (ed.), Cognitive Development and the Acquisition of Language. Academic Press, New York.

Rosch, E. 1975. Universals and cultural specifics in human categorization. In: R. Brislin, S. Bochner and W. Lonner (eds.), Cross-Cultural Perspectives on Learning. Halsted Press, New York.

Rosch, E. 1976. Classifications of real-world objects: origins and replications in cognition. In: S. Ehrlich and E. Tulving (eds.), Bulletin de Psychologie (Special issue on semantic memory).

Rosch, E., and Mervis, C. B. 1975. Family resemblances: studies in the internal structure of categories. Cog. Psychol. 7(4):573–605.

Rosch, E., Mervis, C. B., Gray, W., Johnson, D., and Bayes-Braem, P. 1976. Basic objects in natural categories. Cog. Psychol. 8:382–439.

Ruder, K., and Rice, M. 1977. Comprehension and Production: A Study in the Acquisition of Color Terms. 16mm color film. Bureau of Child Research, University of Kansas, Lawrence.

Sachs, J., and L. Truswell. 1978. Comprehension of two-word instructions by children in the one-word stage. J. Child Lang. 5(1):17–24.

Schiefelbusch, R. L. (ed.). 1978a. Bases of Language Intervention. University Park Press, Baltimore.

Schiefelbusch, R. L. (ed.). 1978b. Language Intervention Strategies. University Park Press, Baltimore.

Schiefelbusch, R. L., Copeland, R. H., and Smith, J. O. 1967. Language and Mental Retardation: Empirical and Conceptual Considerations. Holt, Rinehart & Winston, New York.

Schiefelbusch, R. L., and Lloyd, L. L. (eds.). 1974. Language Perspectives—Acquisition, Retardation, and Intervention. University Park Press, Baltimore.

Schlesinger, I. M. 1971. The production of utterances and language acquisition. In: D. I. Slobin (ed.), The Ontogenesis of Grammar. Academic Press, New York.

Schlesinger, I. M. 1974. Relational concepts underlying language. In: R. L. Schiefelbusch and L. L. Lloyd (eds.), Language Perspectives—Acquisition, Retardation, and Intervention, pp. 129–151. University Park Press, Baltimore.

Schlesinger, I. M. 1977a. The language we learn and the language we think in. Unpublished manuscript.

Schlesinger, I. M. 1977b. The role of cognitive development and linguistic input in language acquisition. J. Child Lang. 4:153–169.

Schlesinger, I. M. Acquisition of words: The first steps. Chapter in preparation.

Shatz, M., and Gelman, R. 1973. The development of communication skills: Modifications in the speech of young children as a function of listener. Monogr. Soc. Res. Child Dev. 38(5), Serial No. 152.

Siegel, G. M., and Spradlin, J. E. 1978. Programming for language and communication therapy. In: R. L. Schiefelbusch (ed.), Language Intervention Strategies, pp. 357–398. University Park Press, Baltimore.

Siegel, L. 1977. The relationship of language and thought in the preoperational child: A reconsideration of nonverbal alternatives to Piagetian tasks. In: L. S. Siegel and C. Brainerd (eds.), Alternatives to Piaget. Academic Press, New York.

Siegel, S. 1956. Nonparametric Statistics for the Behavioral Sciences. McGraw-Hill Book Co., New York.

Skinner, B. F. 1957. Verbal Behavior. Appleton-Century-Crofts, New York.

Sinclair, H. 1971. Sensorimotor action patterns as a condition for the acquisition of syntax. In: R. Huxley and D. Ingram (eds.), Language Acquisition: Models and Methods. Academic Press, New York.

Sinclair-de Zwart, H. 1973. Language acquisition and cognitive development. In: T. E. Moore (ed.), Cognitive Development and the Acquisition of Language. Academic Press, New York.

Slobin, D. I. 1973. Cognitive prerequisites for the development of grammar. In: C. A. Ferguson and D. I. Slobin (eds.), Studies of Child Language Development, pp. 175–208. Holt, Rinehart & Winston, New York.

Snow, C. E., Arlman-Rupp, A., Hassing, Y., Jobse, J., Joosten, J., and Vorster, J. 1976. Mothers' speech in three social classes. J. Psycholing. Res. 5:1–20.

Stokes, T. F. and Baer, D. M. 1977. An implicit technology of generalization. J. Appl. Behav. Anal. 10(2):349–367.

Stremel, K., and Waryas, C. 1974. A behavioral-psycholinguistic approach to language training. In: L. McReynolds (ed.), Developing Systematic Procedures for Training Children's Language. Asha Monogr. 18.

Suchman, R. G., and Trabasso, T. 1966. Color and form preference in young children. J. Exp. Child Psychol. 3:177–187.

Uzgiris, I., and Hunt, J. McV. 1975. Assessment in Infancy: Ordinal Scales of Psychological Development. University of Illinois Press, Urbana, Ill.

Vygotsky, L. S. 1962. Thought and Language. [Trans. by E. Hanfmann and G. Vakar.] The MIT Press, Cambridge, Mass.

Waryas, C. L., and Stremel-Campbell, K. 1978. Grammatical training for the language-delayed child: A new perspective. In: R. L. Schiefelbusch (ed.), Language Intervention Strategies, pp. 145–192. University Park Press, Baltimore.

Wells, G. 1974. Learning to code experience through language. J. Child Lang. 1(2):243–269.

Wetherby, B. 1977. A functional analysis of miniature linguistic system learning in preschool children. Unpublished doctoral dissertation, University of Kansas, Lawrence.

Whorf, B. L. 1956. Language, Thought and Reality: Selected Writings of Benjamin Lee Whorf. The MIT Press, Cambridge, Mass.

Winitz, H., and Reeds, J. 1976. Comprehension and Problem Solving as Strategies for Language Training. Mouton, The Hague.

Index

Current and forthcoming volumes...

LANGUAGE INTERVENTION SERIES

Series Editor: **Richard L. Schiefelbusch, Ph.D.**

Publishing core volumes on major topics in language intervention, this series synthesizes and interprets important developments in language intervention to serve as the central resource for all language practitioners, and emphasizes practical applications by defining organized, validated examples of workable programs. Each volume features a comprehensive academic overview of the title theme, detailed coverage of the technology relating to intervention designs, and explicit descriptions and analyses of intervention strategies, programs, and functions. Each also includes literature reviews and thorough coverage of basic research.

BASES OF LANGUAGE INTERVENTION
Edited by **Richard L. Schiefelbusch, Ph.D.**
486 pages   *Illustrated*   *1978*

LANGUAGE INTERVENTION STRATEGIES
Edited by **Richard L. Schiefelbusch, Ph.D.**
430 pages   *Illustrated*   *1978*

**LANGUAGE INTERVENTION
FROM APE TO CHILD**
Edited by **Richard L. Schiefelbusch, Ph.D.,**
and **John H. Hollis, Ed.D.**
544 pages   *Illustrated*   *1979*

**NONSPEECH LANGUAGE
AND COMMUNICATION**
Analysis and Intervention
Edited by **Richard L. Schiefelbusch, Ph.D.**
544 pages   *Illustrated*   *1979*

**EMERGING LANGUAGE
IN AUTISTIC CHILDREN**
Edited by **Warren H. Fay, Ph.D.,**
and **Adriana Luce Schuler, M.A.**
In press   Summer 1980

DEVELOPMENTAL LANGUAGE INTERVENTION
Psycholinguistic Applications
Edited by **Kenneth F. Ruder, Ph.D.,**
and **Michael D. Smith, Ph.D.**
In preparation   Late 1980

EARLY LANGUAGE INTERVENTION
Edited by **Richard L. Schiefelbusch, Ph.D.,**
and **Diane D. Bricker, Ph.D.**
In preparation   1981

Special 10% Discount on Standing Orders for Series: You may
register your continuation order with University Park Press to receive
each new volume in this series **at 10% off list price** automatically upon
publication on 30-day approval with guaranteed right of return if not
satisfied. Or you may purchase any volume separately in accordance
with your particular interests.

LANGUAGE AND SOCIAL PSYCHOLOGY

Edited by **Howard Giles** and **Robert N. St. Clair**

This book explores the phenomenological world of speakers and hearers and shows that social psychological concepts (such as attitudes, motivations, intentions, expectations, and personalities) are important aspects of the decoding and encoding processes. It shows explicitly some of the interrelationships between social psychology and sociolinguistics in a range of applied social contexts and points out how multidisciplinary work of is nature is of inestimable value to both the linguist and the social scientist.

The first section of the book is concerned with the judgmental aspects of the listener's decoding of language. It presents studies of how speech characteristics affect the hearer's reaction to the speaker and demonstrates that a wide variety of signals from a speaker can affect our evaluations of him or her.

The second section turns to studies of the encoding process. It looks at the psychological processes underlying the development of interpersonal relationships, why non-prestige language forms have survived today, and how ingroup identity pressures affect linguistic style choices. Taken together, these chapters show that encoding involves a complex array of social psychological operations and that the subsequent speech patterns reflect the differing functions the spoken word can have.

Language and Social Psychology is an important text for studies in language and communication, anthropological linguistics, ethnomethodology, secular linguistics, the sociology of language, the ethnography of speaking, discourse analysis, and the social psychology of language. It should be considered an essential acquisition for libraries and departments of sociology, psychology, anthropology, and linguistics.

262 pages   *Illustrated*   *1979*

CHILD LANGUAGE

An Interdisciplinary Guide to Theory and Research

By **Adele A. Abrahamsen, Ph.D.**

This is an unusually broad-based, extensively annotated bibliography of child language research, organized by topic, with introductory material and suggested background reading. It is unquestionably the outstanding compilation of its kind, with many features making it useful for those without experience in child language, and sufficiently comprehensive to serve as a core reference for child language research.

Spanning a period of some sixty years (primarily 1920 to 1976, with selected earlier references), the bibliography is divided into thirteen main sections and forty-eight subsections containing over 1,500 references (more than 500 on background reading) plus numerous cross-references, repetitions, and book reviews, and a complete name index as well as subject index.

The exceptionally well-detailed annotations featured in this bibliography permit quick surveys of research areas by inexperienced as well as sophisticated users—empirical papers are consistently annotated for age of subjects and task, and results are noted unless unusually complex. As a special aid for identifying relevant backgound literature for a research topic, one-third of the entries are selected references from linguistics, cognitive psychology, adult psycholinguistics, Piagetian theory, and artificial intelligence.

Child Language is the definitive, current bibliography for everyone needing access to the literature on child language. It represents an invaluable resource for instructors, advanced students, researchers, administrators, therapists, and librarians. Because so many disciplines touch on child language, this volume is also important for students and professionals in child development and psycholinguistics, education, speech and hearing, sociology, anthropology, and artificial intelligence.

250 pages   *1977*

LANGUAGE AS A SOCIAL SEMIOTIC

The Social Interpretation of Language and Meaning

By M. A. K. Halliday, Ph.D.

This volume presents Professor Halliday's most important recent essays on the functions of language in social communication. It contains revised and updated versions of earlier material drawn from various sources, a new chapter on language and urban society, and an introduction prepared specifically for this text by Professor Halliday.

The essays are organized around five main themes: the sociolinguistic perspective, a sociosemiotic interpretation of language, the social semantics of text, language and social structure, and educational sociolinguistics. Throughout, the approach is ultimately an applied one—a concern with language in relation to the process and experience of education, reflecting the author's conviction about the importance of sociolinguistic background to everything that goes on in the classroom.

Professor Halliday departs from the individualist ideology that has dominated linguistics study for most of the past twenty years to look into language from the outside, and specifically to interpret linguistic processes from the standpoint of the social order. This divergent viewpoint is an immensely helpful supplement and contrast to other linguistics texts and provides a perspective that helps to explain the nature of the linguistic system.

Language as a Social Semiotic is recommended for students of linguistics at all levels as required collateral reading, and as a primary text for courses in applied linguistics, social linguistics, and communication. Engagingly written, it is excellent reading for everyone interested in the nature of how people exchange meanings in interpersonal contexts and how their language is affected by their social roles.

228 pages   *Illustrated*   *1977*